Basic Hunter's Guide

Published By
The National Rifle Association
Of America
Washington, D.C.

The Cover: Deer hunting photograph by Jerry Smith,
Alice, Texas, and quail and duck hunting scenes are by
Joe Reynolds, Catonsville, Maryland.

ISBN 0- 935998-46-2

List of Contents

Introduction . . . . Page   1

Hunting Ethics . . . . Page   5

Role of the Hunter . . . . Page 15

Wildlife Management . . . . Page 19

Wildlife Identification . . . . Page 35

Equipment . . . . Page 133

Firearms . . . . Page 159

Bowhunting . . . . Page 211

Field Techniques . . . . Page 227

Survival . . . . Page 241

Hypothermia . . . . Page 259

First Aid . . . . Page 269

Vision & Physical Fitness . . . . Page 283

Legal Responsibilities . . . . Page 295

The effort and assistance of many people in producing
NRA Basic Hunter's Guide are acknowledged and
appreciated. Without their help and that of the following
organizations, this guide would not have been possible.
- Alberta Energy and Natural Resources
- Alberta Fish and Wildlife Division
- Alberta Conservation and Hunter Education
  Manual Development Committee
- South Dakota Game, Fish and Parks Department

Introduction

Introduction

The primary goal of this NRA Basic Hunter's Guide is to assist you in understanding the important role of modern regulated hunting in wildlife management and conservation. Equally important is the wise and safe use through proper handling of firearms and respect for the property of others. This guide is intended to help you to become a safer and more successful hunter.

The question of whether to hunt or not to hunt is strictly a matter for your decision. Hunting constitutes an important tool of wildlife management. Each year throughout North America over 16,000,000 men and women purchase hunting licenses. Many of these hunters spend many dollars, in travel and purchase of supplies and equipment. Despite its popularity over the years, hunting has proven to be one of the safest forms of outdoor recreation. It is hoped that this guide will enable you to derive more pleasure from North America's great outdoors.

If you choose not to hunt, it is just as important that you understand how modern hunting is used by wildlife managers to help ensure the future well-being of our wildlife species. Hopefully, information in this guide will instill an appreciation of hunting, safe firearm use and respect for property.

HUNTER EDUCATION HISTORY

Hunter safety training became a concern in North America during the late 1940's and early 1950's. New York in 1949 was the first state to pass a law requiring hunter safety training. Soon many state agencies followed with voluntary and mandatory hunter safety training programs.

During the 1970's, hunter safety training was expanded to "hunter education" which included a variety of aspects besides safety such as hunter ethics, sportsmanship, wildlife identification and respect for personal property.

Today, all states and Canadian provinces offer hunter education programs. The NRA joins state and provincial hunter education professionals in an ongoing effort to improve and upgrade hunter education. By continual review of various programs and how they meet the changing needs of the sport of hunting, the NRA will be better able to offer quality hunter education programs. The result will be a better informed group of new hunters and a brighter future for hunting.

Notes

Hunting Ethics

Introduction

People are judged by their actions. How we behave and how we follow the rules affects other people. As a hunter, you must be aware of how your personal behavior and activities, as well as the actions of your companions, will affect others.

When driving a car, we are expected to drive carefully following the rules of the road. When we play any sport we are expected to follow the rules of the game. Hunters, too, are expected to behave responsibly while hunting . . . to hunt according to the rules.

Can you imagine what it would be like if every person driving a car made up his own rules? Can you picture any sport if each player did whatever he pleased? Few people would enjoy living together under such circumstances.

If we are to live, play and work together in harmony then we must conform to the standards of behavior that are expected of us. These standards of conduct or "ethics" are important guidelines for living in peace and friendship with other people.

Definition of Ethics and Laws

Ethics are standards of behavior or conduct which are considered to be morally right. Ethics begin with the standard of behavior of an individual person. Each individual must make a personal judgement about whether certain behavior is right or wrong. If a person truly believes that a specific action is morally right, then it is ethical for him to act that way.

For example, if a hunter truly believes that it is right to shoot a duck with a shotgun while it is sitting on the water, then it is ethical for that particular hunter to do so. His behavior is consistent with his personal code of ethics. If, however, a hunter believes it is wrong to shoot a sitting duck, then it would be wrong for him to do so. Such action would not be ethical for him.

Very often, groups of people share the same ethical beliefs. When a group of hunters have similar ideas concerning ethical hunting behavior, they often form a hunting party, club or association which expects its members to act according to the group code of ethics. In this situation, ethics are similar to laws. The ethics are written down and each member of the group agrees to abide by this code. Any member who violates the ethics agreed upon may be asked to resign from membership in the group or be penalized in some manner.

Sometimes ethics are made laws by state or federal legislatures. When a majority of the people believe a certain ethic or standard of behavior is right for all and they expect everyone to act according to that belief, then that ethic may become law. For an ethic to become a law legislative procedures which are basically the same for creating all laws must be followed.

Most hunters have a personal code of ethics which is very similar to the laws which are associated with hunting. Usually, hunters agree that the hunting laws are fair and just, and find these laws easy to obey. But occasionally, a hunter's personal code of ethics may differ from one of the hunting laws. For example, while hunting on the prairie, a hunter may come upon a doe antelope with a broken leg. According to his personal code of ethics, he believes it is morally right to kill a seriously injured animal in order to end its suffering. However, according to law, it may be illegal to hunt or kill doe antelope except during an open hunting season for antelope and the hunter has a valid permit to hunt doe antelope in the area.

What should he do? One ethical course of action is to advise the nearest Fish and Wildlife Division office or conservation officer as quickly as possible that there is an injured animal and describe its exact location. The officers will then attend to the problem quickly.

A hunter's personal code of ethics, the ethics of others and ethics which are laws sometimes differ widely. These differences of opinion can make some decisions very difficult for a hunter.

Personal Code of Ethics

Personal ethics are "unwritten laws" which govern your behavior at all times—when you are with others, and when you are alone. They are YOUR personal standard of conduct. Your personal code of ethics is based upon your respect for other people and their property, for all living things and their environment, and your own image of yourself.

Aldo Leopold, a pioneer in the field of wildlife management and a respected hunter said, "The hunter ordinarily has no gallery to applaud or disapprove his conduct. Whatever his acts, they are dictated by his own conscience rather than by a mob of onlookers."

The basis of a personal code of ethics is a "sense of decency". You must ask yourself repeatedly, "What if someone else behaved the way I am—would I respect him?"

Chances are you will have developed a personal code of ethics long before you became a hunter. Because you want the respect of your parents and family, your friends and neighbors, you developed a certain standard of acceptable behavior. If you have been on hunting trips, even before you were old enough to hunt game yourself, you gained important insights into how you are expected to act while hunting and learned some hunting ethics. These, and other experiences, will guide your behavior in the future and can help you earn self-respect and the respect of other hunters.

Your personal code of ethics and your hunting behavior may change through the years. It is usual for a hunter to go through five behavior stages.

1) First is the "shooter stage"—a time when shooting firearms is of primary interest.

2) Next is the "limiting-out stage"—when the hunter wants, above all, to bag the legal limit of game he is hunting.

3) The third stage is the "trophy stage"—the hunter is selective, primarily seeking out trophy animals of a particular species.

4) Then the "technique stage"—the emphasis is on HOW rather than WHAT he hunts.

5) The last stage is called the "mellowing-out stage"—this is a time of enjoyment derived from the total hunting experience—the hunt, the companionship of other hunters and an appreciation of the outdoors. When a hunter has reached the mellowing-out stage of his development, bagging game will be more symbolic than essential for his satisfaction.

The hunter's personal code of ethics will change as he passes through each of these five stages, often becoming more strict and imposing more constraints on his behavior and actions when hunting.

These self-imposed restrictions, however, will add to the enjoyment of the hunting experience, for the ethical hunter is the hunter who can most appreciate the sport of hunting. Only he understands the new sense of freedom and independence that comes from hunting legally and ethically.

Ethics for Consideration

Various people have proposed ethical standards which they feel should be adopted by all hunters. These are presented for your consideration in the remaining sections of this chapter. Consider each ethic carefully. Decide whether it is right or wrong in your view. If it is right, incorporate it into your personal code of hunting ethics and practice it when afield. In the final analysis, your standards of conduct while hunting will be the true indicator of your personal code of ethics.

Hunter-Landowner Relations

The ethical hunter realizes he is a guest of the landowner while hunting on private land. He makes sure he is welcome by asking his landowner host for permission before he hunts. On the rare occasions when permission is denied, he accepts the situation gracefully.

To avoid disturbing the landowner early in the morning, an ethical hunter plans ahead and obtains permission to hunt on private land before the season opens. He understands that the landowner usually does not mind if he brings a friend or two along but he will destroy his welcome if he arrives with a carload of companions.

While hunting, the ethical hunter takes extra care to avoid disturbing livestock. If he is hunting with a dog, special precautions are taken to ensure it does not harass cattle, chickens, or other farm animals. He understands that, if disturbed by loud noises or other activity, dairy cows may fail to produce milk and poultry may crowd together in the chicken coop and suffocate. Beef cattle when frightened and forced to run may suffer a weight loss costly to the rancher.

He leaves all gates as he finds them, and if closed, he ensures they are securely latched. He crosses all fences so as to avoid loosening the wires and posts. He only goes on those portions of private land the owner has granted permission to hunt. He never assumes he is welcome on private property simply because other hunters have already been granted permission to hunt there.

An ethical hunter is careful to avoid littering the land with empty shell boxes, sandwich wrappings, pop cans, cigarette packages or other garbage, including empty

shotgun shells. He never drives or walks through standing crops nor does he send his dog through them when crop damage might result. When driving across pastures or plowed fields, he keeps his vehicle on the trail or road at all times. He understands that the ruts left by vehicles on hillsides can cause serious soil erosion when water runs down these tire tracks. He hunts as much private property on foot as possible rather than by driving over it in his vehicle. When parking his vehicle, he is careful not to block the landowner's access to buildings, equipment and roadways. If he notices anything wrong on the property such as open gates, broken fences or injured livestock, he reports it to the landowner as soon as possible.

An ethical hunter limits the amount of game he and his friends take on a landowner's property to less than the bag limit. He realizes the the landowner may accept one man taking his bag limit on a given day but two or three taking their limit is being greedy.

Unless he is a close personal friend of the landowner, an ethical hunter does not hunt on a specific farm or ranch more than two or three times each season. He does not want to wear out his welcome.

Before leaving, he thanks the landowner or a member of his family for the privilege of hunting the property and

he offers a share of his bag if he has been successful. In appreciation of his hospitality, a thoughtful and considerate hunter offers to spend a half hour helping the landowner with his chores. If the offer is accepted, he cheerfully pitches bales, mends fences, forks manure or does whatever else is required. He may even use his special skills if he is a plumber, mechanic, painter or carpenter.

If he owns property elsewhere such as a farm, ranch or lake cottage, an ethical hunter will invite his host to use them. He notes the name and address of his host and sometime later, perhaps around Christmas, he sends a thank you card expressing his appreciation for the landowner's hospitality.

Remember, a landowner has no respect for those who trespass. For the time it takes to ask, why not feel welcome and know you may come back again.

Regard for Other People's Feelings

When hunting on public lands, an ethical hunter shows the same respect for other users of the land and their property as he shows for landowners on private land.

He hunts in areas where his activities will not conflict with other people's enjoyment of the outdoors. And he treats the land with respect—being careful not to litter the back country or seriously damage its vegetation. He limits his use of vehicles to travel to and from his hunting area, always remaining on trails or developed roadways.

He knows that alcoholic beverages can seriously impair his judgement while hunting. He restricts his enjoyment of such drinks to the evening hours after the firearms have been stored away and he can relax with his companions and recollect the enjoyment of his day afield. Even then he limits his drinking to ensure that his actions do not offend others—either his companions or other people who may be sharing the campground with him.

An ethical hunter recognizes that many people are offended by the sight of a bloody deer carcass tied over the hood of a car or a gut pile lying in full view of the road. He knows some people may be offended at the sight of such things. Their senses may be shocked by a vehicle full of hunters with a gun rack full of firearms parading through a campground or the streets of a community. Realizing these things and having respect for the feelings and beliefs of others, the ethical hunter makes a special effort to avoid offending non-hunters. He is constantly aware that many of these people are his friends, neighbors, relatives and even members of his immediate family.

He appreciates the fact that, for a variety of reasons, many people do not hunt nor do they want to hunt in the future. Likewise, he understands some people are opposed to hunting for one reason or another. He does not regard these people as "kooks" and "bambi lovers" or anything else other than normal human beings whose likes and dislikes differ from his own. He accepts the fact that non-hunters and anti-hunters are just as sincere in their beliefs as he is about hunting.

He appreciates that many trappers abide by their own code of ethics. They commonly leave their cabins unlocked in back country areas so someone who is in trouble may use them in a time of need. However, anyone doing so is expected to replace anything they use as soon as possible and advise the owner of their actions. An ethical hunter will never abuse this privilege nor will he tamper with equipment along a trapline.

Relationship With Other Hunters

An ethical hunter shows consideration for his companions. When leaving for a hunt, he ensures he is ready to go at the appointed time and he does not invite others to join the group unexpectedly.

Once in the field, his consideration extends to other hunters as well. He realizes the true satisfaction in hunting does not depend on competing with others for game.

An ethical hunter avoids doing anything that will interfere with another one's hunt or his enjoyment of it. He does not shoot along fencelines adjacent to fields where others are hunting nor does he try to intercept the game they are hunting.

If disputes arise with other hunters, he tries to work out a compromise—perhaps a cooperative hunt—whereby everyone can enjoy themselves.

An ethical hunter does not hog an unfair number of the shots—he does just the opposite. He gives friends the advantage of getting a good shot whenever possible. He shows special consideration for the inexperienced or handicapped hunters by allowing them to hunt from the most advantageous position.

Each hunting season, an ethical hunter invites a novice hunter to accompany him in the field. He takes the time to share his hunting knowledge with his companion and introduces him to the enjoyment of hunting ethically. He realizes that a man learns something very important about his own ethics when he teaches others to hunt.

He respects the limitations of his health and physical fitness. He consults with his family doctor regularly to ensure he is physically capable of coping with the rigor of strenuous hunting activity. If unfit, he builds up his fitness before he goes hunting. He ensures his vision is adequate and, if necessary, wears glasses or contact lenses to correct any visual impairments.

To cope with unexpected outdoor emergencies, an ethical hunter learns and practices the basic skills of first aid and survival and he understands how to recognize and deal with hypothermia.

He does not shoot over his limit to fill the bag limit of others nor does he take his own limit unless he plans to use all he has taken.

He observes the rules of safe gun handling at all times and firmly insists that his companions do the same. He politely lets others know when he thinks their behavior is out of line.

Self-Respect

An ethical hunter realizes it is his responsibility to know how to take care of himself in the outdoors. And he respects his limitations.

He never places his life or that of others in jeopardy by failing to notify someone where he intends to hunt and how long he expects to be gone. If his plans change once he is afield, he leaves a note on his vehicle designating his destination, time of departure and expected time of return.

Respect of Wildlife

An ethical hunter is not just a sportsman, he is also a naturalist. His interest in wildlife extends beyond game animals to the variety of other living things that inhabit the outdoor world. He is just as thrilled by the sight of a bald eagle as a bighorn sheep. He knows and studies nature's ways and realizes that wildlife can be enjoyed year round—not only during the hunting season.

When hunting, his pursuit of game is always governed by the "fair chase" principle. Simply stated, this principle or ethic demands that a hunter shall always give his quarry a "fair" chance to escape being shot.

When hunting big game, an ethical hunter will always attempt to get close enough to his quarry to ensure a quick, clean kill. He realizes that in doing so, his quarry may discover him and escape before he has a chance for a shot. But he always gives his quarry this sporting chance.

Never under any circumstances will an ethical hunter shoot indiscriminately at a flock of game birds or a herd of big game in the hope of hitting one. He will always attempt to kill his quarry quickly and humanely.

Through considerable practice before a hunt, he will learn the distance at which he can be most confident of killing game cleanly. He will ensure his rifle is accurately sighted in and determine the most effective shot size for his shotgun.

Once afield, he will expend extraordinary effort to retrieve and dispatch wounded game—even if it means interrupting his hunting to help another hunter locate a wounded animal. When possible, he will use a trained hunting dog to retrieve wounded game birds.

If it appears he has missed his shot, an ethical hunter will always carefully inspect the spot where his quarry stood to ensure the animal was not hit.

An ethical hunter shows as much respect for his game after it is taken as before he shoots it. He never allows the meat or other usable parts of the animal to be wasted. Even though he may not want the antlers or hide of the animal, he recovers them to give to other people who will use them. The fur and feathers of many game birds and animals are useful, for example, in making flies used by fishermen.

Respect for Laws and Enforcement Officers

An ethical hunter obeys all laws which govern his hunting activities. Although he may occasionally disagree with a specific law, he will not deliberately disobey it. Instead, he will work through his elected representatives to change laws which he feels are unjustified.

An ethical hunter will not condone law breaking by others by ignoring illegal acts he observes when afield. He rightfully insists that all members of his hunting party obey the law and he reports law breaking by other people to the appropriate law enforcement agency. If asked to serve as a witness, he accepts his responsibility as a citizen and sportsman to do so.

When he meets a state or federal wildlife officer, wildlife biologist or technician checking hunters in the field, he is cooperative and provides the information they request concerning his hunting activities. If he does not understand the reason for providing certain information he asks for an explanation.

Importance of Ethics

Future opportunities to enjoy sport hunting in North America will depend upon the hunter's public image. If hunters are viewed as "slobs" who shoot up the countryside, vandalize property, and disregard the rights of landowners and citizens, they will lose the privilege to hunt on private land and public land as well. However, if an increasing number of hunters follow the honorable traditions of their sport and practice a personal code of hunting ethics which meets public expectations, the future of sport hunting will be assured.

Notes

14

Role of the Hunter

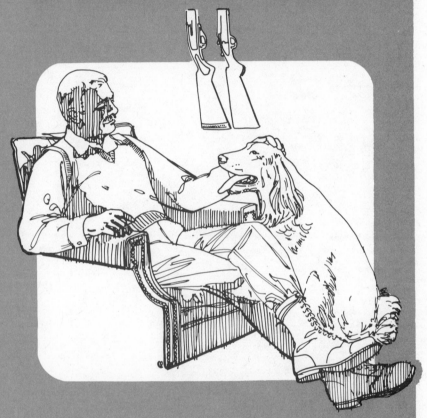

The Role of the Hunter

Throughout history hunting has been a tradition of man. Until recent times man hunted, through necessity, for food. As civilization progressed, man's need to hunt for survival was reduced, so that now, most hunting is recreational. Notwithstanding this change in purpose, hunting has remained as a legitimate and viable activity in today's modern society.

Hunters themselves have long been concerned for the welfare of wildlife. Through their actions, hunters have identified problems such as:

a) pollution and its effect on wildlife

b) habitat loss and abuse

c) helping to focus public attention on the plight of rare and endangered species

For example, hunters have been largely responsible for:

a) initiating wildlife laws and their enforcement

b) wildlife research and management

c) establishment of parks and wildlife preserves

Hunters were instrumental in initiating and organizing institutions such as The Audubon Society and The American Ornithologists' Union. Today, hunters are active supporters of Ducks Unlimited, Wildlife Federations and numerous local sportsmen clubs. These organizations reflect the sincere interest and dedication of hunters to the sound management of our renewable wildlife resources.

In addition, hunters contribute to the welfare of wildlife through their purchases of licenses and state and federal hunting stamps and payment of federal excise taxes on sporting arms and ammunition. The license fees and excise taxes amount to millions of dollars each year which provides nearly 80 percent of the working funds of state wildlife agencies.

Through your role as a hunter, your involvement and dedication will help ensure the continued availability of abundant wildlife resources throughout North America.

Notes

Wildlife Management

Introduction

Everybody likes wildlife of one kind or another.

What is wildlife? Wildlife is any non-domestic mammal, bird, reptile or amphibian. In certain states and provinces, fish are normally regulated by separate legislation. The "Fish and Game" Department is often the title given to the agency responsible for managing these groups of animals.

Many people, particularly hunters, tend to think of wildlife only in terms of game animals—those species which may be legally hunted and harvested. In North America, however, many more of the birds and mammals that occur here are classed as non-game species than are considered game species.

"Fur-bearers", some of which are also game animals, are those forms of wildlife that may be taken and used for their fur.

"Predators" are those animals which prey on and use other animals for food.

Some kinds of wildlife are generally considered as undesirable, particularly by farmers or ranchers. These forms are often called "pest" species and may be given little or no protection by state or federal wildlife laws.

Most wildlife species are native to North America, occurring naturally here before settlers arrived. Some, however, are not native. They have been brought in from another area and introduced here by man. Such non-native, introduced forms of wildlife are often referred to as "exotic species."

Wildlife is a living resource. Living things have a life span and will eventually die to be replaced by others of that kind. Such living animals cannot be "preserved" or stockpiled for future use beyond their normal life span. However, living resources can be "conserved" or used wisely. Wildlife conservation is founded on the principles of planned management and wise use.

Wildlife is a valuable renewable natural resource that can be drawn upon and used in a number of ways. Some uses are "consumptive"; the individual animal is removed from the population through predation, hunting or trapping and used for food or fur. "Non-consumptive uses" of wildlife, which do not result in removing animals from their population, include such activities as bird-watching, wildlife photography or simply enjoying wildlife through observation.

Throughout history, man has developed a fascination with wildlife as a result of his curiosity about animals and his use of them.

This has been intensified in recent times when most people live in cities and are not in daily contact with wild animals. Most of their knowledge about wildlife comes from T.V., movies, newspapers and books, rather than first-hand contact with living things.

To a degree, most people regard themselves as experts when it comes to wildlife matters—certainly the case with many hunters and fishermen. As a result of this many myths have arisen.

However, the science of ecology has dispelled many of these myths and scientists are continually shedding new light on how wild animals and plants interrelate to man and other aspects of their environment. This field of study is called ecology.

Basic Principles of Ecology

In the world around us, the living organisms or communities and the non-living environment function together and interact as an ecological system or ecosystem.

Habitat

Within an ecosystem the kind of "home" or habitat a species of wildlife lives in must provide everything it needs to survive—places for feeding, drinking, resting, breeding and escaping danger.

Habitat is the total environment that supplies everything the animal needs—food, cover, air, water and space. When these habitat factors are in good supply, they contribute to the well-being of wildlife. If any component of habitat is in short supply, it limits the number and distribution of wildlife and is called a limiting factor.

Habitat Change

Habitat, the complex association of soil, water and plants is in itself dynamic and ever changing. These changes can be subtle or dramatic. A forest fire causes a dramatic habitat change. The coniferous forest, cool and shady, disappears. Eventually, on the blackened, but now sunlit ground, fireweed, grasses and other plants appear. Each type of plant appears, grows, matures, and disappears to be replaced by others which also go through their stages and are replaced by still other varieties. This series of changes taking place is not random or haphazard but a predictable, sequential chain of events called succession. Each stage of plant life is succeeded by another. At each successional stage, changes in the plant component of the habitat complex alter that complex in total. With each change, be it subtle or dramatic, habitat is changed. With changes in habitat come changes in the forms of wildlife using that particular habitat.

Bare Soil | Grass and Flowers | Shrubs and Short Trees | Tall Trees and Only Few Shrubs and Grasses

The coniferous forest, burned over, is replaced by a low ground cover of grass and flowering plants. Over the next few years shrubs, bushes, willows, aspens and coniferous trees each in turn, make their appearance. Finally the forest is once again as it was, composed almost entirely of coniferous trees. This final or climax stage will remain until, as a result of fire or logging, the successional cycle is triggered once again.

Wildlife and Plant Succession

Each species of wildlife has unique habitat requirements. Therefore, changes in habitat will effect changes in the kinds of wildlife associated with it.

In the example of coniferous forest succession, elk might be found grazing on the open grass areas made possible by the removal of the trees. As willow and low shrubs take over, moose take advantage of the abundance of their preferred food. The climax coniferous stage accommodates such species as fisher, marten and red squirrels. An older spruce forest with lichen covered trees provides ideal caribou habitat.

Edge Effect

The edges or borders or habitats overlap each other and it is here that change in vegetation is most noticeable.

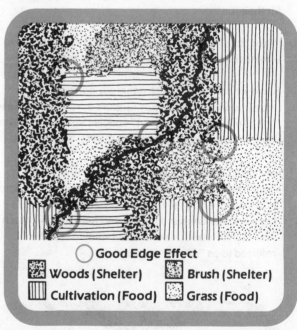

◯ **Good Edge Effect**
▨ **Woods (Shelter)**   ▩ **Brush (Shelter)**
▥ **Cultivation (Food)**   ⬚ **Grass (Food)**

The zone of change or transition offers the greatest mixture of habitat which in turn is utilized by a high diversity of wildlife species. Ideally the best wildlife habitat has an abundance of edge arranged to provide for feeding, escape, shelter, resting and drinking all within close proximity.

Carrying Capacity

Carrying capacity is the ability of a given habitat to support or carry a number of a particular wildlife species. The carrying capacity of habitat changes from place to place, from season to season and from year to year. When carrying capacity is at its lowest, usually in the critical winter period, those animals in excess of that number must either move to new habitat or perish; it usually is the latter which occurs.

The number of ungulates living on a lush summer meadow will be sharply reduced when winter snows flatten cover and lessen the availability of food and shelter. Successional changes over longer periods of time will cause habitat change and alter that habitat's carrying capacity. Because of these changes, both short and long term, carrying capacity cannot support a fixed number of animals of a given species continuously. Over time, nature will maintain a wildlife population balance at or near carrying capacity.

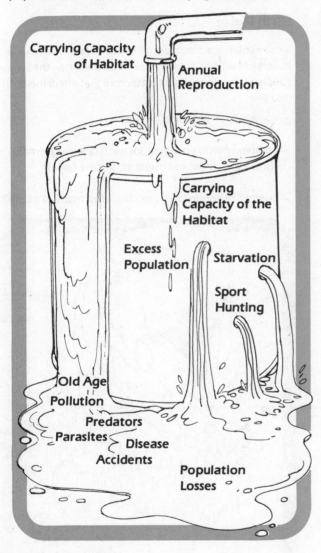

Limiting Factors

Carrying capacity of a habitat is determined by any one of a number of factors. Changes in any of these individual factors may result in either an increase or a reduction of the carrying capacity.

Food:

Each wildlife species eats specific plants or animals, regardless of others that may be available. Some foods have more nutritional value than others which may vary according to the time of year. For this reason, both the quantity and the quality of food may limit the abundance of the wildlife dependent upon it.

Cover:

Wildlife needs cover to shelter and protect it while feeding, sleeping, breeding, roosting, nesting and travelling, or to escape from predators. Cover can take many forms, such as vegetation, burrows, rocks or other features. If a particular kind of cover is in short supply, it may also limit wildlife populations.

Water:

All wildlife needs water. Sources of water are lakes, ponds, streams, dew, snow, and succulent (juicy) vegetation. Some animals can also use metabolic water (water produced by chemical processes in the body). Water may be required only in small amounts for drinking, or in the case of fish and mammals like beaver and otter, in much greater quantities as the principle component of their habitat.

Space:

Wildlife needs space if it is to survive. Overcrowding leads to severe competition for the habitat components essential to life. For this reason, only a specific number of animals can live in an area (carrying capacity).

In addition, wildlife may have territorial requirements associated with mating and/or nesting. Many species of wildlife occupy a home range and spend their entire lives within that range. In the case of white tailed deer, they rarely move beyond the 150 to 200 acres that comprise their home range.

Predation:

Any animal that eats another animal is a predator and the animals they eat are their prey. Predators are generally opportunists. Animals that are either very young or very old, or those weakened by disease, parasites or malnutrition are most likely to first fall prey to predators. When a prey population is low, the predator must find other species to prey on or its numbers will also be affected. Since most predators are well adapted to pursue and take only a few prey species, their numbers are very much dependent on the abundance of their specific prey. This has been dramatically demonstrated by the relationship between lynx and varying hares over a number of years.

Population Dynamics

A population is a group of animals of the same species that occupy a particular area. Dynamics refers to motion or change from within. Population dynamics, therefore, means the changes that occur in a population over time. The study of population dynamics helps explain why wildlife populations must be managed and how.

Two major factors affect the population dynamics of wildlife—the birth rate and the death rate.

Birth Rate:

Most wildlife species have a high birth rate. The smaller species of wildlife have higher birth rates than the larger species. The most important factors that affect the birth rate are:

—age at which breeding begins

—number of births per year for each breeding female (how many times each year young are born)

—number of young born per litter. How many at a time?

Weather:

This is undoubtedly a major factor in determining population numbers. In North America nearly all other limiting factors are directly or indirectly influenced by climatic conditions. Climatic changes (weather) will obviously affect the cover, food, water, space and other components of habitat needed by wildlife.

Human Activities

Human activities such as alteration of habitat, killing of wildlife, impairment of reproduction by pesticides and harassment of wildlife can also serve to limit both numbers and kinds of wildlife in a given area.

Disease and Parasites

The effect of disease and parasites on a wildlife population may range from lethal to debilitating. At the extreme, die-offs of wildlife may occur, thus severely reducing population numbers. At lesser levels of infestation, reproductive capacity may be impaired and the ability of a population to sustain itself can be seriously affected.

Death Rate:

The death rate of most wildlife species is high. The smaller species of wildlife have higher death rates than the larger species. The principal factors affecting the death rate of wildlife in North America are:

—availability of food and cover

—predation

—weather

—human activities

—disease and parasites

Note that these are generally the same factors discussed earlier in relation to limiting the carrying capacity of a habitat.

Principles of Inversity and Compensation:

Two principles of ecology deserve mention at this point. The first is often referred to as the "Law of Inversity." Simply stated, it means that as the survival of breeding populations increases, the survival of their offspring will decrease. The result would be a wildlife population composed mostly of older animals and very few young.

When the breeding population declines, usually the number of young per litter increases. The reverse is also true, as for example with white-tailed deer populations on the prairies. Following a mild winter many adults of breeding age will survive. Under these conditions, the number of fawns produced is low, generally only one per doe. When severe winters have reduced the adult population, twin fawns are commonly seen.

The second principle, applicable to the death rate, is often called the "law of compensation." If one or more factors affecting the death rate decline, others will increase so that overall death rate will not significantly change. Over a given time period, the same number of animals in a population will die due to one cause or another. Thus you cannot stockpile wildlife from one year to the next.

If the birth rate is greater than the death rate, population numbers will increase. If the death rate is greater than the birth rate, population numbers will decrease. If birth and death rates are equal, population numbers will not change. However, populations of wildlife species are not static—they do not remain stable and unchanging.

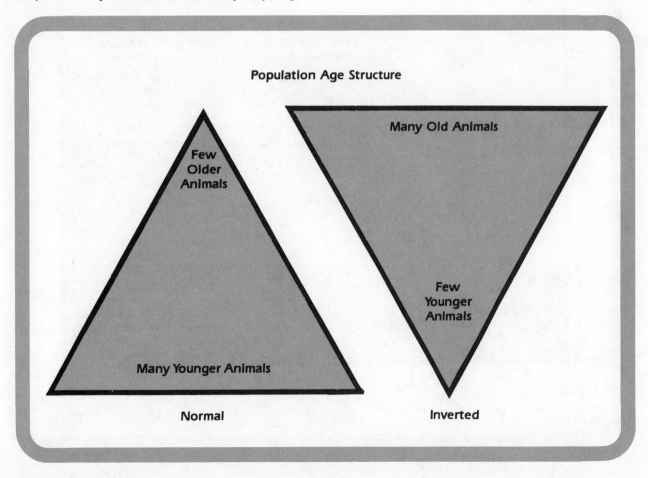

Population Age Structure

Few Older Animals

Many Younger Animals

Normal

Many Old Animals

Few Younger Animals

Inverted

Seasonal Changes:

In addition to the shifts and changes that occur from year to year, populations demonstrate an even greater seasonal fluctuation in numbers.

The most obvious change in population level occurs in the spring when the young of most wildlife species are born. The extent of this immediate increase in population level will depend on the number of breeding females as well as the number of young each female produces. Cow moose and elk may bear one or possibly two calves, while a hen mallard may hatch 12 to 14 new additions to the populations of that species. Not all young will survive, but understandably, populations reach their peak levels in the spring. At this time of the year—habitat is at its best, offering lush new vegetation for the herbivores or plant-eating forms of wildlife and large prey populations for the predators.

Though many animals will die over the spring, summer and fall, the winter period is the period of heaviest mortality.

In winter, the ability of habitat to support a large number of animals is reduced, often drastically. Those animals in excess of the number that the habitat can then support become surplus and may be lost to starvation and other factors. This annual mortality is part of the natural cycle. All that is required in nature is that a sufficient number of animals—the breeding stock—survive until the spring and the cycle starts over.

Surplus wildlife cannot be stockpiled and saved for future use. A surplus is either used or lost.

The average life span of most wildlife species is less than three years. All forms of wildlife are living creatures that will inevitably die and be removed from the population. This loss is replaced by the birth and addition of new individuals to the population.

Man's ability to control and manipulate both the rate of depletion and the factors that influence the rate of production of a wildlife population forms the basis for wildlife management.

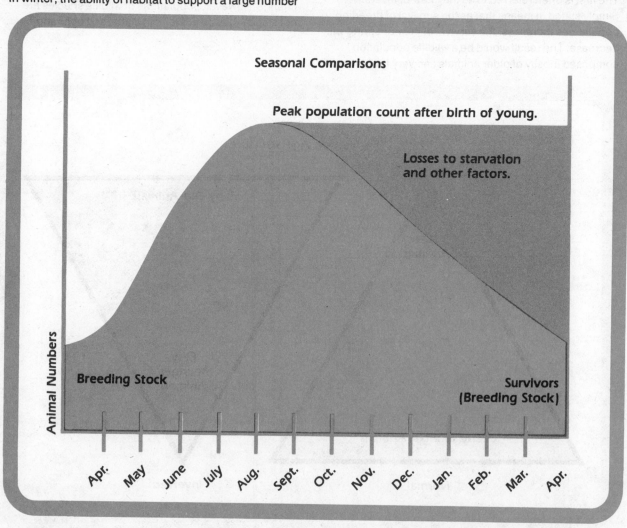

Seasonal Comparisons

Peak population count after birth of young.

Losses to starvation and other factors.

Breeding Stock

Survivors (Breeding Stock)

Animal Numbers

Apr. May June July Aug. Sept. Oct. Nov. Dec. Jan. Feb. Mar. Apr.

Game Management and Conservation

Using the basic principles of ecology, wildlife managers attempt to maintain and manage wildlife populations. Wildlife is one of our valuable resources and in this context wildlife managers are really resource managers. A resource can be defined as "any available supply that can be drawn upon when needed."

Natural resources are those resources supplied to us by nature, for example, plants, water, soil, minerals and wildlife.

Some resources, once drawn upon and used, are then no longer available to us. Coal, gas and oil are examples of natural resources that cannot be replenished or replaced once they have been used. They are called "non-renewable resources." Other kinds of natural resources can replenish themselves through natural means and thus continue to remain available for further use. These resources such as vegetation and wildlife are termed "renewable resources."

Similarly, game managers try to control wildlife populations. A sufficiently high breeding population is maintained to maximize the reproductive potential of that population. As with the rancher, there is a need to remove or harvest a portion of that population to keep it within the ability of the habitat available to support it. In essence, game managers "farm" wildlife just as the rancher manages his herds. Through hunting, the wildlife manager crops portions of game populations just as the rancher removes and markets the surplus portion of his herd.

Game Management

Game management can be thought of as a field of "applied ecology" and is in many respects, very similar to the practice of agriculture or forestry. A forester plants trees, allows them to grow and eventually harvests them. A rancher must continually remove and market animals from his herd to keep it within the carrying capacity of the range he has available for grazing. If he did not do this, the yearly addition of calves to the herd would increase the number of animals to a point beyond the capacity of the land to support them.

The science of game management is more than simply exercising control of population numbers by controlling harvest. Today, the game manager manages not only the species but the ecosystem in which it occurs. Through manipulation of the various factors which affect game species and limit carrying capacity of their habitats, he attempts to maximize the crop of game available for harvesting. This can generally be done by developing habitat to create more space, food, cover or other critical component. Although primarily done to benefit a game species, the creation of new habitat will also benefit many other kinds of non-game wildlife.

Why Manage Game?

Too few people who enjoy the outdoors really understand or fully appreciate the basic objectives and principles of game management. The primary objective of game management is to maintain game species, in sufficient numbers and variety, to meet the present and future economic, recreational and aesthetic needs of the people of the area. Game is a publicly owned resource.

Through their game management programs, state and federal agencies share the responsibility for meeting this objective. The U.S. Fish and Wildlife Service, a federal government agency, has responsibility for all migratory birds in the United States as well as the management of all wildlife occurring within the National Parks. Management responsibilities for migratory birds are shared with Canada and Mexico under the terms of the Migratory Birds Convention Act.

The Fish and Wildlife Agency of each state has responsibility for all other wildlife within its borders.

Together these agencies, in concert with many private organizations, landowners and concerned citizens work actively to ensure the future welfare of North American wildlife.

Who Manages Wildlife?

As shareholders of North America's wildlife, all citizens should be concerned about its welfare. Private landowners are in a position to benefit wildlife through the maintenance of wildlife habitat under their control. Funding from citizens, sportsmen's clubs and conservation organizations also can help maintain wildlife. Everybody can communicate their wildlife concerns to their elected representatives and to state and federal wildlife agencies.

Sportsmen and other users of the resource can also contribute to its welfare by conscientiously following the rules and regulations associated with wildlife management. Through various public communications program most state wildlife agencies work to ensure a better public understanding of wildlife laws.

Public Awareness

Fish and Wildlife agency staff as well as Hunter Education Instructors work with schools and a wide variety of groups and organizations to increase public awareness of wildlife management and the need for resource management. Organizations from the private sector such as State Sportsmen's organizations, Ducks

Unlimited, The National Wild Turkey Federation, The National Rifle Association, and others also cooperate in this effort.

To ensure an opportunity for public organizations concerned about wildlife management to have input and direction for wildlife management, hearings are held annually prior to establishing seasons and bag limits by both state and federal wildlife agencies.

Wildlife Management System Components and Techniques

Biological Research

Across North America, wildlife management systems and techniques used do not vary significantly. Techniques are standardized and differ only in relation to the wildlife species to which they are being applied.

In each case the wildlife manager must be able to accurately determine a number of basic items of information about the resource he is to manage. Biological research provides the foundation for management programs through developing wildlife management techniques and providing basic information on wildlife ecology.

Two of the many biological research needs for managing wildlife are:

1. Techniques for accurately estimating numbers of particular wildlife species in a given area. Since wildlife populations are not static but continually changing, methods for determining and evaluating these changes must also be designed.

Methodology for identifying age and sex classes of populations is also required for predicting birth and death rates. In addition to estimating population size, information is also needed concerning the movement of a species. Animals are captured, marked with distinctive tags or bands and released. Subsequent sightings and information from animals harvested by hunters provides data for determining the range of a population and whether such movement is sporadic and random or of a regular migratory nature. Some individuals are fitted with radio transmitters or transmitter collars enabling biologists to continually monitor their movements.

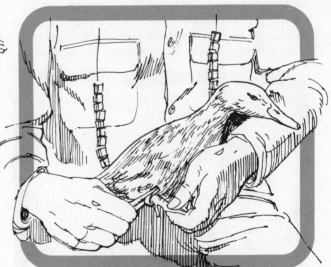

2. Determining the habits and biological needs of various species. This very basic information is needed to be able to determine the habitat requirements and carrying capacities of that habitat for each species.

Inventory

As discussed earlier, it is of prime importance for the game manager to have a reliable count or estimate of the numbers of individuals in populations of wildlife species. This information, when related to an inventory of the area's habitat, will make it possible to estimate the area's carrying capacity and calculate the potential ''surplus'' population. The difficulties encountered in trying to accurately count wild animals are many. Populations may be thinly spread over large areas or may be tightly packed into herds or flocks of hundreds or even thousands of individuals. Most wild animals avoid man and can be difficult to see and count even under ideal conditions.

Difficulties notwithstanding, the most accurate method of determining the number of animals in a given area is to physically count them. Since big game populations are usually surveyed from the air, total counts of every individual of any particular species would be very costly. Attempts to count all, or as many as possible, of the animals present are restricted to only a few species, such as whooping cranes, mountain goats or big horn sheep. Nearly all other game species are censused by first identifying and inventorying the specific habitat appropriate to each species. Small representative portions of this habitat are surveyed and game counts taken. From these sample areas, estimates can then be made as to the number of animals that would be found in other areas of similar habitat and a total population figure for the region arrived at. For example, by counting deer seen from the air on a $\frac{1}{16}$ mile strip on either side of an airplane, the average number of animals can be determined and estimated for larger areas of habitat. This is usually a conservative estimate as not all animals in the survey area will be seen, because of variable cover and terrain. Big game surveys are usually flown during winter months when trees are leafless and the snow on the ground helps to make animals more visible from the air. If possible, surveys are flown at a time when sexual differences are most obvious, as for example, before moose, deer or elk have shed their antlers. Survey personnel are trained and skilled in their ability not only to spot and identify animals but to accurately classify them into their appropriate sex and when possible, age groups.

Other species of game, not as easily observed directly, require different techniques for censusing. Sound counts are used for pheasants and ruffed grouse. Ruffed grouse make a drumming noise on an average of every four minutes in the early morning and late evening during courtship. If a series of four minute stops are made at regular distance intervals, the average number of drums per stop can be counted and then used as an index for spring breeding populations each year. Spring pheasant populations can be monitored similarly by listening for and counting the number of cock pheasants crowing in a given period.

In other circumstances, animal tracks, degree of use of vegetation, or counting scats (animal droppings) can be used to estimate population sizes.

By itself, a single estimate of population, no matter how accurate, is of limited value. However, when surveys are done over a period of years they provide a basis for determining whether populations are on the increase or in a decline.

Nearly all other game species are censused by first identifying and inventorying the specific habitat appropriate to each species. Small representative portions of this habitat are surveyed and game counts taken. From these sample areas, estimates can then be made as to the number of animals that would be found in other areas of similar habitat and a total population figure for the province arrived at.

Estimates of population sizes or numbers of animals present in an area mean little except when used in reference to the carrying capacity of habitat in that area. In order to accomplish this, wildlife habitat must be inventoried as to the wildlife it is capable of supporting. Since the capability of habitat to support wildlife may vary greatly from season to season and year to year. Habitat assessment must take these changes into account.

Many species of wildlife occupy different habitats at different times of the year. In winter, elk move down from the higher open mountain slopes to take advantage of the less severe conditions and greater protection found at lower altitudes. The herds will move back up to the green slopes the following spring and remain through the summer. In cases such as this, both winter and summer habitat must be inventoried and assessed. The seasonal habitat with the lowest carrying capacity, is the most critical and constitutes a limiting factor on the total population.

Waterfowl and other migratory birds make regular annual movements of even greater magnitude. Some species, such as the blue-winged teal, migrate to winter habitat as far away as Central and South America returning to Canada to nest the following spring. In addition to identifying and evaluating the two separate and distant habitats required by the species, the travel routes or flyways between require identification.

These flyways used by waterfowl during their annual migrations have been well studied making it possible to predict where, and to some extent when, various species of waterfowl will be found during migration. These staging or stopping places used during migration are critical habitat areas for waterfowl. Such information is needed in the setting of seasons and bag limits to ensure an equitable sharing of the resource with Canada and Mexico under the Migratory Bird Convention Act.

Habitat Manipulation

Habitat is the complex of soil, water and plants, commonly called "cover" in which wildlife exists. The relationships between soil, water, plants and the

species of wildlife dependent on them are many and varied. One of the greatest influences on habitat is that of seasonal change. The cold, leafless and barren vista of winter is in obvious contrast to the warmth and lush growth of spring and summer. These seasonal changes in habitat have direct relation to the ability of habitat to carry or support game populations.

Man and his activities can cause profound and often irreversible changes on habitat, usually to the detriment of wildlife. In order to maintain produtive wildlife habitat, sound planning programs concerning man's use and future of habitat components are necessary. Both short and long term planning for use of our land and water resources must include a recognition of the need to maintain suitable habitat if native wildlife is to continue to flourish. Agriculture, timber harvest, extraction of coal, oil and gas, as well as our use of water must be based on and guided by sound land and water use planning. Both the private sector and the many agencies of government, including wildlife resource managers, are cooperatively working and planning to minimize man's effect on habitat and the wildlife dependent on it.

Habitat, like wildlife, cannot be "preserved" perpetually in a particular stage or condition. In any natural system, changes are constantly occurring. Plant food used by wildlife germinates, grows, matures and is replaced by other plants. Each stage in the series or succession of changes that occur constitutes a different kind of habitat and results in an accompanying change in the wildlife found there. An area that is diverse in habitat, which offers a variety of different kinds of cover, will maintain the greatest diversity or kinds of wildlife. Habitat provides more than food. It also provides protection and means of escape from predators or the elements. Strip or patch cutting of trees, rather than clear cuts with complete eradication of forest over large areas, will provide food and shelter for wildlife because of the increased amount of "edge" created. The planting or retention of shelter belts will do the same for wildlife in agricultural areas.

Once research has identified the habitat requirements of a game species and inventory has determined the abundance of that habitat, the wildlife manager can decide whether or not to alter or manipulate habitat using various techniques. One method used involves the creating of a particular successional stage of cover for the wildlife species desired and maintaining that stage as long as possible. Fire is used as a management tool to accomplish this. Coniferous areas can be cleared and the growth of willows and dogwoods, browsed by moose, encouraged. The provision of such habitat increases the carrying capacity of the area and game populations for which it was created increase accordingly.

Blasting potholes and controlling water levels by damming has helped create new nesting habitat for waterfowl. Construction of small nesting islands in shallow lakes or sloughs has had a major effect in increasing goose populations in local areas. Planting of shrubs and shelter belts has been used extensively to provide upland overwintering habitat for pheasants.

Much of the funding needed for creating, improving and maintaining wildlife habitat is provided by hunters and other sportsmen through their license fees, hunting stamps and the excise taxes they pay on sporting arms and ammunition.

Wildlife Population Manipulation

In addition to modifying habitat, wildlife managers also use various techniques to alter the abundance and distribution of game populations. Much of this is accomplished through varying the seasons and bag limits associated with the annual sport hunting harvest.

Predators and Problem Wildlife

In the past, game managers placed a heavy emphasis on reducing predator populations in the mistaken belief that, by doing so, game animals would be more abundant. Bounties were used as an incentive to encourage people to shoot or poison predators. Game managers now have a greater appreciation for the true role and value of predators in natural systems. Resource managers now realize that it is most beneficial to maintain a diversity of wildlife including predators to maintain healthy game populations. Towards this end bounties and the poisoning of wildlife have been eliminated and severely restricted in North America.

Wildlife can sometimes conflict with man's interests and activities and may present a problem to the land owner. Damage to grain crops by waterfowl and deer, use of haystacks by feeding elk or destruction of beehives by bears are examples of such conflict. Problem wildlife programs usually emphasize prevention of the problem and involve removal or displacement of wildlife only as a last resort. Current programs include bait or lure stations for waterfowl and protective fencing for haystacks and beehives. In some cases, the farmer or rancher may be partially compensated for his loss through a wildlife damage fund. This fund is maintained by contributions from sportsmen and various levels of government. Hunting can be an effective means of controlling or reducing wildlife damage caused by game species. In some cases it may be possible to increase bag limits or extend seasons in specified damage areas to effectively reduce populations of particular problem species.

Wildlife Rearing and Stocking

Some birds are raised in captivity for release into the wild. This is done to bolster populations of wildlife species in particular areas.

Other wildlife species are trapped and moved to other areas to re-establish them within their former range or expand their natural distribution.

New non-native or exotic species of wildlife have been introduced in the United States on several occasions. The successful introduction of ring-necked pheasants and Hungarian partridge are examples. Primarily, because of habitat loss, natural self-sustaining populations of pheasants have declined substantially in some states over the past few years. To augment natural populations and provide additional sport for the upland bird hunter, additional pheasants are raised at state game farms and released each fall. Licenced private operators may also raise and release game birds for shooting as a commercial enterprise.

Sport Hunting

Sport hunting is used as a tool of wildlife management. Hunting controls are man-made and comparatively easy to manipulate. The effect of hunting varies with the species being hunted and the methods employed. In wildlife management, hunting is used to remove a portion of the annual surplus before it is lost to "natural" causes. The hunter thus serves as a compensatory factor. At the same time, hunting provides the hunter with an opportunity for outdoor recreation. Hunting also provides wildlife biologists with a chance to sample game populations and gather data

relative to distribution, sex, age, and the physical condition of the animals in them.

Sport hunting is useful in helping to alleviate local problems caused by bears, wolves, elk, ducks or other potentially problem species.

An often heard public concern about hunting is that a species may be depleted to the point of becoming endangered or even extinct. The "Law of Diminishing Returns" generally works to prevent the "shooting out" of game animals. As a population decreases, the remaining animals become more wary, widely separated and harder to find. It then takes more effort on the part of the hunter to get game. Beyond a certain level of effort required, most hunters will lose interest and turn to hunting other species, or move to other areas. Even at low population levels the animals taken by hunters are a part of the harvestable surplus. These are animals that, if not taken through hunting, would be removed from the population by some other factor in the environment. Regulated hunting makes it possible to harvest animals when populations are at or close to their highest numbers over the year. By removing animals before the critical habitat conditions of winter occur, more food and cover is left to the remaining population and increases its chance for survival. Pheasant populations, for example, will be reduced by 90% or more due to winter mortality, whether they are hunted or not.

Control over the number of animals harvested can be achieved in several ways. Bag limits (the number of game animals each hunter is allowed to take or possess) can be raised or lowered. Female animals may be taken in some zones and not in others. Hunting seasons for a particular species may vary from a few days to several months depending upon the species. In any particular area or wildlife management zone, a hunting season can be opened for some species and closed for others.

Notes

Wildlife Identification

Introduction

The ability to recognize and accurately identify wildlife is extremely important to the hunter for legal, ethical and recreational reasons.

Hunting laws requires a hunter to accurately identify his quarry. Sometimes the hunter is also required to recognize the sexual and age characteristics.

Many animals are "protected" and must not be hunted. Some wildlife, however, are classified as game and in certain seasons may be legally hunted. A license is required to hunt game animals. Some animals which are neither game species nor "protected" wildlife may be legally hunted without a license (ground squirrels, magpies).

Game species which may legally be hunted and taken in North America are divided into five main categories . . .

1. Ungulates or cloven-hoofed animals
2. Carnivores
3. Upland birds
4. Waterfowl
5. Small game

Techniques of Wildlife Identification

It takes practice to identify wildlife quickly and accurately. The more you practice, the better you will become at it. Take advantage of every opportunity available, at different times of year, to test and improve your skill at identifying the different species of wildlife. It is very helpful to spend time in the field practicing with someone who is experienced in identifying wildlife.

Many excellent wildlife identification field guides are available at libraries and bookstores. There is a list of field guide books at the end of this section. Zoos, game farms, museums of natural history and wildlife parks are excellent places to view wildlife at close range and compare different species of similar animals. Films, television programs and photographs in magazines are also useful in learning to identify wildlife.

Binoculars are extremely useful in making a positive identification, especially at long range. They will help see such details as colors, plumages and patterns of different species of wildlife.

DO NOT USE the telescopic sight on a firearm as a substitute for binoculars to identify wildlife. Remember—never point a firearm at anything you do not intend to shoot.

Each kind of wildlife requires a particular kind of place in which to live, a special "habitat" in which to survive. A hunter must learn which species of wildlife he can expect to find in each type of habitat. Most species of game move from one type of habitat to another on a daily or seasonal basis or under certain weather conditions. Elk will move from open grassy slopes to heavy timber to rest during the day or to seek shelter during a storm.

Maps in this section indicate the general geographic areas where certain species of game occur in North America. Within these ranges, distribution will depend upon the availability of suitable habitat.

Game Identification

In the sections which follow, the identification of various groups of game animals is outlined using descriptive text and illustrations.

The principal identifying characteristics of each animal are highlighted in each illustration. Illustrations depict animals as they appear in the fall. At other times of the year they may differ. These changes can be minor and involve only a slight color variation, or could be a complete change in appearance.

Animal tracks, antlers and the size and shape of scat (animal droppings) may also vary seasonally.

Big Game Cloven-Hoofed Ungulates

All wild ungulates classed as big game in North America are cloven-hoofed. This means that each hoof is split into two parts.

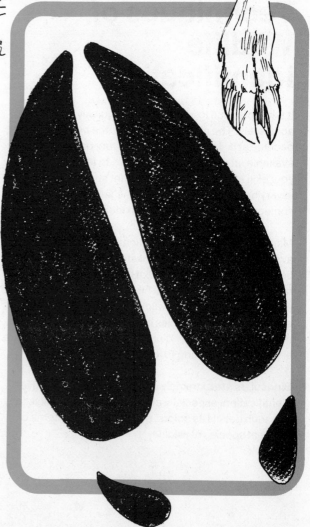

Evidence that a particular game species occurs in the area can be provided by certain signs such as tracks, droppings, feathers, shed antlers, trampled or browsed vegetation.

Spring is a particularly good time to practice identifying waterfowl. Often, they can be approached more closely than in the fall because they are actively involved in nesting and are reluctant to leave their nesting areas.

Also in springtime, male ducks display bright, breeding plumage, and they are unique and distinctive. You will be able to identify each species with certainty, observe its habitat and learn some of its behavior. Remember—it is imperative that you do not harass nesting birds or disturb their nests in any way.

Cloven-Hoofed ungulates are also "cud-chewers" or ruminants. They have a large four-chambered stomach and must chew their food twice to digest it. These animals first chew their food as they feed. Later when the animal is resting and undisturbed, it regurgitates the food, re-chews it and swallows it again.

Ruminants are usually classified as either browsers or grazers although some do both. Browsers are animals which eat mostly shrubs or woody vegetation. Most of the grazers' diet consists of herbs and grasses. Ruminants do not have upper front teeth. Instead, they have a tough pad against which the lower front teeth close.

Ungulates are divided into two major divisions—the horned animals and the antlered animals. Horned animals include bighorn sheep, mountain goats and antelope. Antlered animals include deer, caribou, elk and moose.

Horned Animals

Horns are formed by a sheath of hard, fibrous material developing over a core of solid bone on the skull. As new growth occurs, the old horn is forced up and away from the skull. In bighorn rams, this new growth is very apparent, appearing as a new section each year. These sections can be counted to determine the age of the animal. The bony inner core continues to grow also and determines the shape of the animal horn.

Horns appear on sheep and goats by the time they are six months old and are never shed. Rams grow massive horns that curve and spiral out from the head in contrast to the small sickle-shaped horns of ewes.

Antelope are unique horned animals. Like sheep and goat, their horn forms over a solid core of bone. However, unlike the horns of sheep and goat, antelope horns are shed and regrown each year. A doe antelope's horns are small and not readily noticeable.

Antlered Animals

Antlers are bone structures that grow up from short stubs on the top of the animal's skull. During growth, antlers are covered by a hairy skin called "velvet", which is richly supplied with blood vessels and nerves. Antlers grow during the spring and summer and are fully developed by fall. As growth progresses, the antlers become hard and bony. By rubbing its antlers against trees, the animal is able to remove the dead skin and polish the bony surface of the antlers. All antlers drop off or are shed each year and then regrown.

With one exception, only males of the deer family have antlers. Both sexes of caribou may be antlered but the antlers of the mature male are much larger than those of the female.

As the animal matures, each season's antlers tend to be larger with more points or tines. In an older animal, past maturity, antlers undergo a corresponding decrease in size. Antler growth is closely related to the health or nutritional state of the animal as well as both the quality and quantity of food available.

Moose, deer and caribou may begin to shed their antlers by late December. Elk and female caribou are usually the last to shed antlers. Shedding is caused by a change which weakens the area supporting the antlers.

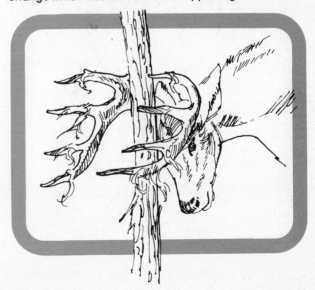

Antler Growth

Shed Antlers

Identifying Features
Mule Deer / White-Tailed Deer

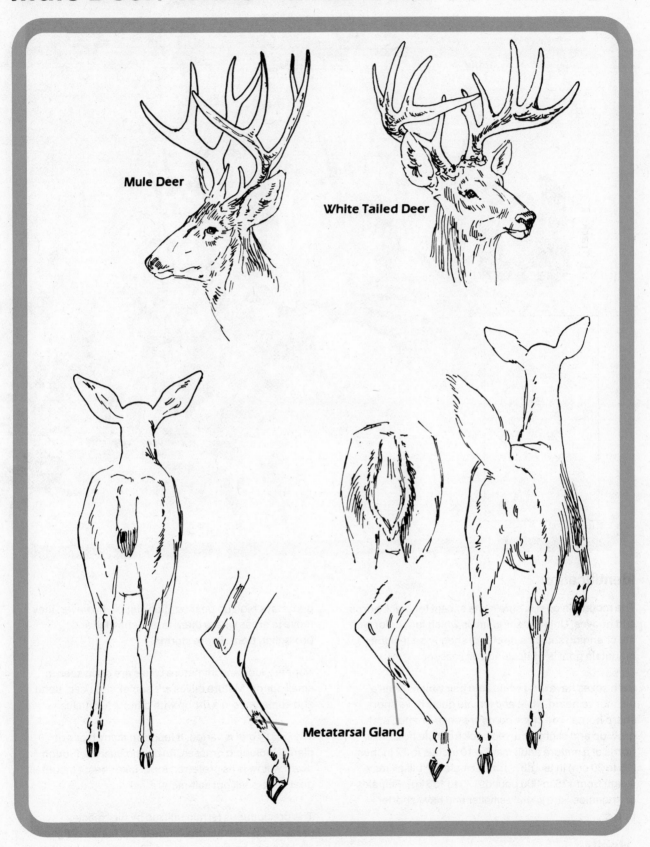

Mule Deer

White Tailed Deer

Metatarsal Gland

Mountain Goat

Billie

Tracks 2"

Identification

The mountain goat is pure white except for black horns and hooves. Unlike many animals which turn color with the changing seasons, the long, shaggy coat of the mountain goat is white during all seasons.

Both sexes have long white chin hair which forms a distinctive beard. Male and female goats have short, sharp horns. The black horns are cone-shaped and grow up and slightly curved back from the head. The horns of a mature adult may be 10 inches to 12 inches (25 to 30 cm) in length. An adult male or "billie" may weigh from 175 to 300 pounds (70 to 136 kg). Females or "nannies" are slightly smaller and have shorter horns.

Habits

Mountain goats generally stay on small home ranges high above timberline. Even in winter, the mountain

goat stays high up on mountain slopes; however, they move to areas where there is less snowfall and protection from severe storms.

Nannies, kids and immature billies are often seen in small bands. Mature billies are sometimes seen alone and sometimes in a group with other adult males.

The goat's diet is varied. It feeds on many types of plants, including grasses, forbs and bushes, though dwarf willow is its preferred food. Like sheep, mountain goats also seek out salt-mineral licks.

The precipituous terrain utilized by this species presents an obvious challenge to the hunter. While stalking can be arduous and difficult, the prospect of retrieving a trophy from some inaccessible rock ledge on a sheer cliff can discourage all but the most dedicated and determined hunter.

Bighorn Sheep

Ram

Ewe

Tracks 3½"

Identification

The color of the bighorn sheep may vary from dark to grayish-brown, but all have yellowish-white underparts. Seen from the rear, the bighorn's creamy-white rump patch around a small brown tail is very distinctive.

Both sexes have horns but the horns of the ewe are seldom longer than 12 inches (30 cm). The spiralled horns of an old ram are massive and may measure up to 45 inches (115 cm) along the front curve and weigh as much as 80 pounds (36 kg). Sheep horns are never shed. Each year the horns grow longer and are marked with a new growth section. The age of a bighorn is determined by counting the growth sections on its horns. Rams may weigh 300-350 pounds (136 to 158 kg); ewes generally weigh about 15 percent less.

Habits

Mountain sheep generally roam the high meadows and rock outcroppings of the mountains. They are usually seen in herds, segregated according to their sex or age.

A solitary sheep is usually sick or injured.

Sheep feed on mountain grasses, forbs, and small bushes such as the dwarf willow. They are attracted to salt-mineral licks.

In the fall, rams compete for the attention of ewes by violently crashing horns head-on, battering at each other until one gives up.

To obtain food during the winter, bighorns usually move to south or southwest slopes which are wind-swept and have little snow. Some herds will go down to the lower foothills and valleys and congregate on snow free areas or winter ranges.

The generally rugged but open terrain along with the difficulty encountered in approaching rams undetected, can make sheep hunting an arduous and challenging experience. Those few hunters who are successful will have expended a considerable effort in pursuit of their trophies.

Dall's Sheep

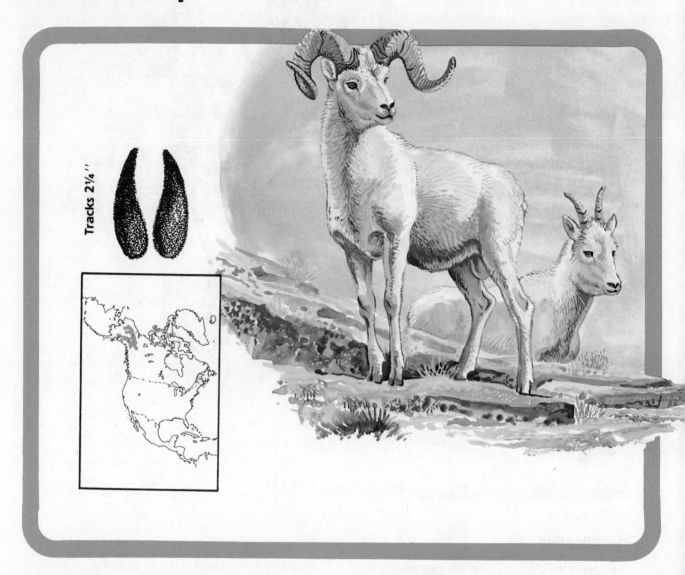

Tracks 2¼''

Identification

Dall's sheep and its subspecies, Stone's sheep, are known as "thinhorns". Dall's sheep are pure white at all seasons of the year. They have amber-brown horns which are much thinner than those of big-horn sheep. Though lighter in build than the bighorn, the thick pelage of Dall's sheep makes it look heavier.

Both rams and ewes have horns but those of the rams are massive at the base and taper to a fine tip. Outside diameters of the curls of adult rams average 10.5 inches (27 centimeters) and the average length of a full-curl ram's horn is 35.5 inches (90.1 centimeters). Horn sizes vary among different sheep populations. Mature ewes average 105 pounds (48 kilograms) in weight while rams average 180 to 220 pounds (82 to 100 kilograms).

Habits

Dall's sheep is found in Alaska, the Yukon, Northwest

Territories and extreme northwest British Columbia. These sheep generally are most active during daylight hours. Their senses of sight and smell are extremely acute.

In the fall, rams compete for ewes but after the breeding season, the rams and ewes spend the remainder of the year in separate groups; the ewes and their young stay apart from the rams. During the move to the spring range, yearling rams leave the groups of ewes and lambs to follow the older rams.

Hunting Dall's sheep is difficult chiefly because of the steep, alpine slopes, mostly above timberline, which the sheep inhabit. Hunting this species, where permitted by federal regulations, is a challenging experience.

Desert Sheep

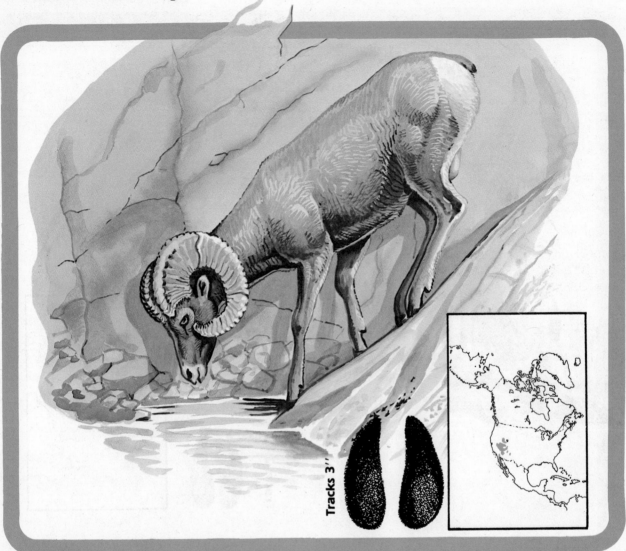

Tracks 3''

Identification

The desert sheep is a subspecies of the bighorn sheep. It inhabits the high, arid lands of southwestern United States and Mexico. Desert sheep are smaller, have larger ears and longer legs and are a darker color than the Rocky Mountain bighorn. White areas on the rump patch and along the rear edges of all four legs also are smaller in the desert sheep. The horns are proportionally larger and have a more open curl than those of Rocky Mountain bighorns.

Adult desert rams weigh 127 to 190 pounds (57.6 to 86.2 kilograms) and ewes weigh 74 to 114 pounds (33.6 to 51.7 kilograms). Average horn length is 40.3 inches (1022.8 millimeters) and the base circumference is 15.8 inches (402.3 millimeters).

Habits

The range of desert sheep extends from Southern California and Southern Arizona to Nevada and New Mexico.

Both male and female desert sheep mature at 18 months of age, although most ewes do not breed until 2½ years of age. The gestation period is 175 to 180 days. Lambing occurs from January to June and single lambs are the rule. Life expectancy for a desert bighorn is 10 to 12 years.

Desert sheep feed on a wide variety of grasses, sedges and forbs. In desert habitat, shrubs and trees are the major foods.

The terrain inhabited by desert sheep is extremely rough and barren, so hunters who seek this sheep must be in excellent physical condition and be able to withstand the harsh conditions of the animals habitat.

Stone's Sheep

Tracks 2¼"

Identification

Stone's sheep is a subspecies of Dall's sheep. It is darker-colored and has thin, amber-colored horns that in the ram spiral outward from the head. Body color varies from light gray to nearly black with the rump patch, underparts and rear edge of the hind legs white. Ewes are similar in color but smaller.

Stone's rams are very similar in size to Dall's sheep but have slightly larger horns which average 35.6 inches (90.5 centimeters) long. Horns of ewes are shorter, smaller and straighter and are oval in cross section while those of rams are more triangular. Average weight of Stone's rams is 220 to 230 pounds (100-104 kilograms).

Habits

Stone's sheep occupy a more limited range than Dall's sheep. They inhabit the western part of British Columbia and the southern part of the Yukon Territory. Their diet consists of sedges, bunchgrass, willow, moss and lichens. Herds of rams as well as those of mixed ewes and lambs move to higher feeding grounds for the spring and summer. At that time the sheep also visit mineral licks. They are heaviest and in their best condition at the end of fall.

Hunting Stone's sheep for most people is a once-in-a-lifetime experience. Breathtaking scenery and hard physical work are part of the hunt, and hunters must be in trim physical condition. Their equipment and clothing also must be suited to the long trip, thin air and rough footing of the high altitudes.

Antelope

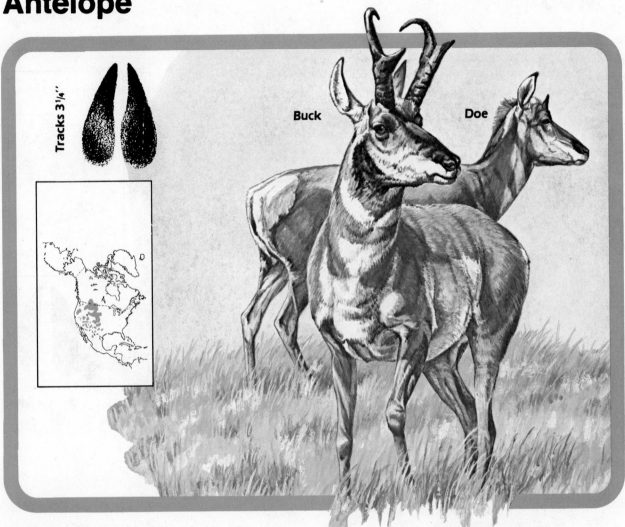

Tracks 3¼"

Buck

Doe

Identification

Pronghorn antelope are a tan color with a distinct dark muzzle and white cheeks. In both sexes, the flashing white rump patch is a reliable identification feature. Bucks have a black patch under the cheek.

Both bucks and does have simple pronged horns which are shed each year. The horns of the doe are generally shorter than the ears, while those of the buck are commonly longer than the ears. The black horns are erect, curved at the tip and have a single wide "prong" which faces forward. After the horns are shed, a skin covered bone core remains. New horns develop over this bony core.

Both buck and doe pronghorns weigh about 110 pounds (50 kg).

Habits

Small and resembling deer, the pronghorn is capable of running as fast as 50 miles (80 km) an hour.

The distribution of pronghorn antelope is shown in the

map insert above. Antelope populations can be drastically affected by severe winters or unfavorable spring weather conditions. Although herds generally remain in local areas, they may sometimes move a hundred miles or more to escape the effects of a very severe winter

Most antelope occur and are hunted on privately owned or leased public land. Management and harvest of the species is largely dependent on the cooperation of ranchers and livestock operators. Since antelope use rough browse and forbs such as sage for food, there is little competition with the cattle that share their range.

Antelope have extremely keen eyesight. Stalking the pronghorn can be a challenging exercise. The hunter must take advantage of hills and low ground for cover to remain hidden from view.

Antelope are curious animals and this characteristic can be used to advantage by the hunter. A handkerchief or piece of cloth left fluttering in the open may bring the antelope into range as it comes to investigate.

Moose

Bull

Cow

Tracks 5¼"

Identification

The moose is the largest member of the deer family in North America. Moose are dark brown in color and have prominent humped shoulders and a large nose. Bull moose, have large, heavy antlers which are wide, flat and rise slightly up and backwards. Hanging under the chin of both bull and cow moose is a piece of loose skin called a "bell".

Moose run with a distinctive long-paced swinging stride.

A mature bull may weigh 1000 pounds (450 kg) or more. Cows weigh 800-900 pounds (380 kg).

Habits

Moose are usually found in those areas shown in the map insert. They browse for food and eat mostly new growth from bushes and trees.

Increased access brought about by land development and associated road construction have increased the susceptibility of the species to hunting. Since moose are normally not a far ranging species, local populations may be quickly depleted because of easy access.

In winter, particularly in years of deep snows, moose tend to concentrate in the willows and shrubs along river valleys or other low areas. At other times of the year moose are solitary although calves will remain with cows for a year or more.

Recognizing this, wildlife managers sometimes create new moose habitat by controlling burning and clearing of old trees. During the fall mating, or rutting season, bull moose will grunt and bellow. Both bulls and cows will respond to a hunter's skilful imitation of these sounds.

Mule Deer

Doe

Buck

Tracks 3¼"

Identification

Mule deer are usually a brownish-grey in color. In late fall and winter their color tends to be more grey than brown. They get their name from their ears which are large and prominent like those of a mule. The mule deer's forehead is dark and its chin and throat are white. The tail of the mule deer is narrow and mostly white except for a solid black tip. The antlers of the buck are tree-like in appearance with tines that are forked or "Y" shaped.

Mule deer bucks average between 200 and 250 pounds (90 to 114 kg) but sometimes weigh as much as 450 pounds (205 kg). Does are much smaller rarely exceeding 160 pounds (75 kg).

When running, mule deer move with stiff-legged bounds with the tail held down.

Habits

Mule deer browse on a wide variety of brush and trees. They depend heavily on the early stages of forest

growth found at the forest edge. Regeneration of plants following forest fires and timber cutting can benefit the species.

Mule deer range further and travel more extensively than do white-tail. They are also more gregarious and will form larger winter bands or herds than white-tail.

Mule deer are more curious than the white-tailed deer and are often seen in open areas. When running for cover, they often pause to look back, giving the hunter a good opportunity for a standing shot.

During the fall rut or mating season bucks compete for and will mate with several does. The rattling of antlers at this time can attract bucks into the area.

Mule deer are most numerous in the mountains and foothills but are also found in many other areas of the west. In the semi-arid southwest they are usually found in the brush areas along rivers and coulees.

White-Tailed Deer

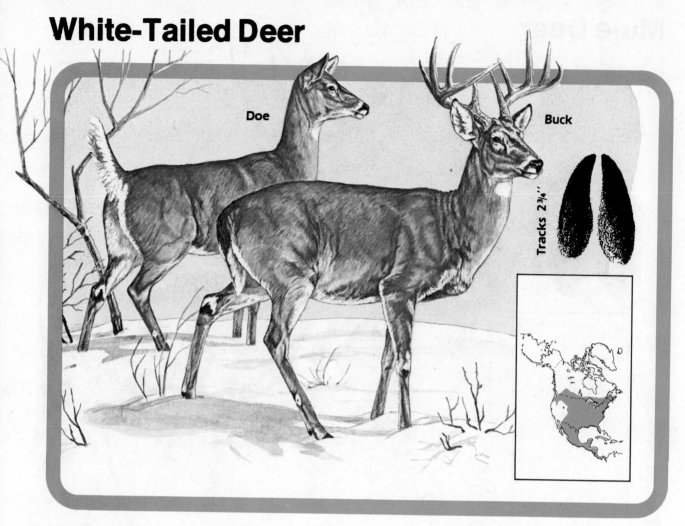

Doe

Buck

Tracks 2¾"

Identification

The body color of the white-tailed deer changes with the seasons varying from grey in winter to reddish brown in summer. However, the underside of its tail, from which this deer gets its name, is always white. When alarmed or running, the deer flashes its tail up showing this solid white underside.

The erect white tail and low running gait of the white-tail distingusih it from the mule deer.

Antlers of bucks grow up and forward with single, unbranched spikes or tines projecting up from the main beam.

An adult white-tailed buck may weigh from 100 to 300 pounds (70 to 140 kg). Does weigh between 85 and 130 pounds (45 to 60 kg).

Habits

Although some grasses and herbs are consumed, white-tail are mainly browsers feeding on such trees as chokecherry, birch, maple, dogwood and aspen.

Land clearing practices since the turn of the century

have enabled the species to spread into formerly unoccupied areas of the continent. White-tail populations have increased rapidly and they now far outnumber the mule deer.

They are generally solitary during most of the year. In late fall and winter small groups may be found on or near favoured feeding grounds. While white-tails do not normally form large winter herds, they may "yard up", in large groups in winters of very deep snow. Home range may vary from 40 to about 300 acres with total movement generally restricted to about one square mile.

White-tailed deer are most often seen in early morning or late afternoon when they move out on the edge of open areas to feed. At other times the white-tailed deer usually stays in thick brush.

Deer mate in late fall. Bucks compete for and, if successful, mate with many different does during this breeding season. Rattling a pair of antlers is a technique hunters use during rutting season to attract competitive bucks in the area.

Elk

Bull

Cow

Tracks 4¼"

Identification

Usually called "elk", this unique North American ungulate is also known as "wapiti", the Indian name for the species.

Elk are generally a yellow-brown color with a distinctive light, cream-colored rump patch. The head, neck and legs are darker than the rest of its body. Cows are more evenly colored than bulls. The antlers of the bull are large and sweep back and upward. A mature bull will have five to seven tines, or points, projecting from each main branch.

Bulls weigh as much as 1000 pounds (450 kg). Cows are smaller and usually weigh between 500 and 600 pounds (225 to 270 kg).

Habits

Elk are now found in those shown in the map insert above.

Because elk are grazers or grass eaters, they must often compete for food with domestic livestock. This is sometimes a serious problem in areas where the elk herds traditionally winter.

In severe winters when grazing is difficult, elk will browse for food and may even strip and eat trees.

Elk mate in early fall. A bull elk will gather together a small herd or harem of cow elk. As part of the mating ritual, other bull elk will challenge him for the herd. This challenge is heard as a high-pitched bugling sound unique to this species. The hunter, adept at imitating this call, may be able to attract a bull into shooting range from as far as a mile away.

During summer and fall elk inhabit open grassy areas at higher altitudes. In later fall, as snow covers these areas, the elk migrate down to lower wintering areas where shelter and food remain available to them. As snow disappears in spring, animals move back up to the meadows at higher altitudes.

Caribou

Bull

Cow

Tracks 4¼"

Identification

The caribou is divided into a number of geographic races, including the barren ground, mountain, woodland, and Quebec-Labrador types. The status is based more on geographic location of separate populations, but certain physical traits are apparent. The Alaskan Barren Ground is generally lighter in color with rather light antlers and long beams and tines. Mountain Caribou in British Columbia and Alberta are darker colored with heavier, more palmato antlers. Quebec-Labrador Caribou is even longer racked, and this woodland caribou is the heaviest and darkest, with generally a smaller rack. The distribution of these three races is illustrated in the insert map above.

Caribou are dark brown in color and have distinctive markings—a thick white neck mane, white tail and rump, and a light leg band just above the hooves. Caribou antlers are different than those of other deer in that one or two heavy tines called "shovels" extend outward from the animal's brow. The main stem of the antler extends back, up and out to the side. Caribou antlers

are flatter and wider than those of mule and white tailed deer. Cow caribou may also have antlers. If so they are smaller than those of the bulls.

Bulls weigh from 200 to 300 pounds (90 to 136 kg) and cows weigh about 25 percent less.

Caribou hunting is challenging due to the nomadic nature of the animals. The caribou is a stylish, impressive trophy animal with delicious meat. Once found, they are not so hard to kill as moose or elk, and can be dispatched by any cartridge that would handle a mule deer.

Habits

Woodland caribou are generally found in mature forests or tundra where they feed year round on lichens and ground mosses. Logging, forest fire and other removal of old forest growth may result in a decrease of caribou numbers. They are probably the most migratory of big game animals.

Big Game Carnivores

Carnivores are meat-eating mammals which have teeth along the sides of their jaws for cutting, or more accurately, "shearing" their food.

Bear teeth are different from those of other carnivores. The teeth of bears are similar to human teeth which are flat-topped and crush, rather than shear, food.

Certain of the large species of carnivores found in North America are classed as game animals. Included in this group are the cougar or mountain lion; black or brown bear; and the grizzly. Other carnivores such as the lynx, weasels, mink, fox and fisher are hunted or trapped for their fur.

In some areas of the country, certain carnivores are protected while in other areas they are not. Before hunting or trapping for them check the current game regulations for your area.

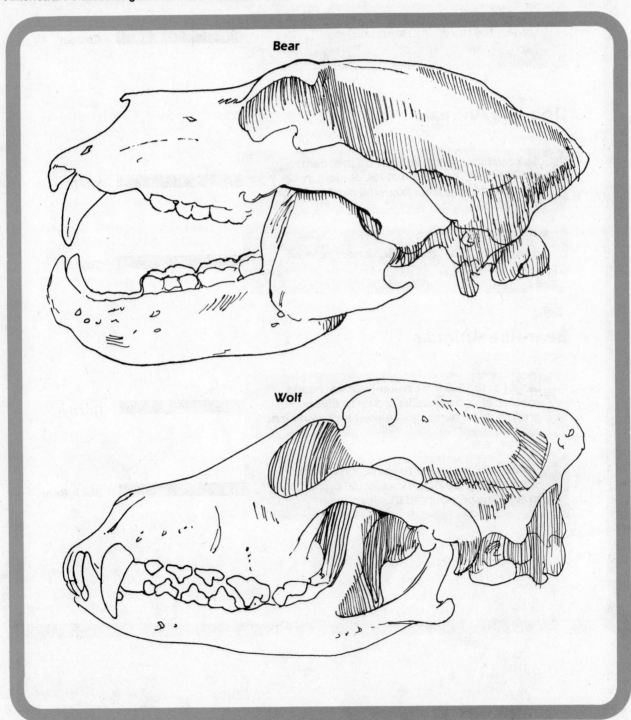

Bear

Wolf

Large Carnivores

The larger carnivorous forms of North American wildlife are generally recognizable as those that are cat-like, dog-like, bear-like or none of these. This short key will use these groupings to help you identify the animal in question.

Cat-like Animals

Large, (100 to 200 lbs.) long tail. — **Cougar**

Dog-like Animals

Color variable, ashy white through brown, grey to black, large, 75-100 lbs. or more, nose elongated blunt; thick powerful neck bushy tail. — **Wolf**

Smaller 20-40 lbs., thick hair, slender pointed nose, bushy tail. — **Coyote**

Bear-like Animals

Large (up to 1000 lbs. or more) massive head, concave of dished profile, brown to silvery grey, shoulder hump pronounced and prominent. — **Grizzly**

Smaller (300 lbs.) black to cinnamon brown, often with white chest patch, facial profile straight, no pronounced shoulder hump. — **Black Bear**

Grizzly Bear

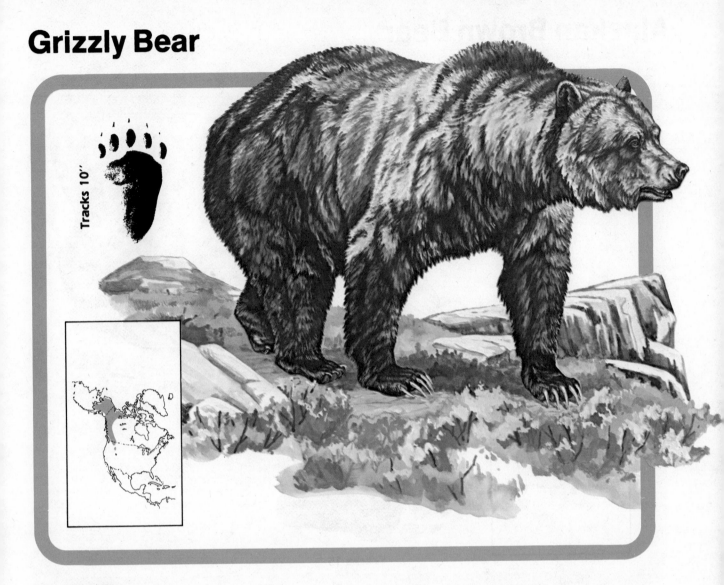

Tracks 10"

Identification

The grizzly bear is the largest and most powerful of the North American carnivores. A boar or male bear may weigh 500 pounds (227 kg) or more. Sows or female grizzly bears are usually smaller and weigh an average of 400 pounds (182 kg).

Grizzly bears are usually brown although their color may vary from blonde to black with a grizzled "silver tip" appearance. The pronounced shoulder hump, large muscular body and massive head with its dished, concave profile are all distinctive characteristics.

The grizzly's tracks will show claw markings, distinguishing them from the tracks of black bears which usually do not.

Habits

The grizzly is found in remote mountainous and foothill terrain. The distribution of the grizzly bear in North America is shown in the insert map.

Grizzlies live on roots, berries and other vegetation as well as small mammals. They also eat dead animals and will occasionally kill a large ungulate.

Young grizzlies can climb trees easily but the adults have more difficulty in doing so because of their long claws.

Grizzly bears are inactive during the winter when they hibernate in dens. Hibernation usually extends from December to March.

In most regions of North America grizzly bear populations have decreased substantially in recent years and where that has occurred this species is considered endangered.

Grizzlies, particularly males or boars, are solitary animals but cubs will remain with the female or sow for up to three years. Cubs and sows with cubs cannot be hunted. The home range of a grizzly may be from three to ten square miles (eight to 26 km²) but bears have been known to range up to 50 to 60 miles (80 to 100 km).

Alaskan Brown Bear

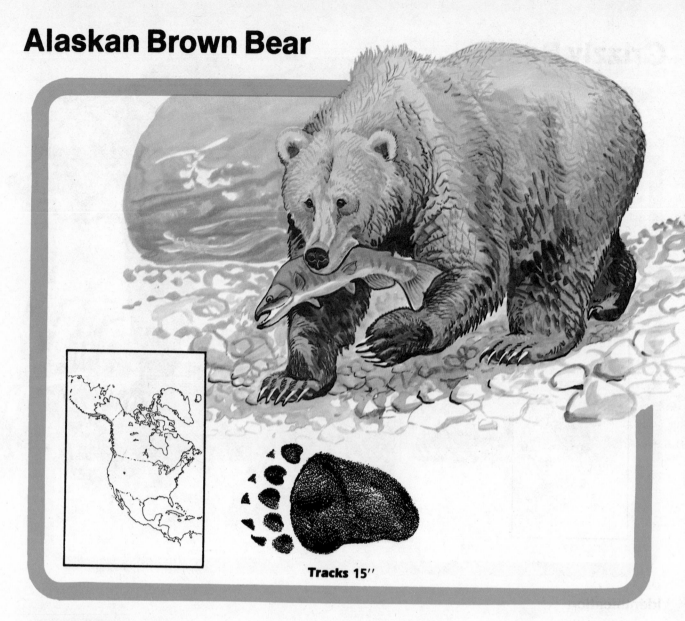

Tracks 15″

Identification

The Alaskan brown bear's pelage varies from very dark brown to blond, but lacks the silver-tipped guard hairs of the grizzly bear. This species has a short tail and shorter and less curved claws on the forefeet than a grizzly. The brown bear's powerful build, prominent, heavy canine teeth and aggressive disposition make it a potentially dangerous game animal. The adult male is 8 to 9 feet long (240 to 270 centimeters) and as high as 4½ feet (135 centimeters) at the shoulder. His weight may be from 800 to 1200 pounds (340 to 510 kilograms), although occasional individuals will exceed 1,500 pounds (695 kilograms).

Habits

The Alaskan brown bear ranges over most of Coastal Alaska. Their habitat includes slopes where deep grass and spongy moss grows as well as upland timber areas.

The brown bear is omnivorous. It feeds heavily on salmon and trout in the coastal areas. Other foods include berries, carrion, fresh green grass, eggs of nesting waterfowl and large animals such as caribou.

The breeding season is from spring to midsummer. Females breed in alternate years, some only every third year. The gestation period is six to eight months, and one to three cubs, which are unable to see at birth, are born during the last weeks of the hibernation period.

Most of the movements of the brown bear are related to obtaining food. This animal is a fine swimmer, but it is not noted as a tree climber because of its size and the nature of its claws which are not adapted to climbing.

Although the Alaskan brown bear has very poor eyesight, it has a keen sense of smell. Individuals who hunt brown bears must be in top physical condition and be prepared to cope with the animals keen sense of smell.

Black Bear

Tracks 7''

Identification

Black bears usually have a deep glossy black coat, but other color variations including cinnamon and brown occur. The average weight for adults of either sex is 250 to 300 pounds (115 kg to 135 kg). In the fall, bears have a heavy accumulation of fat and may weigh considerably more.

The smaller size, absence of a shoulder hump and straight or slightly bulging facial profile help to distinguish black bears from the grizzly.

Unlike the grizzly, black bear tracks do not normally show claw marks.

Habits

Black bear are found in forest regions and foothills. Like the grizzly bear they feed on roots, berries, other vegetation, insects, fish, small mammals and the flesh of dead animals. The distribution of the black bear in North

America is illustrated in the insert map.

Black bears are excellent swimmers and tree climbers. In early winter they den up and emerge the following spring.

Homes ranges for black bear vary from one to 16 square miles (three to 40 km²) but individuals may travel 60 miles (80 km) or more.

Black bears are normally solitary animals but cubs remain with the sow for a year or more. Cubs and sows with cubs cannot be hunted.

In some areas, black bears have become dependent on humans for their food. The bears feed on garbage, oat crops and raid beehives. In such instances bears can become a problem of economic importance and can be a hazard to human safety.

Wolf

Tracks 4³/₄″

Identification

Wolves are the largest wild members of the dog family in North America. The wolf's long, dense fur is usually a pale ash or creamy white color often overlaid with shades of brown or grey though color may vary from black to white.

An average adult wolf weighs about 100 pounds (45 kg) with little difference in either size or appearance between sexes. Both look much like a German Shepherd dog.

It is sometimes difficult for the inexperienced hunter to distinguish a wolf from a coyote. Wolves are larger, heavier and more powerful in appearance than the coyote. The wolf's nose is bluntly pointed; the coyote's nose is elongated and sharply pointed.

Habits

At one time wolves were found throughout much of

North America. The regions in which they are now found are shown in the map insert.

The number of wolves in an area varies from year to year depending on the availability of game to feed on and the territorial needs of the pack. The size of a pack may vary from four to 20 or more. If there is sufficient food to sustain the pack, it will be large. When the food supply is low, the pack is smaller.

In summer when the pups are young, wolves seldom travel far and are usually seen alone or in pairs. Packs of wolves travelling and hunting together occur most often in winter. At this time, packs may range and travel over territories of 100 square miles (260 km) or more.

Wolves may eat birds and small mammals but they depend primarily on the large ungulates such as deer, elk and moose for food.

Coyote

Tracks 2½''

Identification

The coyote is similar in appearence to the wolf but is smaller. Weighing about 30 pounds (14 kg) it is more slender in body shape and has a more sharply pointed nose than the wolf.

Coyotes are generally a tawny grey with lighter, yellowish legs, paws, muzzle and ears. Paler or much darker animals are also frequently seen.

Habits

The coyote is the most numerous of the wild dogs in North America and is found over much of the United States as shown in the map insert. It is an extremely adaptable animal and has adjusted to many of the changes that man has made to its habitat.

Considered a pest by many landowners, the coyote has survived poisoning, bounty programs and other efforts by man to erradicate it.

Over most of its territory the home range of the coyote is about 10 to 15 square miles (25-40 km). Adult males may travel much further.

Coyotes are usually seen alone or in pairs with their young. Primarily a carnivore, rodents make up about 75 percent of a coyote's diet. They also eat eggs, birds, insects, snakes, frogs, fish and some vegetation.

Cougar

Tracks 3"

Identification

The cougar or mountain lion is the largest of the North American wild cats. Males average 160 pounds (75 kg) but may weigh as much as 250 pounds (115 kg). Both sexes look alike, but the female is smaller, weighing about 100 pounds (45 kg).

Cougars are tawny brown with a light colored belly. Their long, round, black-tipped tail is the most reliable identification feature.

Habits

Cougars are now found mainly in the mountain and foothills region as shown in the insert map. Cougars are solitary animals occupying firmly established territories

of up to 40 or 50 square miles (105 or 130 km).

Cougars have no special breeding season but young are usually born in spring and late summer.

A cougar's prey is primarily deer or elk but other small mammals and birds are also eaten.

Although cougars are more active at night than during daylight, they rely more on sight and hearing than on scent for locating and stalking prey.

Cougars are usually hunted using dogs to track and tree the animal.

Upland Game Birds Introduction

The upland game birds of North America include the wild turkey, several varieties of grouse and grouse-like birds, quail, partridges and pheasant. All are "gallinaceous" or chicken-like ground birds with heavy bodies, short, heavy bills and short rounded wings. And all but three—the ring-necked pheasant, chukar partridge and Hungarian partridge—are native species.

In no one area of the country are all of these game birds to be found. The ruffed grouse, ring-necked pheasant and bobwhite quail are the upland game birds of the East and Midwest. The other grouse and grouse-like species are found in the Northwest and over much of Canada. The several species of western quail occupy the mixed woodlands of the Pacific Coast (California and mountain quail) and the drier regions of the Southwest (scaled, Gambel's and Harlequin quail).

The most nearly ubiquitous of the upland game birds in the United States is the wild turkey. Currently, huntable populations are found in most states due mainly to the reintroduction of wild turkeys through the release of birds trapped from wild flocks into suitable, unoccupied habitat.

Each of these upland game birds offers its own challenge to the upland game hunter.

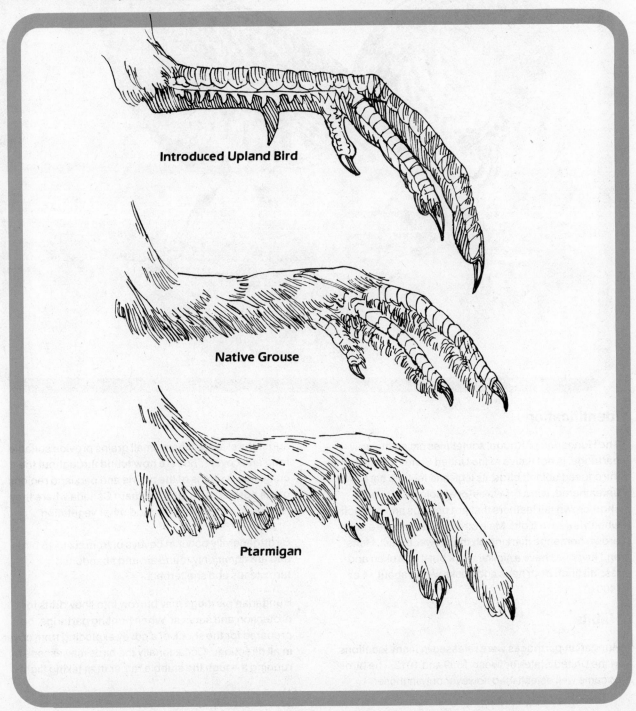

Introduced Upland Bird

Native Grouse

Ptarmigan

Hungarian Partridge

Detail of Scapular Feathers

Female   Male

Identification

The Hungarian partridge, sometimes called the gray partridge, is not native to the United States. Like other introduced upland birds, its legs and feet are bare and unfeathered. It is a brownish-grey colored bird with short brown tail feathers that are obvious and distinctive when viewed in flight. Male birds or cocks have a solid brown horsehoe marking on their lower breast. Hens and juveniles have a similar mark but it is broken and less distinct. Both hens and cocks weigh about 14 oz. (400 g).

Habits

Hungarian partridges were released in many locations in the United States between 1899 and 1912. The birds became well established however only in those agricultural areas where small grains provide suitable food and cover. They are now found throughout the cultivated portions of the prairie and parkland regions of the northern U.S. and southern Canada where they feed on grain, grass seeds and other vegetation.

Birds generally occur in coveys of from six to 15 birds and are commonly found around abandoned farmsteads and shelterbelts.

Hungarian partridge may burrow into snowdrifts for protection and survival. When hunting partridge, be prepared for the shock of a covey exploding from cover in all directions. Occasionally the birds may escape by running through the stubble rather than taking flight.

Ring-Necked Pheasant

Indentification

The male or cock, ring-necked pheasant is unlikely to be confused with other game birds because of its brilliant markings. The cock is brightly colored and has a distinctive red eye patch on an iridescent purple head. The long, tapered tail may reach 15 to 18 inches (38 to 45 cm). Cocks are also distinguished by the presence of pointed spurs on the back of each scaly, unfeathered leg. The spurs on the adult cock are longer and more pointed than those of the young cock.

The hen pheasant is a more subdued, pale-brown color and resembles the sharp-tailed grouse. The tail of the hen pheasant is longer than that of the sharp-tailed grouse.

A mature cock weighs about three pounds (1300 g); a hen weighs about two pounds (900 g).

Habits

The ring-necked pheasant is not native to North America. It was introduced to the U.S. in 1818 and released in other areas later. Pheasants spread rapidly, and quickly occupied much of the corn and grain producing areas of the U.S. and southern Canada. A number of color variations of ring-necked pheasants have also been released. Occasionally, hunters may take birds of this species that vary in color from dark black to almost white.

Pheasants can usually be seen feeding in open cultivated fields during early morning and late afternoons. Young birds feed exclusively on insects while older birds feed on grass seeds and grain.

One of the wariest birds, pheasants normally take advantage of ground cover to run from the approaching hunter. Hunters using a well trained dog will have a decided advantage over those who do not. When forced to flush, cocks take to the air with a noisy cackling sound.

Unlike the Hungarian partridge, pheasants will not burrow into snow drifts for protection during severe blizzards. Unless they can find dense cover, they may perish.

Willow Ptarmigan

Winter Plumage

Indentification

In winter, the willow ptarmigan is white except for a black tail, beak and eyes. In this winter plumage both sexes look alike and cannot readily be distinguished.

A cock in summer plumage has a brown head, neck and breast. The female is mottled yellowish brown. White wings are good field marks for summer identification.

Mature adults of both sexes weigh slightly over one pound (450 g). Ptarmigan have a completely feathered foot.

Habits

Willow ptarmigan are found in the northwest and northen provinces of Canada and in Alaska. Although willow ptarmigan gather in large flocks in fall and winter, they are difficult to find. Against the snow, their white plumage makes them almost invisible. They are easiest to locate while perched in bushes. Ptarmigan are extremely curious and can often be closely approached. The willow ptarmigan feeds extensively on buds of the willow although its diet also includes alder, birch buds and twigs, and the flowers of many plants. Much of their range is not easily accessible, and therefore the species is not heavily hunted.

White-Tailed Ptarmigan

Winter Plumage

Identification

In both summer and winter plumages, both sexes are similar in appearance. In summer, they are a mottled brown with patches of black and white. Unlike the willow ptarmigan, they are completely white in winter except for the black beak and eyes. The white tail of this species is thus a distinctive feature of both summer and winter plumages.

Both sexes weigh the same at about 10 to 12 ounces (280-340 g).

Habits

White-tailed ptarmigan are found in the higher mountain regions of several western and northwestern states, the northwestern provinces of Canada and in Alaska. Their diet consists of flowers, berries, buds and twigs.

Throughout the summer they occur in small family groups. By fall, the family groups have merged into larger flocks. Protective coloration and seasonal changes in plumage add to the difficulty of hunting ptarmigan. Perhaps because of their reliance on this excellent camouflage, they may be easily approached before flushing.

Because of the relative inaccessibility of its habitat, it is not often seen and is rarely taken by hunters.

Ruffed Grouse

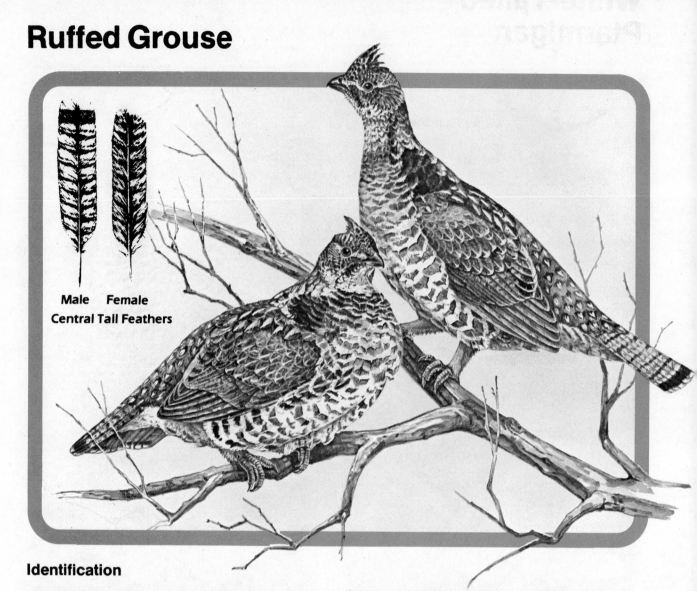

Male Female
Central Tail Feathers

Identification

The ruffed grouse gets it name from the "ruff" of dark feathers on each side of its neck. The ruff is more prominent on the cock than the hen. The bird's color may be either grey or reddish brown; both color phases are common. The head is crested. The long, slightly rounded, fan-shaped tail is barred and has a broad, black band near the outer edge. The band on the cock's tail is usually complete and distinct, while on the hen it is broken by central unbanded tail feathers. An adult cock weigh about one and a half pounds (680 g), slightly more than the mature hen.

Habits

Ruffed grouse are found in northwestern New England, the eastern and Great Lakes states and most of Canada. They usually occur in association with aspen and willow cover or in areas of mixed hardwood and conifers and occasionally they may be found around cultivated fields.

The low muffled "drumming" of the ruffed grouse is a familiar spring sound in North America. As part of the mating ritual display, the cock finds a suitable "drumming log" within the established territory.

Standing on the log, he beats his wings, slowly at first, then much more rapidly. The drumming sound so produced can be heard for up to half a mile.

Family groups, after remaining together through summer, break up and disperse in the fall. Through most of the hunting season the birds are found singly, but some regrouping takes place in early winter.

In summer and fall, the diet of the ruffed grouse is green plants such as clover and a variety of seeds and berries. In winter, when these foods are scarce, the ruffed grouse eats poplar and willow buds.

Ruffed grouse are a popular game bird over most of their range in the U.S. While they can be approached quite closely in areas where they are not hunted extensively, grouse are much more wary when they are subjected to constant hunting. Their abrupt erratic flight provides a challenge to even the most practised hunter.

Ruffed grouse are the only native grouse that may be commonly found in urban areas.

Sharp-Tailed Grouse

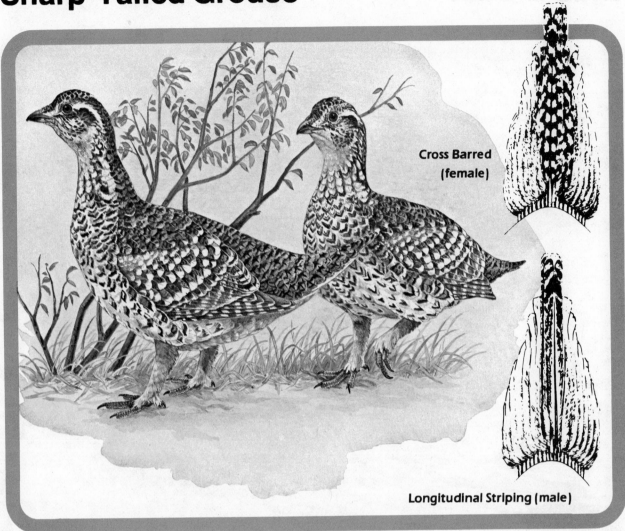

Cross Barred (female)

Longitudinal Striping (male)

Identification

Sharp-tailed grouse are a pale-brown color, speckled with black and white. In flight, the short, white tail distinguishes this bird from the ruffed grouse. Mature birds of either sex weigh slightly less than two pounds (900 g).

The cock has a yellow comb over the eyes. Two sharp, tail feathers extend beyond the rest of the short tail. The markings on these feathers differ between the cock and the hen. These tail feathers give the sharp-tailed grouse its name.

Habits

Sharp-tailed grouse are found in the northern states of the mid-west and in central Canada. They prefer brush to open areas. Patches of bush scattered throughout grain and grassland areas are ideal habitat.

In early fall the birds are found in small family groups. By late fall they have merged into large flocks containing as many as 100 birds.

The sharp-tailed grouse may often be seen feeding in grain or stubble fields in early morning. Later in the day they commonly roost and sun themselves on bales, stacks or in trees. On cold frosty mornings, they often sit motionless in tall trees or bushes.

When flushed, birds usually make a "clucking" sound as they fly away.

Hunters who are aware of the importance of traditional "dancing grounds" to the species can use this knowledge to help locate sharp-tail flocks during the hunting season.

Blue Grouse

Identification

Blue grouse have no well defined markings but their slate grey color, solid black tail and large size are distinguishing features. Adult birds commonly weigh two and three-quarter to three and a half pounds (1250 g - 1590 g). Their color is darkest on the back and brownish on the wings. The long, square tail of the blue grouse is usually tipped with a band of grey.

In some areas, blue grouse and spruce grouse share similar habitats and the two are sometimes confused. Blue grouse are much larger than spruce grouse and have a white or greyish throat and plain grey breast. Both sexes of blue grouse are similar in appearance.

Habits

Blue grouse are found in the mountains and foothills of the western United States and northwestern Canada. These birds winter in the high coniferous forests near timberline. They eat the needles and buds of trees, and when available, the leaves of shrubs. In spring, blue grouse move down to lightly wooded mountain valleys or to aspen forests of the foothills to nest and raise their young. Family groups break up before fall. The birds make their way back, singly or in small groups, to the high coniferous forests where they will stay all winter.

During the fall, blue grouse are usually found alone at the high elevations near timberline. For this reason, few hunters pursue them. When flushed, they will invariably fly downhill.

Spruce Grouse

Identification

Spruce Grouse cocks have a black breast and white spots on the sides. The hen is a dark rusty brown. Both sexes have black and white barring on the breast and a tail tipped with pale brown.

Franklin's grouse, a variety of spruce grouse, does not have this brown tipped tail. It has white spots on the sides of the base of the tail.

Adults of both sexes weigh about one and a half pounds (545 g)—about half the size of the Blue grouse.

Habits

Spruce grouse are found throughout most of the coniferous forests of the northwestern United States and Canada. In spring and summer they feed on the ground, eating insects, leaves and berries. In fall and winter, they feed almost exclusively on conifer needles. This change in the birds' diet strongly flavours the meat.

When flushed, the spruce grouse will usually flutter up into a spruce tree and sit, relying on its coloration for camouflage and protection. Because of its apparent lack of fear, the spruce grouse is often called "fool hen".

Spruce grouse are generally found singly or in small groups during the hunting season. They frequent lower elevations than do blue grouse.

Sage Grouse

Identification

A large upland bird, a mature cock may weigh as much as seven pounds (3000 g). Hens are smaller at three to four and a half pounds (1300-2000 g). Both sexes are similar in appearance. Their backs and wings are brownish-grey while their undersides are lighter in coloration. The large, black abdominal patch and long pointed tail feathers of equal length are distinctive characteristics of the species.

Habits

Distribution of sage grouse is restricted to the sage brush plains of the northwestern and western regions of the United States. During the fall, sage leaves and buds form the major part of its diet, imparting a strong flavour to the flesh. At other times of the year, a variety of plants and insects are also eaten.

Sage grouse use traditional dancing grounds for their elaborate spring mating ritual. By late fall, small family groups will have merged into large coveys and can usually be found on or near these same dancing grounds.

Sage grouse will often try to elude the hunter by running through the sage rather than taking flight.

Their large size and striking appearance make the sage grouse a handsome trophy.

Bobwhite Quail

Identification

The sexes are very different in appearance. The Bobwhite is a chunky reddish-brown bird with a gray tail. A mature bird will measure 9.5–10.6 inches. (24-27 cm) in length. Males have a white throat and eye-stripe that extends back to the base of the neck, and a black collar. Females have buffy colored plumage on the chin, throat and eye-stripe in place of the white coloration of the males. The females also lack the black collars of the male.

Habits

The range of this bird covers virtually all of the eastern United States north to southern Maine, New York, southern Ontario, Central Wisconsin, and Central Minnesota, west to Wyoming, Colorado, and New Mexico and south to parts of Mexico. The bobwhite quail is mainly a farmland game bird. Ideal habitat for this species is a combination of cultivated fields, brush and weed patches and wood lots. Brushy fence rows and brush piles are conducive to high populations. The food of Bobwhite includes seeds, such as lespedeza, corn, ragweed, sorghum, and oats, supplemented with small insects.

Breeding begins as early as January in the south, and early March in the north. The average clutch size is 12-15 eggs, and the incubation period is 23 days.

Bobwhite quail is the number one game bird of eastern and southern United States. The exploding flush of coveys and singles and fast darting flight make this bird a challenge for the hunter.

Western Quail

Mountain Quail

Scaled Quail

Valley Quail

Gambel's Quail

Mearn's Quail

Identification

The Valley or California quail is the most popular game bird among the different western quail due to its abundance, its readiness to fly, and its habit of holding to a point. Native to the foothills of the Southwest, this quail has been introduced to many parts of the West. Males and females have distinctive, forward curved crests; the belly plumage contains black scaled markings.

The Gambel's quail which is slightly smaller and lighter in weight than the California, inhabits the Sonoran Desert regions of the southwest. Recognized by its black belly, it is similar in outline to the Valley Quail.

Scaled or Blue Quail share some habitat with the

western Bobwhite, and gets the name "cottontop" from the white tip of its short crest. It prefers arid grassland habitats.

The Mountain Quail are larger than the other western quail; and prefer the brushy clearings of the Pacific Northwest. The straight-plumed crest of this species is distinctive.

Mearn's or Montezuma Quail, also known as Harlequin or Fool Quail is found in Texas, New Mexico and Arizona. It tends to freeze and remain motionless until nearly stepped on using its black, spotted feathers as camouflage.

Chukar

Identification

An Adult Chukar may range from 13-15.5 inches (31.5-40 cm) in length. The sexes are identical in appearance, with white or buffy-white cheeks and throat separated from the breast by a black collar that passes through the eyes. The upper parts are grayish brown to olive, while the under parts are shades of black and chestnut. The bill, feet, and legs are reddish, and mature males have slight spurs on the legs.

Habits

The first introductions of this game bird to the United States were made in the mountains of the western states. The present range of the species is from southern British Columbia southwards through eastern Washington, Oregon and California and east through Nevada, Idaho, Utah, western Colorado and Montana. Chukars are found on talus slopes, cliffs and bluffs with surrounding sagebrush and cheatgrass. These birds can survive bitter cold temperatures but not large amounts of snow.

They feed on grasses, especially cheatgrass, seeds, grains and insects.

Breeding takes place between February and mid-March. The egg clutch is from 14 to 20 eggs and the incubation period is 24 days.

Hunting this game bird requires top physical condition and excellent shooting ability.

Wild Turkey

Gobbler

Hen

Identification

The wild turkey is the largest upland game bird in the United States. An adult bird weighs between 13-20 pounds (4.8-7.4 kilograms) with some exceptional individuals weighing 24 pounds (8.9 kilograms) or better.

Plumage of the wild turkey is basically the same in both the hen and gobbler, with shades of dark brown, brown and black predominant in the feathers. The most colorful part of the turkey is the head, which varies from hues of bluish gray and red, to neutral gray and purple; the appearance of the variations depending on the season and the degree of excitement of the bird.

The legs, wings and tails are proportionately longer than those of domestic turkeys. Spurs of about 1 inch (2.5 centimeters) in length are characteristic of adult gobbler. The second most prominent characteristic of the gobbler is the beard; beards, however, occasionally are found on hens, too. The beard of a mature gobbler will measure 3.5-9 inches (8.7-22.5 centimeters.)

Habits

Mixed hardwood forests with scattered openings are ideal habitats for wild turkeys. The exact composition of the forest will vary with the geographical location. Recent experiences with transplanting wild turkeys into new areas show that this species also flourishes in woodlot and stream valley type habitat. As a result of modern game management practices and game restoration programs, healthy, huntable and self-sustaining turkey populations now exist in almost every state in the nation.

The primary food of the wild turkey is nuts, berries, seeds, tubers and insects. Wild turkeys are polygamous. Mating takes place in April and May. Hens lay 4 to 10 eggs in ground nests and incubate them for 28-30 days before they hatch.

Depending on the state, turkeys of either sex may be hunted in the fall and gobblers only in the spring. Certain states have just a spring gobbler season, during which the gobblers can be hunted only by calling so that nesting hens are not disturbed.

Waterfowl Introduction

This large and important group of game birds includes the wild ducks and geese that occur in North America. They nest each spring, raise their young over the summer, and migrate south in the fall. Many other waterfowl are non-game, protected species, which include: loons, grebes, whooping cranes and a wide variety of shore birds. Care must be taken not to confuse these birds with the migratory game birds that may be legally hunted—ducks and geese. Coots, rails and snipe are other game birds that may be taken by the hunter.

All hunters have a responsibility to correctly identify their targets before shooting. When hunting waterfowl, the ability to accurately identify and recognize each species can provide additional enjoyment to the hunt.

What to Look for

Several characterists can be used to distinguish one waterfowl species from another. Among these are habitat, action, color, shape and sound.

Habitat

Each species of waterfowl usually has special habitat requirements. Being familiar with these requirements will aid you in identifying waterfowl in their various habitats. Some species, such as dabbling ducks like the mallard, prefer shallow marshes and small potholes. Others, such as the canvasback, prefer deeper bodies of water. Mallards and pintails are usually the only ducks feeding in stubble or on swathed grain fields.

Action

Wing beat and flocking behavior are also useful identification characteristics. Flying mallards and pintails form long lines and have a slow wing beat characteristic of pond or dabbling ducks. Canvasbacks fly in shifting, waving lines and have a fast wing beat common to diving ducks. Shovelers and teal flash by in small bunches.

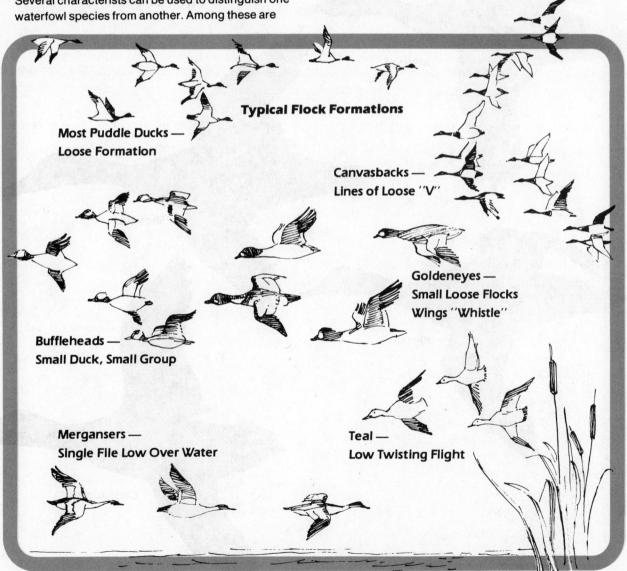

Typical Flock Formations

Most Puddle Ducks — Loose Formation

Canvasbacks — Lines of Loose "V"

Goldeneyes — Small Loose Flocks Wings "Whistle"

Buffleheads — Small Duck, Small Group

Mergansers — Single File Low Over Water

Teal — Low Twisting Flight

Color and Shape

Waterfowl silhouettes will vary, showing large or small heads, broad or narrow bills, fat or slender bodies, long or short tails. Colors can be seen at close range. Depending on light conditions, birds may not appear in their true color, but color patterns can be a key to their identity.

Sound

The sound of their voice or the noise made by their wings when in flight may both be used as aids in identifying waterfowl. Wings of goldeneye whistle in flight while those of most other ducks do not. Not all ducks quack. Many whistle or squeal. Experience can help you to identify waterfowl from their sounds.

Green Wing Teal

Mallard

Shoveler

Pintail

Canvasback

Eclipse Plumage

Most ducks shed their body feathers twice each year. Nearly all adult drakes lose their bright plumage after mating and for a few weeks resemble adult females. This hen-like appearance is called the "eclipse plumage." Return to breeding coloration varies between species. Blue-winged teal and shovelers retain eclipse plumage into the winter.

Wing feathers are only shed once a year. Wing colors are always the same and are the most reliable feature for identifying a duck in hand.

Plumage of juvenile ducks early in the fall is very similar to that of the adult female. During the fall, juvenile males start to change to their first adult breeding plumage. Therefore, a juvenile drake mallard with green feathers on the head may be confused with an adult drake coming out of eclipse plumage.

Age Determination

A simple technique for accurately identifying juvenile ducks is to closely examine the tips of the bird's tail feathers. If any of the feathers have notched tips, the bird is a juvenile. By late fall however, these juvenile tail feathers will have molted and been replaced by pointed feathers. Other methods will then be needed for accurate ageing.

Drake Full Eclipse

Emerging From Eclipse

Fall Plumage

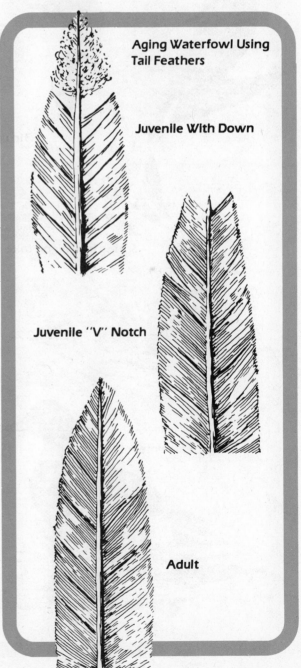

Aging Waterfowl Using Tail Feathers

Juvenile With Down

Juvenile "V" Notch

Adult

Ducks

Based on their habitats ducks are commonly separated into two broad groups—puddle ducks and diving ducks.

Puddle Ducks

Puddle ducks usually frequent shallow marshes and river edges rather than large lakes and bays. They usually feed by "dabbling" or dunking their heads in the water. They ride high on the water and jump directly upward when taking off.

The colored wing patch, called the "speculum", is generally iridescent and bright.

Ducks feeding on croplands will probably be puddle ducks because this group can walk and run on land. Their diet is mostly vegetable.

Puddle Duck Characteristics

Tip up to feed, rarely dive.

Spring into air on take-off.

Generally have metallic speculum.

Legs near center of body.

Usually swim with tail held clear of water.

Smaller foot than in diving ducks.
Hind toe not lobed.

Diving Ducks

Diving Ducks usually frequent large, deeper lakes and rivers. They feed by diving, often to considerable depths. To escape danger they can swim a considerable distance underwater. They may then emerge only far enough to expose their head or bill before submerging again.

Wing patches of diving ducks lack the iridescence of those of puddle ducks. To compensate for their short tails, they use their large paddle shaped feet as rudders in flight. These are often visible when they are flying. When launching into flight, most of this group run or patter along the water before becoming airborne. Because their wings are small in proportion to their bodies, they have a rapid wingbeat in comparison to that of puddle ducks.

Their diet is chiefly fish, shellfish, and aquatic plants. The flavor of their meat is often different than that of puddle ducks, which feed on grain.

Diving Duck Characteristics

Dive completely underwater to feed.

Patter along surface for some distance to take-off.

Usually swim with tail close to water.

Legs set near rear of body.

Hind toe lobed.

Key to Waterfowl

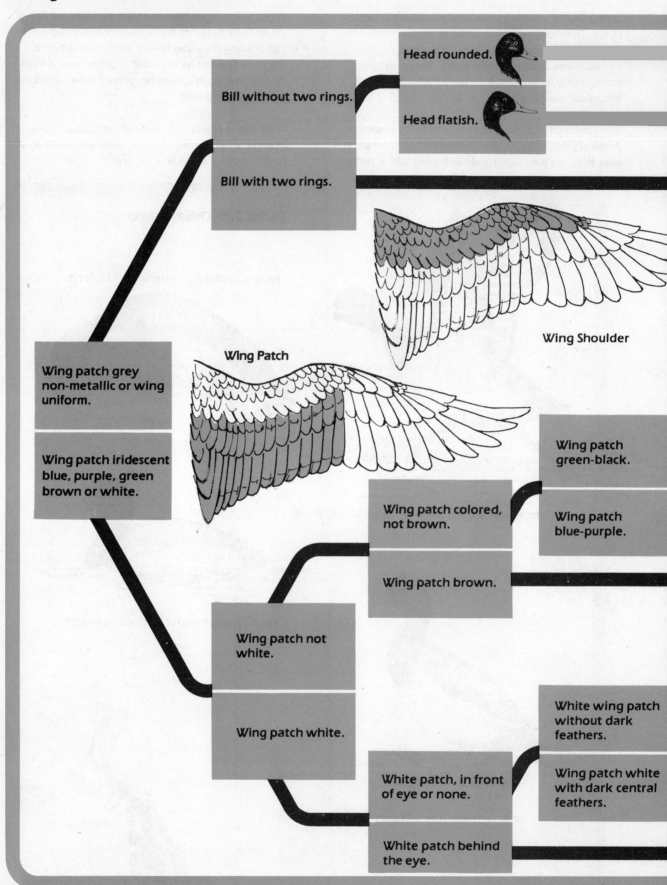

Bill without two rings.

Head rounded.

Head flatish.

Bill with two rings.

Wing Shoulder

Wing patch grey non-metallic or wing uniform.

Wing Patch

Wing patch green-black.

Wing patch iridescent blue, purple, green brown or white.

Wing patch colored, not brown.

Wing patch blue-purple.

Wing patch brown.

Wing patch not white.

White wing patch without dark feathers.

Wing patch white.

White patch, in front of eye or none.

Wing patch white with dark central feathers.

White patch behind the eye.

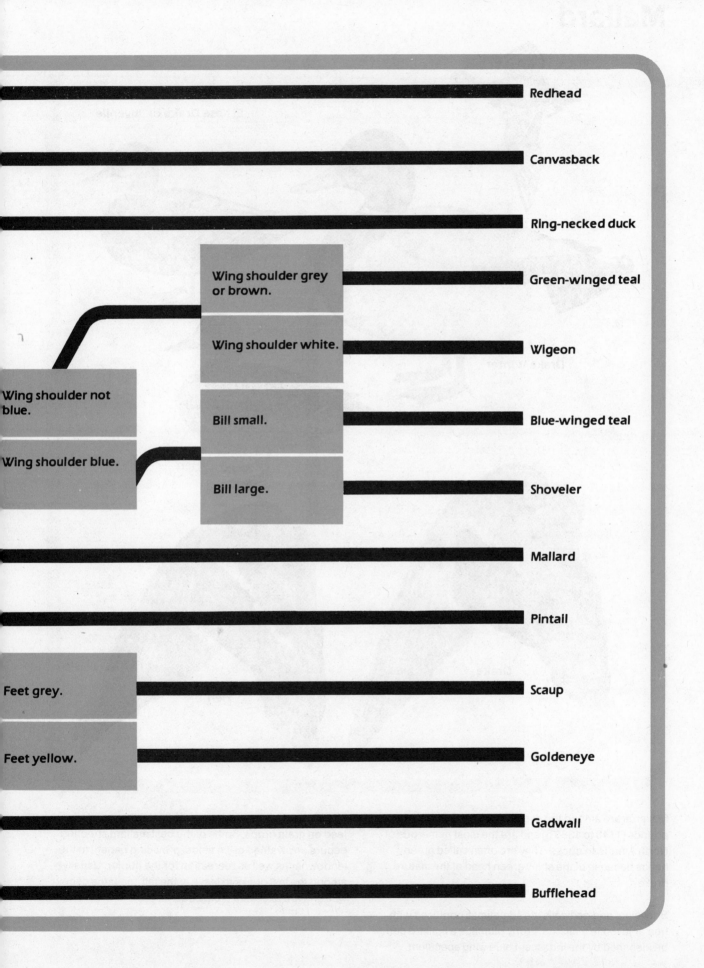

Redhead

Canvasback

Ring-necked duck

Wing shoulder grey or brown. — Green-winged teal

Wing shoulder white. — Wigeon

Wing shoulder not blue.

Bill small. — Blue-winged teal

Wing shoulder blue.

Bill large. — Shoveler

Mallard

Pintail

Feet grey. — Scaup

Feet yellow. — Goldeneye

Gadwall

Bufflehead

Mallard

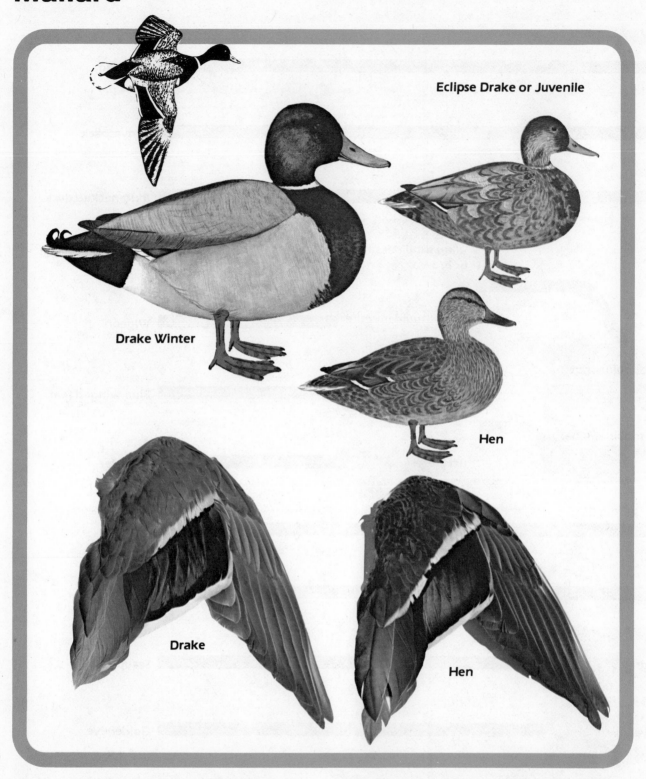

Eclipse Drake or Juvenile

Drake Winter

Hen

Drake

Hen

Mallards are among the largest—two and a half to three pounds (1140 to 1360 g) and are the most numerous of North American ducks. They are often called green heads because of the shiny green head of the mature drake.

Shovelers and gadwalls are sometimes confused with hen or juvenile mallards. In any plumage a mallard can be identified by the iridescent blue wing speculum.

Mallards and pintails are the only ducks that regularly feed on grain crops. Some of the best mallard shooting occurs on swathed grain fields, providing benefit to the landowner as well as recreation for the hunter. Usually among the last ducks to leave in the fall, mallards decoy well and are excellent table birds.

Pintail

Drake Winter

Drake

Eclipse Drake or Juvenile

Hen

Hen

A large duck weighing from two to two and a half pounds (910 to 1140 g), the pintail is smaller than a mallard, and, not as numerous. In flight or in hand, the long neck and sharp tail are distinctive characteristics. The colorful male breeding plumage is seldom seen in fall birds since pintails are a relatively early migrant and most will have moved south from the northern nesting grounds by late October.

Like the mallard, pintails feed on swathed grain and can cause considerable crop damage. Field shooting provides excellent sport and helps to protect crops. Pintails, with slightly darker flesh than the mallard, are an excellent bird.

Green-Winged Teal

Eclipse Drake or Juvenile

Drake Winter

Hen

Drake

Hen

Green-winged teal are the smallest of North American ducks, seldom exceeding 12 oz. (340 g). Their erratic, twisting flight and small size give the impression of great speed and a difficult target. Fall birds are mottled brown with little indication of the colorful male winter plumage. Although green-winged teal are a late migrant, most will have left before the latter plumage develops.

The species can easily be confused with blue-winged teal, particularly in the early plumages. In hand the iridescent green wing speculum provides positive identification.

Cinnamon Teal

Drake Winter

Eclipse or Juvenile

Hen

Drake

Hen

This duck, true to its name, has cinnamon body plumage. The lesser and middle coverts of the wings are sky blue, while the greater coverts form a distinct white bar. The body of a mature Cinnamon Teal is about 16 inches (40cm) in length and approximately 15 ounces (.4 kg.) in weight. The small size of this species and its twisting, turning flight creates the illusion of great speed.

Small compact flocks of Cinnamon Teal commonly fly low over the marshes, often taking the hunter by surprise. It is more vocal than most ducks; its high pitched peeping and nasal quacking is heard commonly in the spring. The Cinnamon is among the first to migrate in the fall.

Blue-Winged Teal

Eclipse Drake or Juvenile

Drake Winter

Hen

Drake

Hen

One of three species of teal in North America, the blue-wing is a small duck weighing slightly less than a pound (450 g). Their small size combined with a rapid, twisting, flight pattern can provide a challenge to the hunter. Numerous in early fall, the species are among the earliest to leave, some migrating as far as South America. By late September, blue-wings are fat, plump and in spite of their small size, a table bird to be desired.

Shoveler

Drake Winter

Eclipse Drake or Juvenile

Hen

Drake

Hen

The shoveler is a small to medium bird of up to about one and a half pounds (680 g) in weight. The large spoon-shaped bill is a feature distinctive enough to make identification of the shoveler or "spoonbill" relatively quick and easy. Mallards are similarly colored, but lack the large bill. Shovelers are not particularly wary and their steady, direct flight makes them a relatively easy target. This species usually migrates early in the fall. As table birds they are not highly regarded perhaps because of the large numbers of snails and aquatic insects used as food.

Gadwall

Eclipse Drake or Juvenile

Drake Winter

Hen

Drake

Hen

Gadwall is a medium sized duck of up to two pounds (910 g). They are common early in the fall. By October, most have migrated south. Hunters may confuse gadwall with hen mallards. The white-wing speculum is unique to this puddle duck species and in hand should be positive identification.

Gadwall fly in small compact flocks and are easily decoyed within range. After a shot they will often circle back and make a second pass over the hunter and his decoys.

Wigeon

Eclipse Drake or Juvenile

Drake Winter

Hen

Drake

Hen

Wigeon is a medium sized duck seldom exceeding two pounds (910 g). They are also often called "baldpate" because of the white crown on the head of the winter male. In addition to wing markings, the bluish bill and feet are reliable characteristics for identification. Even in early plumages, males will generally show some trace of the green eye mask so prominent in breeding plumage. Wigeon are largely vegetarian in their diet and remain in the northern nesting grounds until mid-fall — often well into October. Usually seen in small tightly bunched flocks, their flight is fast and erratic.

Bufflehead

Eclipse Drake or Juvenile

Drake Winter

Hen

Drake

Hen

The bufflehead is one of the smallest diving ducks; it weighs no more than a pound (450 g). Like the goldeneye, the bufflehead nests in tree cavities. Bufflehead are late fall migrants, occasionally remaining all winter on open water areas where available. Late in the fall, males are seen in their distinctive winter plumage. The large iridescent head with a fan-shaped, white patch behind the eye is outstanding. Typical of ducks that eat animal food, their flesh may have a rather strong taste.

Red Head

Eclipse Drake or Juvenile

Drake Winter

Hen

Drake

Hen

The red head is similar in appearance to the canvasback but smaller, two to two and a half pounds (910 to 1140 g). It has a rounded head shape rather than the flat sloping forehead of the canvasback. Hens may be confused with lesser scaup but they lack the yellow eye and white wing speculum of that species.

Red heads are fairly common in localized areas, particularly around the larger sloughs or lakes. The species is an early migrant and birds are generally gone from the northern nesting areas by late October.

Canvasback

Eclipse Drake or Juvenile

Drake Winter

Hen

Drake

Hen

One of the larger ducks, canvasbacks weigh up to three pounds (1360 g). The large head with its straight flat profile is a reliable identification feature and may be used to distinguish the species from the redhead. Reputed to be the fastest of our ducks, the canvasback has a very rapid wing beat typical of a diving duck.

Canvasbacks are no longer common throughout North America. Hunters are most likely to encounter these ducks when around deeper lakes and reservoirs.

The canvasback is an excellent table bird, considered by many to be gourmet fare.

Lesser Scaup

Drake Winter

Eclipse Drake or Juvenile

Hen

Drake

Hen

These are medium sized ducks of up to two pounds (910 g). As with other diving ducks, scaup are more likely to be encountered around larger areas of deeper water.

Although it closely resembles the ring-necked duck, scaup do not have the white ring on the bill characteristic of the ring-neck. Both sexes have blue colored bills, hence the common name "Blue Bill" is often used for the species. Scaup migrate at about the same time as canvasbacks, when ice begins to cover the lakes.

Flying in tight compact groups, the species decoys will provide hunters with excellent shooting opportunities.

Ring-Necked Duck

Eclipse Drake or Juvenile

Drake Winter

Hen

Drake

Hen

Similar in habits and general appearance to the scaup, ring-necked ducks are slightly smaller in size, averaging a little over one and a half pounds (680 g). In hand, the white band on the bill and pearly grey speculum will confirm identification.

Ring-necked ducks are essentially vegetarian in their food preference.

Black Duck

The Black Duck has a dark sooty appearance with a lighter head. Its feet are orange to reddish orange. Average length of the Black Duck is 24 inches (60 cm). It attains a weight of 2¾ pounds (1.2 kg.). It is a very shy and wary bird, being considered the elusive of all the ducks.

Often seen in the company of mallards, Black Ducks frequent the salt marshes and ocean much more than mallards along the Atlantic Coast.

Their flight is swift, and they usually travel in small flocks. Their white wing lining in contrast to very dark body plumage is a good identification clue for the waterfowl hunter.

Black Ducks inhabit the Eastern Seaboard, primarily the Atlantic flyway, and to a lesser extent the Mississippi flyway.

Wood Duck

Drake Winter

Eclipse or Juvenile

Hen

Drake

Hen

The wood duck is one of the most colorful of the waterfowl. It is a medium sized bird ranging in weight up to 1½ pounds (.7 kg.). Its about 15-18 inches long (38-46 cm). It has dark cinnamon-colored iridescent plumage on the chest with white flecking. The sides are tan and the belly is white. The male has distinct white stripes on its head crest. The eyes are red, the bill is short and multicolored, and the feet are a dull gold color.

The wood duck is found along all flyways, but primarily in the Atlantic and Mississippi flyways. It frequents wooded streams and ponds and nest in natural tree cavities. It can fly through thick timber with speed and ease. It feeds on acorns, berries and grapes. In the flight, wood ducks make a rustling, swishing sound with their wings.

Oldsquaw

Drake Winter

Eclipse or Juvenile

Hen

Drake

Hen

The Oldsquaw is a slim, brightly plumaged sea duck, smaller than the scoters or eiders. A mature Oldsquaw will be about 20½ inches (52 cm) long weigh around 2 pounds (.9 kg.).

Flocks of this sea duck fly swiftly and low, constantly changing formations. The species is found along both coasts and in the Great Lakes area. It is one of the most vocal of the ducks. The plumage of the drake is black and white. The chest, breast, hindback, and wings are black; the foreback, sides, flanks, belly and lower tail coverts are white. The head is white with a large brown-black patch extending from the cheek down the side of the neck.

Common Merganser

Drake Winter

Eclipse or Juvenile

Hen

Drake

Hen

This species, which is larger than the red-breasted merganser, is one of the largest of our ducks. It will weigh about 3¼ pounds (1.5 kg.) and attain a length of about 25 inches (65 cm). The merganser has a black back, and a white belly, chest and sides tinted with pink. It has a greenish, black head and a narrow, serrated dusky red bill.

It is among the last of the waterfowl to migrate south. Flocks fly in a "follow-the-leader" style, low over the water. Their flight is strong and direct. It is an excellent bird to hunt, although the flesh may have a fishy taste.

Red-Breasted Merganser

Drake Winter

Hen

Drake

Hen

Eclipse or Juvenile

Slightly smaller than the common merganser, the Red-breasted Merganser attains a length of about 23 inches (59 cm), and an average weight of about 2½ pounds (1.1 kg). The drake has a black back, a grayish white belly, and an orange chest speckled with black. It has a greenish black head with narrow, serrated dusky red bill. Hens have chestnut-red heads and gray body plumage.

This species winters most abundantly in coastal waters including the Gulf of Mexico, and to a lesser extent, the Great Lakes area. Its flight is strong and direct, usually low over the water. It is difficult to distinguish in flight from the common merganser.

Hooded Merganser

Eclipse or Juvenile

Drake Winter

Drake

Hen

This is the smallest merganser. A mature bird measures about 18 inches (46 cm) in length and weighs about 1½ pounds (.6 kg.). It has the characteristic black back with two prominent black bars between its chest and sides. The belly plumage is white, while the sides are tan. The drake has a dark, greenish black head with a distinct hood and fan-shaped white area. Its eyes are yellow and the bill is black, narrow and serrated.

Hooded Mergansers often are seen in pairs, or very small flocks. Their short rapid wingstrokes create an illusion of great speed. This species winters in the inland waters of all coastal states; very seldom is it seen in salt-water.

Scoters

Hen

Surf Scoter

Drake

Surf Scoter Hen

Common Scoter Drake

Common Scoter Hen

White-Winged Scoter

Eclipse or Juvenile

Drake

Hen

Scoters are large, chunky sea ducks weighing 2.2-3.5 pounds (1-1.6 kg). Plumage of the males is solid black while the females tend to be dusky brown, as are the immature birds. Three species, common, surf, and white-winged, may be seen together during the winter months on both Atlantic and Pacific coasts, flying in long lines just over the waves. The Common Scoter is smallest.

The male is recognized by the butter-yellow knob on its black bill, and by its dark eyes and feet. Other male scoters have pinkish feet, light or whitish eyes, and their bills are brightly colored with yellow, pink, white, black and red markings. White-winged scoters have white patches in the secondary wing feathers, and surf scoters are recognized by their outlandish bill configurations.

Scoters are most often hunted from a boat. They are easily attracted to decoys, and their rapid flight offers a challenging shoot.

Eiders

Pacific Eider

King Eider

Spectacled Eider

Common Eider

Drake

Hen

Steller's Eider

Drake

Hen

Largest of the sea ducks, Eiders range in weight from 2.9-5.5 pounds (1.3-2.5 kg). The male plumage is black and white, while that of the female is rich brown, barred with black. The Common Eider breeds in coastal areas of the arctic region, together with others of its races, the Pacific and Northern Eiders.

King Eiders, the most majestic of this group, breed in the northern Arctic and winter in the north Atlantic and Pacific coasts, as far north as open water permits. The distinctive black-bordered orange lobes on the bill that cover the front of the face of the male are characteristic of this species.

The Spectacled Eider, named for the circular feather formations and markings about its eye, is slightly smaller than Common or King Eiders, and is one of the rarest of North American ducks.

Its breeding range is along the Bering coast in northwest Alaska. Steller's Eider is the smallest of the Eiders, breeding along the coast of Alaska and wintering along the Alaska panhandle and the Aleutian islands. The male's chestnut breast and belly plumage and the more mottled plumage of the female make this eider more distinctive than the others.

Common Goldeneye

Eclipse Drake or Juvenile

Drake Winter

Hen

Drake

Hen

One of the larger diving ducks, goldeneye may weigh up to two and three quarter pounds (1250 g). In flight, their distinctive wing-whistling sound has earned them the name of "whistler" by many hunters.

Goldeneye, along with the much smaller bufflehead, are unique in their nesting requirements. Both species nest in tree cavities such as abandoned woodpecker holes. Goldeneye are commonly found on deep water bodies in wooded areas.

Geese

Geese and ducks are waterfowl, and as such they have many similar characteristics. For example, both have webbed feet, similar feathers, and bills of similar shape.

However, geese are generally larger than most ducks. Geese have no eclipse plumage and both sexes are identical. Most species of ducks mature by their first spring while geese take two years or more before reaching maturity.

Pairs of geese mate for life and both the gander and the goose help to rear their young.

Canada Goose

A number of varieties of Canada geese occur in North America. All are similar in appearance but vary considerably in size. The smallest are under three pounds (1400 g) with others weighing as much as 12 pounds (5500 g). Both sexes look alike, having a dark head and neck with a distinctive white chin strap.

The distinctive honking of these geese can often be heard even before the "V" shaped flocks are sighted. Although they may nest in various regions, a great many Canada geese nest in Canada and migrate south during the fall.

In the fall, geese feed on grain stubble or summer-fallowed fields. Usually twice a day, in the morning and afternoon, they fly from nearby water bodies to these feeding areas. If undisturbed, flocks will usually return to the same location for several days. Goose hunters try to "spot" or locate feeding flocks. When the geese are finished feeding and have gone back to the water, pits are dug or blinds constructed near the feeding areas. Decoys are set out and the concealed hunters wait for the geese to return.

White-Fronted Goose

Juvenile

Adult

White-fronted geese are medium sized geese, weighing about six pounds (2700 g). The name is derived from the white band around the face at the base of the bill of adult birds. Both sexes are similar in appearance. They are also called "speckle-bellies" in reference to the irregular black marking across their bellies. Juveniles are more uniformly grey and lack the bill and belly markings.

White-fronts migrate south during the fall. Flocks are generally large and "V" shaped. Their call, a high pitched cackling or laughing sound can easily be distinguished from the deep honking of Canada geese.

Feeding habits and hunting techniques are similar to those of other geese.

Snow Goose

Snow goose are all white with black wing tips and weigh about six pounds (2700 g). Both sexes are similar in appearance but juveniles are more grey than white. Head and neck feathers are usually stained with rusty orange. A dark color phase of the snow goose exists and is called a blue goose. At one time it was believed to be a separate species.

Care must be taken not to confuse snow geese with protected species like whooping cranes, pelicans or swans. Swans lack the black wing tip. Cranes trail legs and feet in flight. Pelicans fly with the neck curved and have a distinctively large head and bill.

Snow geese fly in loose "V" formations but the lines tend to shift and change. A popular common name for the species is "wavey". The call of the snow goose is a distinctive, shrill, high pitched "yelp" rather than a honk.

Snow geese are generally less predictable in their feeding habits than Canada geese and will not usually return to the same feeding area for extended periods.

Flesh of snow geese is much darker than that of other geese.

Ross's Goose

In appearance Ross's geese are very similar to snow geese but smaller (about four pounds or 1800 g). In hand, their size and lack of a "grinning patch" distinguish them from snow geese.

While not a plentiful species, there has been a significant increase in the number of Ross's geese in North America in the last 25 years.

Brant

Black Brant　　　　　　　　**Atlantic Brant**

The Brant is a small, dark goose with a short neck and lacking the white cheek of the Canada. The average size of this bird is 3¼-4 pounds (1.5-1.8 kg.); the normal length is 24-25 inches (6.2-6.4 cm).

The Black Brant is a small dark western goose very similar in plumage, size, habits and voice to the Brant but it has black rather than gray plumage on the breast and belly. Black Brants winter south to Baja California.

The Brant winters from Virginia northward. Its flight is swift, with irregular and changing flock patterns. Hunters must take special care to heed the Federal regulations regarding the seasons and bag limits of this species.

Whistling Swan

Drake　　　　　**Juvenile**

Whistling swans are now common and increasing. They are hunted by special permit in certain Western States. The adult is entirely snow white, with black feet. Its bill is black with a yellow spot in front of the eye.

Mature birds are very large, weighing from 11-20 pounds (5-9 kg.) and measuring 48-57 inches (120-140 cm.) in length. In flight their long necks and their black bills and feet are evident. They have a loud and musical call.

Migratory Birds Introduction

The migratory game birds of North America are a heterogenous group made up of rails, gallinules, woodcock, snipe and doves. The rails and gallinules are long-legged wading birds which favor the shallow shorelines of lakes and freshwater and saltwater tidal marshes. The snipe and woodcock are inhabitants of inland marshes and bogs and the doves are pigeonlike birds of the open woods and fields.

Rails, and to a lesser extent gallinules, were hunted fairly heavily along the Eastern Seaboard in former years. Hunters either waded the marshes or had a guide with a light skiff pole them through, flushing the birds ahead of them. The best shooting occurs when the tide waters flood the marsh grasses so that the birds are not able to run and must fly when the hunter approaches.

Today, the woodcock and doves are the most hunted of the migratory birds. Southward migrations of woodcock take place in late September and October. Alder thickets and bottomlands barren of birds one day may fill up overnight. The same thickets which yield scores of birds one day also may empty overnight as the birds move on, leaving only their tell-tale, chalky white droppings to mark their passing.

Because of their habit of roosting and feeding in flocks and traveling flyways to and from their roosting and feeding areas; their speed and agility on the wing; their abundance and their wide distribution, doves are by far the most heavily hunted of the migratory birds today. They are the most difficult and challenging of this group of game birds for the hunter to down.

Mourning Dove

The mourning dove is a handsome streamlined bird with a small head and long pointed tail. Adult birds measure about 11-13 inches (27.9–33 cm) in length. The plumage is slaty blue above and reddish fawn below, with large white spots on the tail. It has a black spot behind the eye, a black bill, and the legs and feet are red. Its flight is direct and rapid and its wings produce a noticeable whistle when the bird is in flight.

The mourning dove is found throughout the continental United States, southern Canada, and Mexico. Some populations of mourning doves are migratory, while others remain in the south during the summer and winter. This dove frequents woodland areas, farm fields and residential areas. It feeds primarily on small grains and weeds.

Nesting takes place from March or April to September. Nests are flimsily constructed and are usually located in trees and shrubs, although occasionally a dove will be found nesting on the ground. The normal clutch size is 2 eggs, but on rare occasions a nest will contain 3. Incubation requires 14 days.

The mourning dove is a popular game bird in some states while it is protected in other states. The hunting of mourning doves provides fast and challenging shooting.

Band-Tailed Pigeon
White-Winged Dove

Band-tailed Pigeon

White-Winged Dove

The name band-tailed is derived from the wide, pale gray band across the tail bordered with black. Band-tails are somewhat longer than domestic pigeons reaching a length of about 13 to 15 inches (350–380 mm). They have slightly shorter wings and are lighter in weight than the domestic pigeon. They are blue-gray in color with a white neck crescent above an iridescent nape.

The habitat of the band-tailed pigeon is in the oak-conifer forests of Western North America. It is a migratory bird and remains in flocks during the winter.

The breeding cycle ranges from mid-May to late August. The female lays one or two eggs per clutch, but may lay and hatch several clutches a year. Incubation requires 18 to 20 days.

This species feeds primarily on small grain and berries.

The white-winged dove is more chunky in build and larger in head size than the mourning dove. A band of white across the middle of each wing is an identifying field mark. The eyes of this species have a bright red iris with a patch of blue skin surrounding it.

The white-winged dove is a sub-tropical species, found primarily in southern Texas and Arizona. It is more likely to be found in dense, thicket-like forests of subtropical trees, and thorny shrubs.

Nesting occurs in late May through early June; the normal clutch size is two eggs. Incubation is complete in about 14 days.

White-winged doves feed primarily on small grain and also the fruits of certain cactus plants.

Common Snipe

The Common Snipe reaches an average length, including the bill, of 10.4-11.6 inches (265-295 mm). The bill is 2.5 inches (64 mm) long, flesh colored, though darkening to a deep brown. An adult bird weighs between 2.5-5.5 ounces (70-155 gr.). The legs and feet are greenish-gray to yellow green. There are broad, blackish, sometimes flecked, crown stripes and also a dark stripe through the eyes and a dark patch on the lower cheek.

The snipe is a migratory bird. Its summer range extends across the central southern region of the United States up to the coast of Alaska, Canada, and California. The winter range runs across the central southern United States as far south as the northern areas of South America.

Breeding takes place in early spring. Clutches consist of four heavily blotched, buffy eggs. The incubation period for the eggs is 19 days.

The diet consists mainly of animal matter, largely insects, earthworms, crustacea, arachnids, and mollusks. Supplementary foods include plant matter, such as seeds, fibers and grit.

The main habitat areas are wetland areas, near bogs and swamps. Snipe frequently are bagged by waterfowl hunters.

Woodcock

The woodcock is a stocky, brown bird with short, rounded wings which enable it to fly in dense cover. The color pattern of its plumage blends with the dry leaf pattern of the forest floor. Distinguishing characteristics are the darker bands on the top of the head, short legs, large eyes set high and far back on the head and a long bill. The bill approximately 2.5 inches (6.4 cm) in length is used for probing the soil for earthworms and grubs. A mature woodcock weighs .3-.4 pounds (125-190 grams).

Although classified as a shorebird, the woodcock is physically adapted to a forested habitat. Its distribution covers the forested regions in the eastern half of the United States. It is a migratory bird, nesting in the northern regions and wintering in their southern areas.

The woodcock prefers forested areas of alder, aspen or birch trees bordering fields or recently logged areas.

The primary diet of the woodcock is earthworms, supplemented with beetle, and fly larvae and some plant life.

Mating which is preceded by a unique courtship display occurs in mid-spring. Nests are located within a few yards of brushy field edges. The nest consists of a well-formed cup on the ground and usually contains about 4 eggs. Incubation takes 21 days.

Hunting this bird with a well-trained bird dog is an experience enjoyed by at least half a million hunters today.

Rails

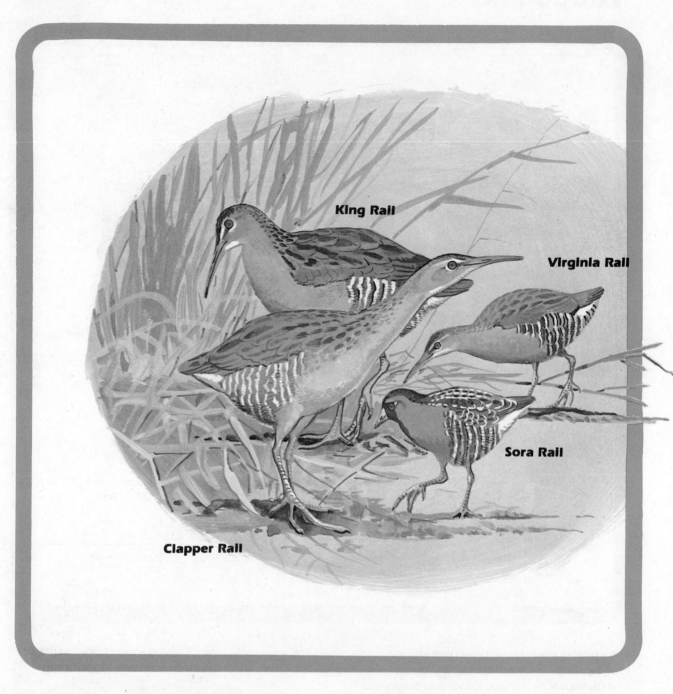

King Rail

Virginia Rail

Sora Rail

Clapper Rail

The two larger rails, the King and the Clapper, inhabit coastal marshlands. Nearer the size of small ducks, (18-22 inches) they are very easily overlooked. They are able to swim and dive as well as hide in the thick marsh grasses. The Clapper rail is pale tan or grayish brown with white-barred flanks and a down-curved bill. It prefers tidal marsh bordered by salt or brackish water. The King is a similar but more brightly-colored, reddish rail which inhabits freshwater marshlands of the Eastern United States.

Rails are hunted by walking through the marshes on foot or they are hunted from a flat boat poled through the marshes at high tide.

Virginia rail is a medium sized bird 8-11 inches 20-28 cm) in length. Unless flushed from the sedges in its marshland habitat, it is difficult to observe. Its thin, flattened body enables it to move through thick marsh growth, and its barred plumage of chestnut, gray, brown and black make it nearly invisible. The sora is about the same size. It is more common perhaps than the Virginia rail, and is fonder of cattail marshes. Its gray, barred plumage is set off by a chicken-like yellow bill.

Common Gallinule
Purple Gallinule

Common Gallinule

Purple Gallinule

The Common Gallinule is a large rail with a wide distribution throughout the United States. It has the body form of a small coot, but differs in having a red bill and a white line on each side of its body.

The secretive behavior of the common gallinule and its choice of vegitated areas, rather than open water, make it a rarely seen bird. Breeding takes place from early April, through early May. Nests are built of dead vegetation. Clutch size may vary from 2 to 17 eggs; 8-10 being the average size. Incubation periods last between 4-10 days.

Gallinules inhabit bogs and shallow marshes. They feed mainly on aquatic vegetation which is supplemented by some grains.

Gallinules are not hunted extensively in North America.

The Purple Gallinule is a brightly colored bird with a bluish purple neck and underparts and a brassy green back. The frontal shield is light blue; the bill is red but tipped with yellow. Its legs are bright yellow.

This species inhabits lowland marshes of Florida and Texas north to South Carolina and Tennessee. It frequents deep water if lily pads are present, and feeds on aquatic insects, water plants, and the seeds of wild rice and millet.

Sandhill Cranes

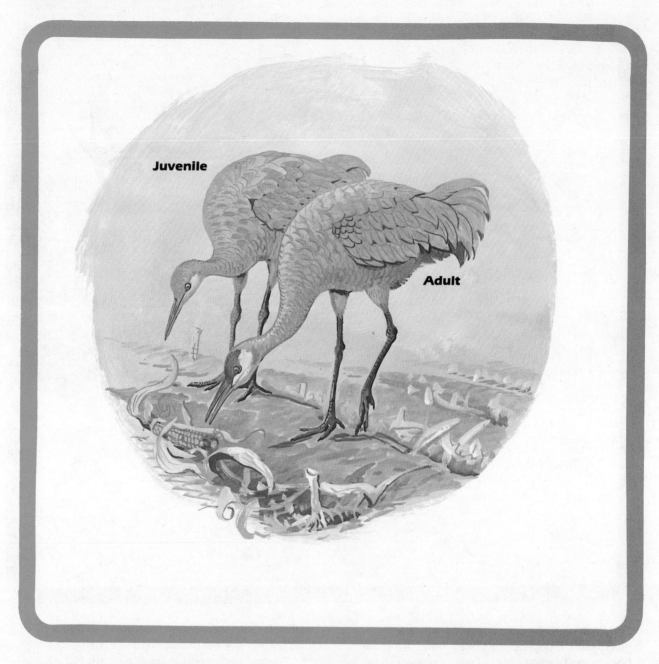

Juvenile

Adult

Sandhill cranes, or one of their six subspecies, are found in the northwestern United States, Mississippi, Florida and Georgia. Their primary habitat is in tundra areas, dunes, shallow marshes, and bogs.

Sandhill cranes have long legs, necks and bills. They attain an average weight of about 6-12 pounds (2.72-5.44 kg). The adult has a dark red skin on the crown. Body plumage is slate gray except in summer when it is stained a rusty brown from having been preened with marsh debris. Immature birds lack the bare patch of crimson red skin which adults have on the forehead.

The sandhill crane will nest on dry land but prefers to be near the water. Nesting begins in the latter part of spring. Clutches usually contain two eggs and the incubation period is 28 to 31 days.

The prime food of the sandhill crane is almost exclusively small rodents, frogs and insects, however the young may supplement their food supply with grain in the autumn months.

Hunting the sandhill crane is limited to only a few states and regulations governing this game bird are strictly enforced.

Small Game Animals Introduction

The smaller mammals which are hunted in North America include a variety of animals, some of which are classified traditionally as small game and others which are more often referred to as "varmits", even though many of them in recent years have been assigned a game animal status. All of these small mammals are native to the United States.

Throughout their range in the Eastern and Midwestern states, the fox squirrel, gray squirrel and cottontail rabbit are popular and much sought after game species. Also hunted over much of their home range as varmints are the woodchuck and its counterpart in the talus slopes and rocky outcropping of the West, the rock chuck. Several small mammals which are valued for their fur are hunted as small game in some parts of the country and as varmints in other regions. Included in this group are the red and gray fox, raccoon and opossum, all of which are found throughout much of the United States today. Though more restricted in distribution, other small mammals which are hunted as game or varmints are the lynx, wolverine and bobcat.

The predators among this group of small game animals often are hunted with the aid of a predator call. By mimicking the sounds of a prey animal in distress, the calls lure the predators into the area from which the hunter is calling.

Gray, Red and Fox Squirrels

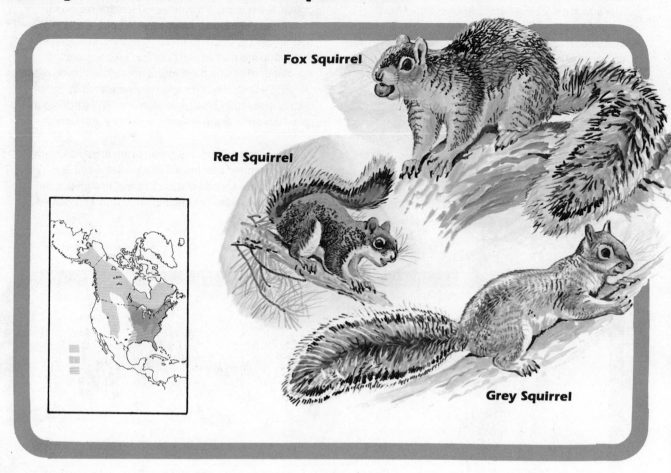

Fox Squirrel

Red Squirrel

Grey Squirrel

Identification

Squirrels are probably the favorite among young small game hunters and they are found throughout North America wherever forests occur. Fox squirrels are the largest, weighing from 1–3 pounds (453-1,360 grams) and vary greatly in color. The grayish form with rust-colored underparts as illustrated here is the most common in the east and midwest. In the southeast the head is often black, with white muzzle and paws. In the deep south, black is the predominant color while the nose remains white. Gray squirrels are medium-sized, weighing from ¾-1½ pounds (340-680 grams) and are uniform grayish with white underparts and white edged tails. Red squirrels are the smallest weighing from 7-8⅕ ounces. They vary in color from rust-red with white underparts in summer, to grayish with red on back and tail in winter. The tail is edged in buff and there is a black stripe along the side in summer. Black or albino squirrels of all three species are locally common.

Habits

Fox squirrels are found in open deciduous woodlands, and spend a good deal of time foraging on the ground. When disturbed, they usually head for the tree that holds their den, a leafy structure in summer and a cavity in winter. The gray squirrel, by contrast, is more adept at climbing and often escapes by running through the treetops, using its tail for balance or to help brake an occasional fall. Red squirrels are small but aggressive, and frequent cone-bearing trees. Their noise often serves as a warning to other birds and animals. Both red and gray squirrels construct leaf nests in upper tree branches for summer use, and resort to leaf-lined tree cavities in winter.

Squirrels of all three species feed on a variety of plant material, including mast from oak and nut trees, seeds, fungi, and bark and buds of trees. Red squirrels may cause some damage to eggs and nesting birds.

Home range of fox squirrel is 2-3 acres, while grays may venture over 7 acres. Red squirrel's entire range is less than 200 yards across.

Fox squirrels, because of their superior size, are widely hunted, but the elusive gray is a challenging target as well as excellent table fare. Red squirrels are too small to be considered a major game species but are often shot as pests. Squirrels may be hunted during late summer in certain states, but are mainly a fall game animal. A dog may be used to help locate and distract squirrels.

Cottontail Rabbit

Tracks 4''

Identification

The cottontail is one of the most hunted small game animals in the United States. The body coat color is brownish or grayish with a cottony-white tail. The nape patch is rusty and the leg pelage is white. Coat color may vary from area to area.

Cottontails are 14 to 17 inches (35 to 44 centimeters) long and weigh from 2 to 4 pounds (.74 to 1.5 kilograms) when mature.

Habits

The cottontail rabbit, or any of its related subspecies, can be found throughout the United States. It's habitat varies with the subspecies and may include heavy brush, strips of forest with open areas nearby, edges of swamps, weed patches, rocky foot hills, marshes and canebrake swamps.

Cottontails are most active from early evening to late morning. They spend most of the day in partial concealment, underground, beneath brush piles or among rocks. Green vegetation is their main food in the spring and summer and bark, twigs and buds are the primary winter foods. Home range for a cottontail may take in 3 to 20 acres.

Young are born between March and May, but litters may be dropped as late as September. A doe may have 3 to 4 litters each year with 4 to 7 young per litter. Gestation takes 26½ to 30 days and the young are born with their eyes closed. Nesting areas usually are depressions in the ground which the doe lines with her body fur.

The cottontail rabbit is a favorite with the young hunter and it provides excellent table fare.

Snowshoe Hare

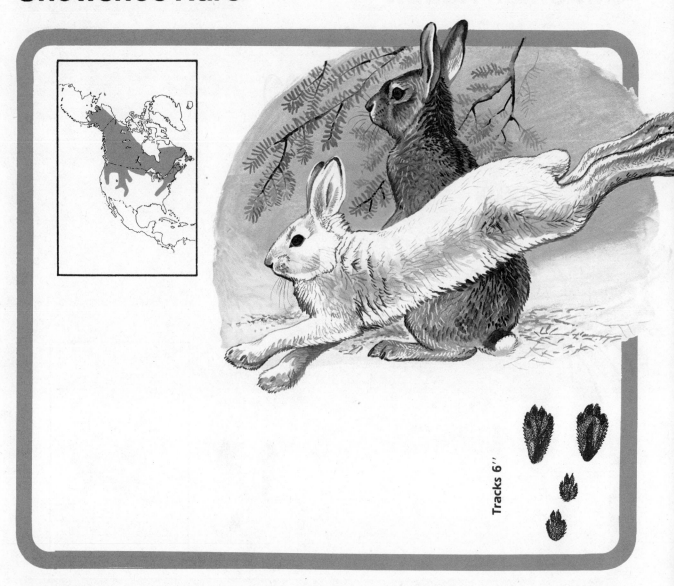

Tracks 6"

Identification

The snowshoe hare is dark brown in summer and almost pure white in winter. The winter pelage, however, is only white on the tips of the hairs while the band of hair beneath is a yellowish color.

The snowshoe rabbit is 13 to 18 inches long (33 to 46 centimeters) and weighs between 2 to 4 pounds (.74 to 1.5 kilograms). It is named for its large, heavily-furred hind feet. The snowshoe's ears are 3½ to 4 inches (8.7 to 10 centimeters) long.

Habits

The snowshoe hare is found in the northern, western and eastern portions of the United States. In the northern and eastern areas, it lives in swamps, forests and thickets. In the western areas, it is found in mountainous sections. A nocturnal animal, the snowshoe remains quiet during the day, concealed among brush and trees.

Snowshoe hares feed on green vegetation during the summer and on twigs, buds and bark during the winter months. They also are fond of frozen meat. Home range for the snowshoe is about 10 acres, but it may travel as far as a mile.

The gestation period is 36 to 37 days. The does usually have 2 to 3 litters a year with 2 to 4 young in each litter. The young are born with their eyes open. Snowshoe hare populations fluctuate greatly, with population peaks about every 11 years.

The flesh of the snowshoe hare is excellent and hunting this animal is truly sporting. It is well to remember that the snowshoe will run in a very large circle when pursued by trailing hounds.

Raccoon

Tracks 4½''

Identification

The raccoon is a medium sized, stocky mammal with a prominent, black mask around its eyes and a heavily furred, ringed tail about half the length of the head and body. The adults are grizzled brown and black strongly mixed with yellow on the back. The underparts are dull brown, grizzled with yellowish-gray. The dark rings on the tail vary in number from 4 to 7 and are more pronounced above than they are below.

An adult raccoon is 26 to 38 inches long (66 to 96.5 centimeters) and has a tail 8 to 12 inches (20 to 30.4 centimeters) long. Males will weigh 8 to 25 pounds (3.6 to 11.3 kilograms), while females will weigh 7 to 18 pounds (3.0 to 7.9 kilograms).

Habits

The raccoon is found from the northern areas of Canada to as far south as South America, with the exception of the Rocky Mountain region. They thrive along stream and lake borders where there are wooded areas and rock cliffs nearby. Raccoons are expert climbers and they swim well.

Both plant and animal matter is eaten, depending on what is available. The plant food includes grapes, plums, chokecherries and blackberries, corn, acorns and other nuts. The animal food consists of birds, bird eggs, crayfish, clams, fish and various insects.

The gestation period is 63 days and the young are born from April through May. There is one litter a year, with 2 to 7 young in a litter.

Raccoons are hunted with dogs and about three-quarters of the harvest is taken in that manner; the remainder is trapped. They are hunted and trapped for their fur as well as the excellent meat they provide.

Bobcat

Tracks 2½''

Identification

The bobcat varies from reddish-brown to tawny gray in color with an overlay of variable darker markings or spots. The tail has several dark bars across the top and a broad, black bar or spot bordering the tip which is white. The ear tufts are short and not conspicuous.

The body length of a mature bobcat is 25 to 30 inches (62.5 to 75 centimeters) and the tail length will be about 5 inches (12.5 centimeters). An adult animal will weigh 15 to 35 pounds (5.6 to 13.1 kilograms).

Habits

The bobcat is found throughout the United States except in the northcentral region of the country. The major habitat for bobcats are chaparral areas in the western part of the country and swamps and forests in the East.

The bobcat preys heavily on small game, especially rabbits. However, because of population fluctuations of the rabbit, it supplements its diet with mice, rats, squirrels and birds such as grouse, woodcock and wild turkeys. The bobcat prefers fresh meat and it rarely stores a kill for consumption later.

The breeding season differs with the location but usually occurs during the first quarter of the year. From 2 to 4 young are born following a gestation period of 60 days.

All of the senses of the bobcat are sharp but it relies mainly on its keen eyesight and hearing to avoid detection. This animal is hunted for its fur.

Lynx

Tracks 4"

Identification

The lynx is the northern counterpart of the bobcat. It is distinguished by its short tail which is black at the tip and its tufted ears. The gray to pale yellow or tan coat color of the lynx is lighter than that of the bobcat.

An adult lynx will be 32 to 36 inches (80 to 90 centimeters) long, its tail will be about 4 inches (10 centimeters) in length and it will weigh 15 to 30 pounds (5.9 to 11.2 kilograms). The females are usually smaller.

Habits

The lynx is found in the northern most regions of the United States and in the Canadian provinces. Forested areas and swamps make up the prime habitat of this species. The lynx is a nocturnal, solitary animal. It has extremely large feet padded with fur, enabling it to move swiftly and easily in deep snow.

The diet of the lynx is made up mainly of snowshoe hares and supplemented with rodents and birds when the snowshoe population is low. The lynx mates in January or February and after a gestation period of some 62 days bears its young in March or April. Dens are located in hollow logs, large tree stumps or other sheltered areas.

Lynx populations fluctuate over the years with peak populations occuring every 9 to 10 years. These population fluctuations appear to parallel but lag slightly behind population fluctuations of the snowshoe hare, the lynx's prime food source.

The lynx is hunted or trapped primarily for its fur.

125

Wolverine

Tracks 5''

Identification

The wolverine somewhat resembles a small bear. Its pelage is a dark-brown, paler on the head, with two yellowish stripes running down the back, starting at the shoulders and joining at the rump. The feet are large for the size of the animal.

A mature individual will be 29 to 32 inches (72.5 to 80 centimeters) long with a tail about 7 to 9 inches (17.5 to 22.5 centimeters). The animal will weigh from 35 to 60 pounds (13.1 to 22.4 kilograms).

Habits

The wolverine inhabits the high mountains of western North America, near the timberline and as far as the tundra in the far northern reaches of the continent.

A solitary animal, the wolverine may be active any time of the day or night. Its diet consists of small birds and animals supplemented with eggs and berries. It has a reputation as a robber of traps and a destroyer of food caches. The wolverine will travel extensively in search of food.

The mating season is from April through August. Females bear a litter every 2 to 3 years on the average and give birth to 2 to 3 young in each litter. Dens are located in sheltered areas such as root depressions of large trees and undercut ledges.

Wolverines are hunted for their fur and they are hunted by trappers to prevent the animals from damaging their traplines.

Gray Fox

Tracks 2⅛"

Identification

The gray fox has a feline-like appearance. Its coat is a pepper and salt color with buff-colored underfur. The tail is long and bushy with a median black stripe down its length and a black tip. The rusty-yellowish sides of the animal's neck, the back of its ears, legs and feet serve to distinguish it from other foxes.

A mature gray fox will measure 21 to 29 inches (52.5 to 72.5 centimeters) long. It will weigh 7 to 13 pounds (2.6 to 4.8 kilograms) and its tail will be 11 to 16 inches (27.5 to 40 centimeters) in length.

Habits

The gray fox is found in the southern, eastern and western parts of the United States. It prefers brushy forests and rimrock country for its habitat. It dens in hollow logs, beneath boulders and sometimes in ground burrows.

Chiefly nocturnal and very secretive, the gray fox will climb trees to escape pursuit. Its major food is small animals but it also feeds on insects, fruits, acorns, birds and bird eggs.

Mating occurs in February and March. The gestation period lasts about 51 days. The young, which are born with their eyes closed, arrive between April and May. There usually are 3 to 7 pups in a litter.

Gray fox are hunted for sport and for their fur, which in most years is less valuable than that of the red fox.

Red Fox

Tracks 2½''

Identification

The red fox is dog-like in appearance. Its pelage is reddish yellow. The coat is darkest on the back, the underparts are light and the bushy tail has a blend of black hairs and it is tipped with white. The legs, feet and ears are black. Many color variations may be seen from area to area, ranging from reddish-yellow to black.

A mature red fox is 22 to 25 inches (55 to 62.5 centimeters) long. Its tail will measure 14 to 16 inches (35 to 40 centimeters) in length and the animal will weigh 10 to 15 pounds (37.3 to 55.9 kilograms).

Habits

The red fox ranges over most of the United States with the exception of an area just east of the Rocky Mountains, extending north and south from the Canadian border to Mexico. This species prefers a mixture of forest and open country.

The red fox is most active during the night, early morning and late evening. Its food consists of prey animals ranging in size from insects to hares. Berries and fruits round out the animal's diet.

The young are born in March or April, depending on the part of the country. Vixens bear one litter per year with 4 to 9 pups in the litter. Gestation lasts about 51 days. Nests are located in dens dug usually on slopes in porous soil.

Home range for the red fox is 1 to 2 square miles but individuals have been known to travel greater distances, especially during the winter. Red fox are hunted with hounds or with the aid of a predator call which is used to lure the fox to the hunter. The animal is hunted and trapped for sport and for its fur.

Javelina

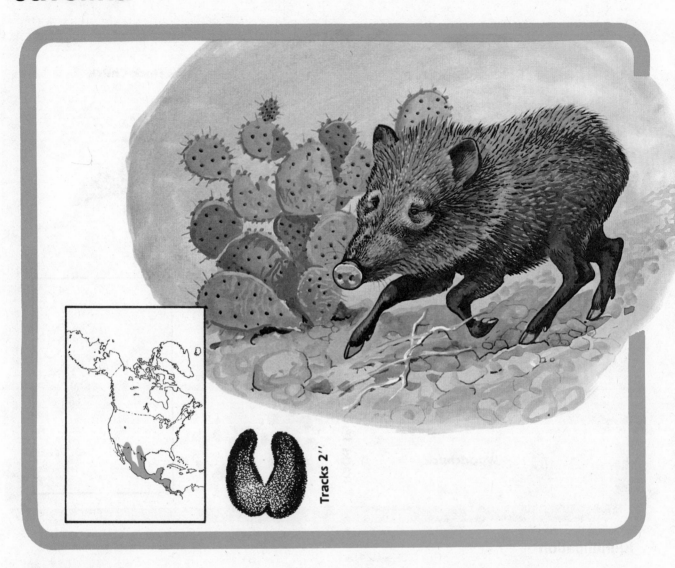

Tracks 2''

Identification

The javelina is a small, dark, pig-like mammal inhabiting southwestern United States and Mexico. It has thick, bristly hair which grows particularly long about the head and neck where it forms a whitish collar.

Sometimes called the collared peccary, the javelina is 18 to 22 inches (45.7 to 55.9 centimeters) at the shoulder and weighs 30 to 60 pounds (13.6 to 27.2 kilograms). The hair on the neck may grow to a length of 6 inches (15.2 centimeters), making the animal appear much larger than it is. Both sexes have a musk gland located beneath the long hair in the middle of the back which produces a strong scent.

Habits

Javelinas move about in herds of 6 to 20 animals. In the arid Southwest climate, the animals bed down in shaded thickets during the heat of the day and forage for food early and late in the day or at night. They feed on cactus fruits, desert beans and berries, acorns, pine nuts and tubers which they root out of the ground. Javelinas obtain water by eating succulent desert plants and they also frequent water holes where they are available.

While their sense of smell and hearing are acute, their eyesight is poor. When alarmed, javelinas make clicking sounds with their teeth. Although nervous and excitable, the only attacks upon man have come in the form of bites from animals kept as pets.

Javelinas are legal game in Texas, Arizona and New Mexico. They are difficult to find and are more often bagged incidentally by deer hunters. The meat is excellent and not affected by the scent glands which can be removed with the skin.

Woodchucks and Rock Chucks

Rock Chuck

Woodchuck

Tracks 1½''

Identification

Woodchucks and rock chucks are similar in size and appearance, and both are heavy-bodied, burrowing rodents with grizzled gray fur. The eastern woodchuck is browner on the belly with a yellowish or reddish cast and black feet. The western rock chuck is more yellowish brown underneath and has a white area between the eyes, and brownish or yellowish feet. Individuals of both species may be either all black or all white. Both woodchuck and rock chuck weigh from 4-14 pounds (1.8-6.3 kilograms), and are much heavier in the summer than when emerging from hibernation in the spring. Woodchucks are often called "groundhog," while rock chucks are more often referred to as "yellow-bellied marmot."

Habits

The woodchuck is found in forested and farming country throughout eastern North America. Originally a forest animal, it has benefitted by the opening of the land to agriculture, and its burrows are found on the edges of many farm fields. Rock chucks are restricted to the Rocky Mountain region, and burrow among the talus slopes and foothills, usually near a large boulder.

Chucks are considered pests by most landholders due to their fondness for hay and garden crops as well as their burrowing tendencies. They have the habit of sitting upright looking for danger, and when alarmed give a shrill chirp or whistle. Between 2 and 6 young are born in spring and remain with the mother until midsummer. Woodchuck hibernates October through February; Rock chuck between September and May. Both are active mainly during daylight hours, and often sun themselves in an open spot with a good view of danger.

Chucks offer the big game hunter an excellent opportunity to test his marksmanship before the big game season, while doing the landowner a service by eliminating a pest species.

Opossum

Tracks 2''

Identification

The opossum is a medium-sized animal. It has long, coarse fur, a long, prehensile tail which is scaly and naked, a slender muzzle, thin, naked ears and short legs. The female has a prominent fur-lined pouch on her belly. The fur is grayish-white but the front and hind quarters are darker and the belly lighter in color.

An adult is 24 to 34 inches long (60.9 to 86.3 centimeters) and the tail is 9.5 to 15 inches (24.1 to 38.1 centimeters) in length. Opossums reach a weight of 4 to 15 pounds (1.8 to 6.8 kilograms). Males are larger than the females.

Habits

The opossum is distributed throughout most of the eastern, central and southern regions of the United States. It prefers wooded areas near streams but is at home anywhere it is dry, sheltered and safe. This shy, nocturnal animal is most often observed by roadsides. It is well-adapted to climbing and can hang by its tail for short periods.

Opossums eat a variety of food but prefer animal matter. Their diet includes grasshoppers, crickets, beetles and ants, birds and bird eggs, crayfish, earthworms and carrion. Fruits are eaten in the fall and early winter.

Mating takes place about the first three weeks of February and the gestation period is only 12 to 13 days. Up to 14 young are born at one time. There may be two or more litters a year. The young are not able to see at birth and are incompletely developed.

Opossum are hunted for their fur and, in some parts of the country, for their flesh.

Notes

Only a limited number of North America's many species of wildlife have been treated in this section. For further information on North American wildlife, the following publications are among those that would be useful:

Game Birds of North America — Rue and Allen
Big Game of North America — Wildlife Management Institute
North American Big Game — Nesbitt and Parker
Wildlife and America — Brokaw

Various field guides such as those in the Peterson Field Guides Series

Vertebrates of the United States — Blair
The Alien Animals — Laycock
Ducks, Geese and Swans of North America — Frank C. Bellrose

The duck illustrations in this text have been reproduced with the permission of the South Dakota Department of Wildlife, Parks and Forestry.

Equipment

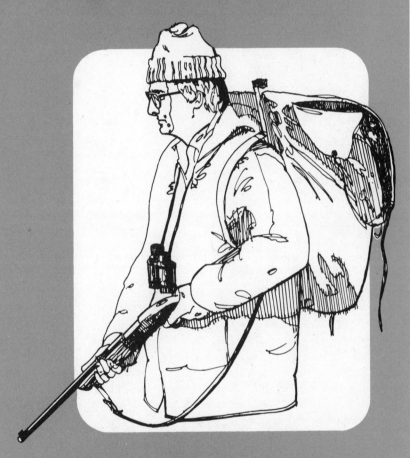

Introduction

The veteran hunter has learned from experience exactly what equipment to take on a hunting trip. He plans ahead, then takes only what is needed, reduced to the smallest practical weight and bulk.

Knowing what to expect in the way of terrain, weather, shelter and water, and taking steps to meet these conditions are essential to the success of the hunt.

For the newcomer to hunting, advance planning will ensure comfort and safety right from the start. This chapter suggests how to select, use and take care of equipment, clothes, personal items, camping gear and food; and how to plan ahead to avoid pitfalls that could get you into trouble.

Clothing

Function of Clothing

Clothes by themselves are neither "warm" nor "cold". It is your body heat and what happens to that heat when wearing clothing that makes you feel warm or cold.

Clothes which make you feel warm keep your body heat inside the clothing. "Warm" clothes keep out the cold air surrounding your body and trap your body heat in, in the same way that insulation between the inside and outside walls of your house keeps it warm in winter.

Clothes in which you feel cold let your body heat escape. Clothes dampened by sweat or wet weather are "cold" clothes. Wind, though it dries up dampness by evaporating moisture, chills as it dries and can thus make you cold.

A hunter's clothing must provide a layer of insulation for warmth, be thick enough to absorb perspiration and be able to shed rain and cut the wind.

Clothing which is completely waterproof will shed rain and wet weather, but it does not provide insulation or absorb perspiration. Without insulation to keep you warm and absorbency to help keep you dry, depending on weather conditions, you will feel either very cold or extremely hot while wearing totally waterproof garments.

Clothes should be loose enough for comfort. They should not restrict movements. New clothing, no matter how well it fits when first worn, needs to be "broken in". Plan to buy any new hunting clothes well before the hunt so any alterations can be made before wearing them afield.

The big game hunter must be specially careful selecting clothes for the hunt. The temperature in mountain areas can rise and fall several degrees in a few minutes even as he walks from sunlight into shadow. Hunting big game is strenuous exercise. The hunter may get hot and perspire during the chase, but his body will cool off quickly when he stops to rest. There is a very real danger of becoming chilled.

Advice from outfitters, experienced sportsmen or those who live in the territory can be most helpful to the hunter in choosing the proper clothes for the hunt.

Underwear

During warm weather, wear regular cotton underwear. If you expect to hunt in thick brush at a high altitude or during cold weather, however, you will need the extra protection and insulation of long underwear.

For cool fall days and frosty nights, thermal knit undergarments are ideal. The quilted knit fabric provides extra insulation and absorbency and is easily laundered and dried in camp.

In cold weather, snow and freezing conditions, you will require undergarments having an outer layer of wool for insulation and an inner layer of cotton for absorbency and to prevent itching. The two-piece style with separate bottoms and under-vests is most practical, allowing you to wear them separately or together, whichever is suitable to your activities and the weather.

Quilted undergarments of down or Dacron will keep you warm in extreme cold.

Down is the soft, inner breast feathering of mature geese or ducks. Down filled garments have excellent insulating qualities and because of their very light weight and small bulk, allow great freedom of motion. Down is expensive, however, and not easily laundered when camping.

Dacron, a synthetic fibre, has similar qualities to down but does not provide as much insulation or as little bulk as down. Dacron filled garments, on the other hand, are more easily laundered and less expensive.

Pants and Shirts

Unless you are planning to hunt in subzero temperatures, pants of any hardy fabric, cotton twill, duck, denim or wool, will be suitable for hunting.

Denim jeans are practical for hunting, inexpensive and tough enough to withstand thorns and brambles in brush country. If horse-back riding will be part of your activities, denim jeans make comfortable riding pants.

Heavy-weight woollen pants are best for walking in snow. Even when wet, wool provides some insulation against the cold. Unlike denim when it gets wet, wool does not make a noisy swishing sound which could frighten your quarry as you walk.

For winter hunts or treks through mountainous terrain, down insulated pants will keep you warm even in severely cold temperatures.

Light cotton shirts with short sleeves are ideal for warm climates, shirts of heavy cotton are suitable for hunting during mild weather, but in cold weather woollen shirts should be your choice.

Two light woollen shirts are more versatile than one of heavy wool. They can be adapted to changing weather conditions, wearing both when it is cold and one when it is mild.

Boots and Socks

Care and conditioning of the feet and proper fitting boots are essential to the hunter's well-being. Unconditioned feet may swell and bruise. Boots which do not fit can cause painful blisters and a blister can be considered a major injury when walking far from camp.

Inner Lining

Leather uppers treated for water resistance.

Steel Shank

Cushioned Insole

The most common cause of blisters is chafing from socks and boots which rub against the skin. This friction occurs when boots are too large or loosely laced and if socks are lumpy or wrinkled.

You should not wear everyday socks for hiking or hunting. Most hunters wear two pairs of socks — thin lightweight ones next to the feet and heavier socks overtop. Socks should be wool, Orlon, or wool-Orlon mix not cotton. Cotton socks will make your feet wet, clammy and uncomfortable after walking a long distance. They can even cause blisters. Wool socks are warm and they soak up sweat. The thickness of two pairs will act as a cushion between boot and foot. Orlon is a synthetic fabric. Like wool, it absorbs moisture well and is thick enough to cushion the sole. Orlon and wool-Orlon mix socks are preferred by many hikers because they wear longer than woollen ones, they wash easier and dry more quickly.

When pulling on socks, be sure to smooth them out. Remove all wrinkles or bunching at the toes or heels. When trying on boots, remember to wear your hiking socks. If two pairs of socks do not give a snug fit, try wearing a third pair.

Experienced walkers know that loose boots can cause blisters. To prevent this, boots should be laced fairly snug around the foot but less tight around the ankle. To do this, lace the boot firmly to the top of the instep and tie a reef knot here to hold the tension and prevent the laces from loosening. The laces can then be comfortably laced from the instep to the top of the boot.

The weight of your boots is very important. Even a few ounces of extra weight carried for many miles can be equal to several hundred pounds of physical exertion. Boots should be sturdy, but avoid wearing boots heavier than you need.

Because hunters need boots that will last through long and hard usage, most prefer leather boots between 8 (20 cm) and 10 inches (25 cm) high. Leather is sturdy yet supple and molds to your foot shape with wear. Leather breathes letting in air and carrying off heat. It also has good insulating properties.

On a rocky trail or uneven surface, you need boots which will not slip and slide. Soles should be made of neoprene, a synthetic material most often sold under the trade name Vibram, For hunting in rain, light snow or in marshy areas, soles of heavy gauge rubber can be an advantage.

When walking through bush or along dusty or gravelled roads, twigs, burrs and small stones can collect in your socks and boots. Such bits of dirt and debris can rub and irritate your skin causing painful sores and blisters. Socks and boots should be removed ocassionally to shake out any objects which have been picked up on the trail.

Boots bought for hunting should be a half size larger than your regular shoe size to allow room for thick socks and innersoles and for some swelling of feet which is normal during hard walking.

For hunting through marshy areas during mild weather, moccasin style boots made of heavy moosehide are a good choice. When wet, moosehide moccasins will dry throughly overnight and dry without stiffening, ready to wear in the morning.

Moccasins with cleated soles which can be worn over thick socks are also suitable in mild weather. They will grip slick surfaces and are better suited for walking on rocky or uneven terrain than moosehide moccasins.

The duck hunter, who must often wade through swamp and water to retrieve his quarry, needs hip-high rubber boots with ridged or corrugated soles. They should be large enough to be worn with thick socks and felt insoles.

Gloves and Mitts

Gloves are a necessary part of a hunter's cold weather gear. But gloves can do much more than keep the hands and fingers warm in cold weather. When handling horses and saddles, riding, working with ropes, setting up camp and doing other rough work during the hunt, hands and fingers need protection against cuts, blisters, splinters and other injuries.

In mild weather, short buckskin gloves are best. Avoid gauntlet style gloves because they will collect twigs, leaves and debris.

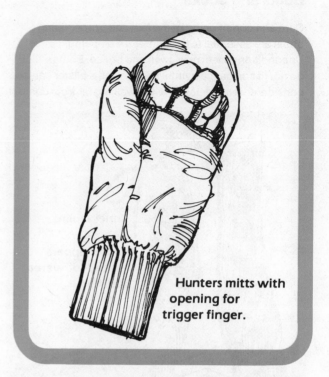

Hunters mitts with opening for trigger finger.

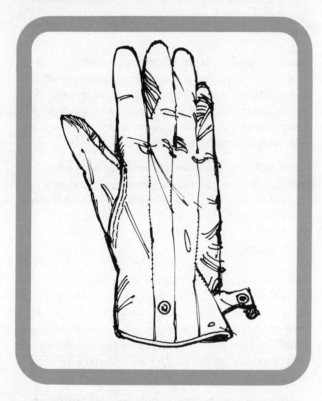

Less expensive than buckskin, yet very durable and practical are the jersey-knit work gloves available from most department stores and super-markets and wherever hardware or garden supplies are sold. As well as their lower price, these gloves are warmer than buckskin. However, they are not waterproof and are impractical for wear in rain, snow and other wet conditions. In cold weather, these jersey-knit gloves worn inside leather mitts will keep hands warm and dry.

For extra warmth in very cold weather, many hunters wear knitted wool mitts inside tough leather mitts. This combination is warm, durable and inexpensive.

For winter hunts in sub-zero cold, down-filled mitts provide the most warmth. Most down-filled mitts are designed with long gauntlets to keep out snow and wind, and some have mouton backs as a convenience for wiping snow and moisture from your face.

Hunting Coats

A lightweight sleeveless cotton hunting vest is ideal for warm weather. In mild weather, a denim jacket is a wise choice. Like denim jeans and riding pants, a denim jacket is trim, light-weight and hard-wearing. Denim resists snagging on branches and underbrush better than most other materials and it is not an expensive fabric.

A long-sleeved lumberjack shirt of heavy wool is suitable for mild weather hunting. The shirt should have pockets, preferably with button-down flaps.

Down vests are popular because they retain body heat to keep you warm and at the same time allow great freedom of movement. For extremely cold weather conditions a down-filled jacket with hood is the ultimate in warmth and comfort.

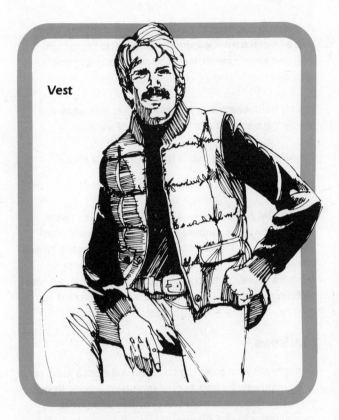

Vest

On a big game hunt a rubber rain coat and water-proof trousers are a must. If the raincoat does not have an attached hood, you will need a rain hat.

There are coats designed specifically for duck hunters. Usually made of light canvas or khaki. The bird hunter's coat has many pockets in which to carry a supply of shells, and a large pocket in the rear in which to carry his game. This coat is ideal for wearing in spring, summer and fall. When the weather is warm it can be worn with a light shirt. In cool weather, it is comfortable worn over a woollen shirt or sweaters.

Coat

A mackinaw is a practical coat for the big game hunter because it is made with double thickness at the shoulders and cuffs which adds extra warmth and protection from the wind.

Parka

Headgear

No matter what the weather, a hat should be included with the hunter's gear.

You should have headgear that will not be easily knocked off or nudged over your eyes by tree branches. In bright sunlight, your hat should shade your eyes and protect your neck and ears from sunburn. In cold weather, it should keep your head warm and protect your ears from frost-bite.

Body heat is lost rapidly when the head is exposed to cold. Because body heat escapes faster through the head than from anywhere else on the body, it is vital to keep your head covered in extreme cold. Your hands and feet will remain warm longer if your head is covered and warm.

Change of Clothes

Hunters who expect to be camping for several days away from showers and other sanitary facilities should pack a complete change of clothes. Wet, torn and dirty clothing are common on a hunting trip and changing into clean clothes adds greatly to a hunter's comfort.

Bedding

Sleeping Bag

The most convenient, practical and warmest bedding for the hunter is a sturdy sleeping bag.

A sleeping bag makes a comfortable bed and also helps to limit the loss of body heat while you sleep. The warmth of a sleeping bag depends on the thickness, not the weight, of its insulating material.

For camping in mild weather, filler material of manmade polyester such as Dacron or Fortrel provides adequate insulation and is lightweight.

In the fall, even though the days may be warm, night-time temperatures can drop drastically and you will need a bag which provides maximum insulation to keep you warm. A down filled bag will keep the hunter warm even when camping in the snow or in Arctic conditions.

A sleeping bag should have a flannel inner liner, which you can make from a flannelette sheet, to protect the bag and keep it clean. It can be removed easily for washing.

In very cold weather, it's a good idea to fold a blanket inside the bag for extra insulation and warmth.

Be sure to get a bag that is the right size for you.

Pillow

Your pillow should be small enough to roll up inside your sleeping bag. Inflatable rubber pillows are often used with sleeping bags and some air mattresses have a pillow attached. There are also pillows filled with feathers or foam which are made especially for use with sleeping bags. If you do not have a pillow, a rolled up coat or jacket is a good substitute.

Mattress

Underneath your sleeping bag, you will want a foam pad or air mattress. As well as cushioning your body from the rough ground, a mattress provides additional insulation.

An air mattress should not be over-inflated. Blow it up just enough so that when lying on your side your hipbone will bump the ground when you bounce gently up and down.

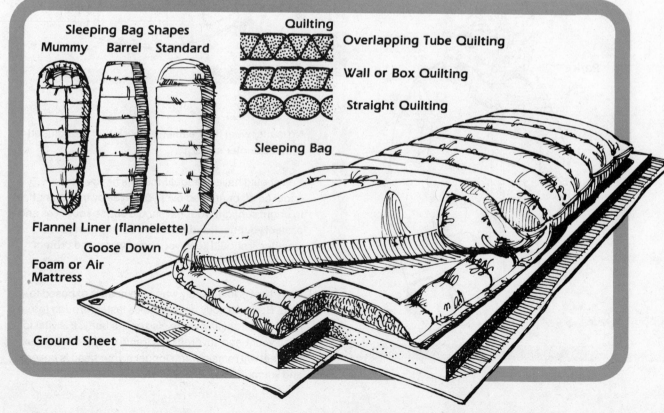

Sleeping Bag Shapes
Mummy Barrel Standard

Quilting
Overlapping Tube Quilting
Wall or Box Quilting
Straight Quilting

Sleeping Bag

Flannel Liner (flannelette)
Goose Down
Foam or Air Mattress

Ground Sheet

Tents

Tents are made from several kinds of fabrics including canvas and water repellent cotton but most recreational tents today are made of nylon. Nylon is exceptionally strong, easy to repair if torn, will not rot, is water resistant and weighs only a few ounces per square yard.

A tent keeps you and your gear dry, warm and sheltered, and it protects you from insects when on a hunting trip. There are many styles, sizes and weights of tents available. The tent your hunting party should take should be practical for the kind of camping you plan to do. It should provide snug shelter from strong winds, rain and snow.

Wall Tent

A large wall tent, 12 × 14 feet (3.5 × 4 m), will accommodate four hunters comfortably. It has room enough for moving about inside and plenty of head room. With a wood burning tent stove, it will keep the party warm in any weather.

When a stove will be used to heat the tent, it is better to have a canvas tent. Although much heavier, canvas is less flammable than nylon. If a wood burning stove is to be used, the tent must have an asbestos ring for the stovepipe to exit without scorching the tent fabric. The stovepipe must project a foot above the ridge of the tent so the wind will not blow sparks onto the roof.

A smaller wall tent, 8 × 10 feet (2 × 3 m), is suitable for two hunters, but it will be a little cramped. Sleeping bags should be rolled up during the day to make more room inside the cooking and eating tent.

Asbestos Collar

Forester's Tent

A forester's tent makes use of nylon fabric and aluminum pegs and poles to save weight. A campfire built outside the tent opening will provide enough heat to keep the tent warm and comfortable even in extremely cold weather.

Because of this tent's design, a fire can be built quite close to it. A forester's tent is set up with three poles—

two poles of equal length and a longer ridge pole. The ridge pole is erected at the rear of the tent. It is an easy tent to set up and take down. If rain or snow blows through the tent's front opening, the tent can be quickly turned to another direction by changing the position of the ridge pole.

142

Mountaineer's Tent

A mountaineer's tent is useful for the hunter who requires only a place to sleep and protection from the weather. It is small and very light in weight. The tent floor is sewn to its walls, which keeps out drafts, mosquitoes and other bugs, as well as rain and snow. The tent is not high enough to stand up in and there is very little room for gear other than a sleeping bag.

Lean-to Tent

A lean-to or tarp tent makes a convenient and comfortable shelter. The tarp is simply a rectangle of water-proof cloth with rings called grommets every two or three feet along the sides and at each corner. The grommets are used to tie and erect the tent. The tarp can be any size which is adequate for shelter. Several different lengths of line for tying will give you the flexibility you require to set up a lean-to.

A lean-to tent pitched at a 40 degree angle will provide good protection for beds and gear stored under it. It will shed a driving rain. With a fire in front, a lean-to can be warm and comfortable. This type of tent is particularly suitable in the woods where trees are readily available for use as tent poles and where there is shelter from the wind.

To keep out rain or gusts of wind, small spruce trees and evergreen boughs may be cut down and stood up at the open ends of the lean-to tent.

A tarp has many other uses around camp and at least one should be included on every trip where space is available. A tarp can be used to cover food supplies and protect saddles and equipment. It can be set up as a roof to provide overhead shelter from rain or shade the sun or it can serve as a windscreen.

Selection and Care of Tents

Most tents on the market today are manufactured with waterproof canvas floors sewn in, mosquito screening at the entrance and vents which make them completely bug, wind and waterproof.

Although these features are important, there are some disadvantages to such models. The sewn-in floor adds considerably to the tent's weight and bulk. A wood-burning stove must not be used in tents with floors. The tent can only be pitched on smooth level ground and mud and dirt tracked inside on a hunter's boot makes housekeeping a problem.

Sod Cloth

If your tent is floorless, you will need a sod cloth. A sod cloth is a strip of canvas about 12 inches (30 cm) wide, sewn completely around the bottom of the tent. The sod cloth is stretched out on the ground inside the tent and weighted down with stones or logs. This provides a wind and bugproof seal between the bottom of the tent and the ground.

A tarp, spread over the ground inside the tent makes a suitable carpet for a floorless tent.

Mosquito Screen

Tents can be kept mosquito-free with a curtain of mosquito netting or cheesecloth. The curtain should cover the entire front entrance of the tent. The netting should be very full and long. It should be sewn to the tent where the roof and walls meet.

When in use, the bottom of the netting is weighted down with a pole or tucked under the sod cloth. When the mosquito curtain is not needed, it can be tied to the top of the tent.

Color

Tents today come in a variety of colors. Light green or khaki colored tents are cooler in hot weather than those in brilliant colors. Some very dark green tents, especially those made of canvas, require a lantern when working inside even in daylight. White lets light through the fabric and makes the tent interior much cheerier than dark colors.

Waterproofing

Tents which have not been treated to resist water will shrink when wet and unless guy ropes are loosened the tent pegs could be pulled out of the ground. Tents of closely woven cotton or canvas become very heavy when wet and are difficult to handle if you must break camp during a storm or immediately after a heavy rain.

Most nylon tents are treated to make them water repellent and some are completely waterproof.

Untreated cotton and canvas tents can be made waterproof by painting them with a waterproofing solution available from tent and awning manufacturers. You can make a similar solution by dissolving paraffin in gasoline. After painting or soaking the fabric in this solution, hang up the tent until the gasoline evaporates.

If a spot on the tent is no longer waterproof and needs recoating, it should be rubbed with a block of paraffin wax.

Do not build a fire near tents that have been treated for waterproofing with paraffin and gasoline.

Repairs

Tears in cotton and canvas tents can be repaired by gluing a piece of waterproofed fabric over the tear, using fabric cement or canoe glue.

If a nylon tent is torn, it can be repaired with nylon sail-repair tape.

Storing Tents

Before packing a tent away, shake out all the dirt, twigs, grass, pebbles and bits of food. Be sure the tent is thoroughly dry before storing. Canvas and cotton will rot if stored wet. Nylon won't rot, even if put away wet, but it may become mildewed.

Knives and Axes

Knives

Some hunters prefer a sheath knife, others like a pocket knife. It is often wise to carry both when hunting in case one is broken or lost.

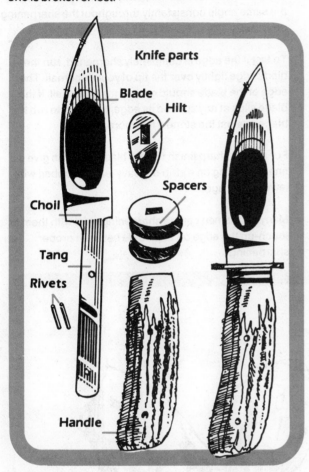

Knife parts

Blade
Hilt
Choil
Spacers
Tang
Rivets
Handle

The blade of any knife should be of good quality steel so it will keep its edge for a reasonable time. With regular use around camp, a knife will need to be sharpened every three or four days.

Knife blades should not be used to pry, chop or bore holes.

Sheath Knife

The blade of a sheath knife, to be effective for hunting purposes, should be no longer than 4 inches (10 cm). Longer knives are clumsy and not as versatile as a 4 inch (10 cm) blade which can be used for many chores such as butchering, skinning and whittling.

Sheath knives should remain in their scabbards at all times when not in use. The sheath, or scabbard, should be made of durable leather, reinforced at the tip with wire or copper rivets.

To keep your sheath in good condition, clean it with saddle soap, never oil. Saddle soap will keep the leather supple.

Pocket Knife

A pocket knife for hunting should have two strong blades, each between 2½ to 3 inches (6 cm to 8 cm) long. A pen knife is not suitable for such use.

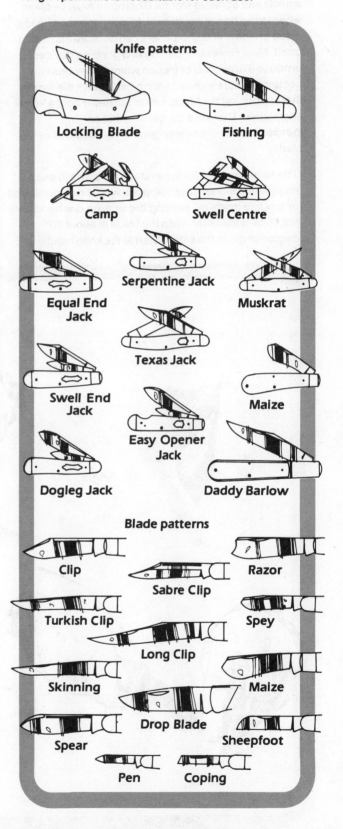

Knife patterns

Locking Blade
Fishing
Camp
Swell Centre
Equal End Jack
Serpentine Jack
Muskrat
Texas Jack
Swell End Jack
Maize
Easy Opener Jack
Dogleg Jack
Daddy Barlow

Blade patterns

Clip
Razor
Sabre Clip
Turkish Clip
Spey
Long Clip
Skinning
Maize
Drop Blade
Spear
Sheepfoot
Pen
Coping

Pocket knives should be kept folded when not in use.

Sharpening a Knife

Knives must be kept sharp to perform their functions properly. Present day sharpening and grinding implements include a variety of electric-powered wheels and abrasive stones. Great care must be taken when using power equipment. In inexperienced hands, these grinders and sharpeners can do more harm than good. Most power sharpening and grinding devices produce a great deal of friction which generates very hot temperatures. Over-heating will "draw" the temper, thereby ruining the blade, which will never hold a keen edge again. There is a danger too, that an inexperienced person may grind away too much of the blade.

The safest method for the average person is to use a sharpening stone. Keep the stone wet using a honing oil or any fine grade oil. Holding the stone in one hand and the knife in the other, keep the blade at about 30° degree angle to the stone. Start at the knife handle end of the blade and, in a sweeping motion, rub the stone against the blade to the tip. Turn the blade over and sharpen the other side. Maintain an even pressure and the same angle consistently throughout the sharpening process.

To test if the edge is completely sharpened, run the blade edge lightly over the tip of your fingernail. The edge of the blade should grab at the fingernail. If the blade slips at any spot on its edge, continue to rub the blade against the stone a few more times.

For a razor sharp finish to your blade, you can give it a final stropping on a strip of heavy leather rubbed with jeweller's rouge.

Many sportsmen carry a sharpening steel with them to touch-up the edge on their knife between proper sharpenings.

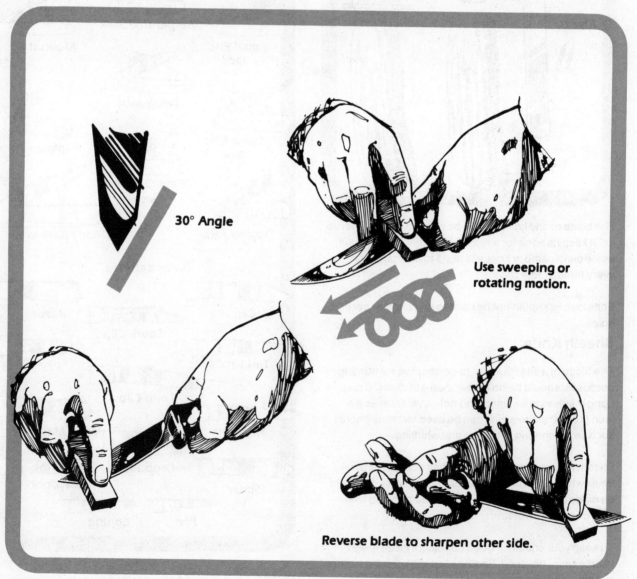

30° Angle

Use sweeping or rotating motion.

Reverse blade to sharpen other side.

146

Axes

The modern outdoorsman will find an axe is his most useful tool. Besides felling trees and chopping wood for fire and shelter, a well sharpened axe can skin and clean game and, if necessary, the steel axe-head can be used with a piece of flint to start a fire.

Selection of Axes

Axes come in different sizes to perform many different jobs. Axes are categorized as small, medium and large according to the weight of the axe-head and the length of the handle.

A camp axe is a small axe with a head weighing about 2 or 2½ pounds (.9 kg. or 1 kg.) and a handle between 20 and 28 inches (50 cm to 71 cm) long. It will chop small to medium size logs easily and can be used for bigger jobs if the edge is kept razor sharp. The camp axe takes up very little space and is ideal when horsepacking or when camping in small quarters.

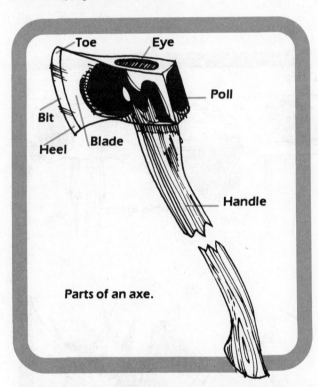

Parts of an axe.

No matter what size axe you choose, it should have a forged steel rather than cast steel head. Cast steel does not hold a sharp edge and breaks more readily than forged steel.

The best axes are made from high quality carbon steel which has been tempered to resist brittleness.

When selecting a wood-handled axe, be sure the grain of the wood is straight for the entire length of the handle. Hickory is considered the best wood for axe handles.

Care and Use of Axes

Replace a cracked or splintered axe handle. Do not attempt to patch it.

When replacing a wood axe-handle, cut off the old handle as close to the metal head as possible. The remaining wood can be dug out of the eye of the axe-head in small pieces. Insert the new handle in the eye and tap it into place. Cut two hardwood wedges and insert them in the axe-head next to the handle. Drive the wedges in as far as they will go so the handle is seated snugly in position and is as tight as possible.

To protect the handle, rub linseed oil into the wood of the handle along its entire length using a soft cloth. Never varnish or paint an axe-handle. Painted or varnished handles can cause your hands to blister.

If an axe-head is loose, do not use it until it has been tightened. You can tighten a loose handle by driving the hardwood wedges in further to fit more snugly, or you can soak the axe-head in water which will cause the wood to swell and the handle will then fit more tightly.

In extremely cold weather, always warm an axe before starting to cut. Cold makes the metal brittle which could cause the axe-blade to snap.

When using an axe, always work on a chopping block. A stump or log makes a satisfactory chopping block.

Always be sure no one is standing in line with the swing of your axe. Be careful when using an axe to insure that the area of the entire swing is clear of all obstructions.

Sharpening an Axe

A dull axe is dangerous. A sharp blade will bite into a log, but a dull edge may glance off the mark and cause a serious mishap.

To sharpen an axe you will need a file, and if available, a vise. Place the axe-head in a vise with the blade up. Clamp the axe-head in the vise close to where the handle is inserted in the eye. Holding the file flat, file from the eye along the entire edge. File on the outgoing stroke only, maintaining the same pressure and the same angle throughout the stroke. Turn the axe-head to the opposite direction to file the other side of the blade. Be sure to file both sides evenly.

In the field, where a vise is not available, extend the edge of the blade over a log or stump and hold the axe-head securely with your knee or foot while you file.

To check if you have sharpened the blade evenly, sight down the edge. There should be a fine bur on the blade edge. If you notice any bright or white spots, file the edge again until these dull patches disappear.

A final rubbing with a fine emery stone will hone the edge to razor sharpness.

An axe should never be thinned, that is, ground or filed to a thinner shape than when it comes from the factory. Grind or file the axe in a fan-shape, leaving a little more metal at the corners. The cutting edge of an axe should be rounded, not wedge-shape. The rounded edge will throw wood chips outward, away from the blade.

An axe is the outdoorsman's most useful tool. Select a quality axe and care for it properly. Keep it sharp. Take proper care of the handle, keeping the head tight and the handle smooth. Never use your axe to drive or pound on anything more than a tent peg. Axes are not designed to be used as a sledge hammer or as a wedge and should not be used for these purposes. With care, an axe will give the outdoorsman years of useful service.

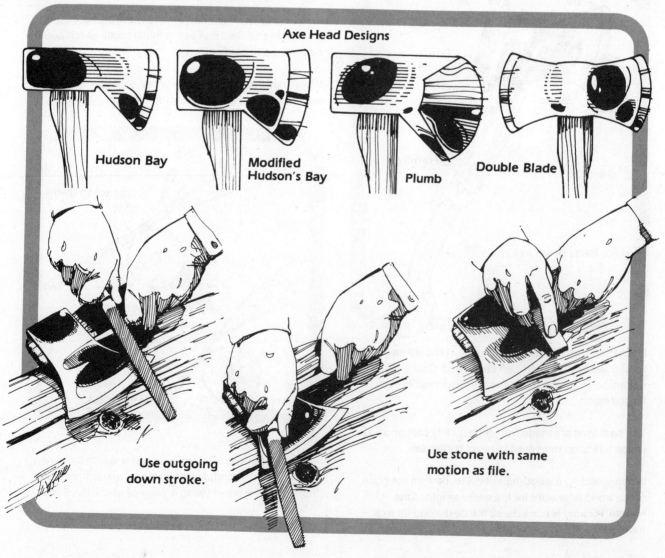

Axe Head Designs

Hudson Bay

Modified
Hudson's Bay

Plumb

Double Blade

Use outgoing
down stroke.

Use stone with same
motion as file.

Compass and Maps
Compasses

A compass and a map of the region around camp should always be carried when hunting in unfamiliar country.

There are many types of compasses available. They range from a simple pocket compass which shows general directions, to complex models with sights and sighting lines, useful for drawing maps or navigating exactly to specific locations.

A pocket compass is satisfactory when the hunter just needs to know north, south, east and west directions to find his destination. There are two types of pocket compass. One has a magnetized needle which pivots at its balance point and swings around the dial. The other has a revolving dial instead of a magnetic needle, which turns as the compass is moved.

A compass dial is divided into 360 degrees, numbered clockwise on the dial. The degree numbers shown on the dial are called azimuth directions. The letter N for NORTH is marked at the 0 degree point on the dial. South is at 180 degrees, east at 90 degrees, west at 270 degrees.

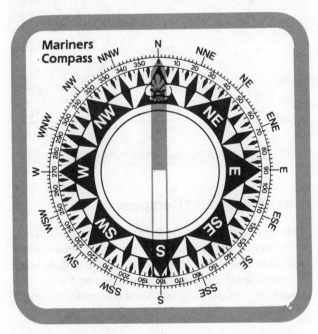

Usually one end of the needle is colored or one end is shaped like an arrowhead so you can tell which end of the needle is pointing to the north.

Do not rely on memory to tell you which end of the needle is the north end. In the confusion which sometimes happens when a person realizes he is lost, or if someone is injured, it is easy to forget which end points north.

If there is any chance you will forget which is the north end of the needle, scratch a mark on it. Write on a piece of tape and tape it to the back of the compass, or inside the cover, "north gray" or "north red" or "north arrow", or whatever applies to your particular instrument.

To tell which end of the needle points north, test it at home on objects and places where you know which is the true direction.

Be sure to hold the compass horizontally and flat. Otherwise the needle may stick or show an inaccurate reading. The compass must be kept away from metal

objects. Stand several feet away from any firearms, axes, or knives when taking a compass bearing. Even a metal belt buckle can distort the needle's action. If you are near bridge girders or railroad tracks, move to a different position that is distant from the metal structure.

When hunting game, a compass is used to guide the hunter back to camp. For example, if the hunter decides to stalk deer in a range of hills about two miles distant, he would take a compass reading before leaving camp. If the compass showed the direction of the hills is southwest of camp, he would know that after hunting in the hills he must walk north-east from the hills to get back to camp. The direction should be checked at intervals along the way.

Should the hunter, on reaching the hills, walk several more miles, he must take this into account when reading the compass for directions back to camp. If he had turned to the right when he reached the hills and walked in that direction for several miles, he would then be almost directly west of camp, not southwest as he was on leaving camp. To reach camp, he must now travel east.

General compass directions such as these, although not exact, are accurate enough to direct a hunter who has travelled only a few miles distance, back to the campsite. Following the compass directions will bring him back to the general area where he began his trek and he will then be able to recognize landmarks which tell him exactly where camp is.

When camp has been set up beside a "base-line" such as river, road or railway, the hunter can easily find his way back to camp with a compass. If he is hunting north of the base-line, he knows that as long as he doesn't cross that base-line, all he needs to do to find camp is walk south from where he is and he will be in line with camp.

A compass is best used in combination with a map. The map will show which directions to take to get to a specific location. The compass will keep you walking in the right direction.

Maps

Hunters use three main types of maps for finding their way in wilderness country:

a) printed maps prepared and published by governments or private mapping firms;

b) hand drawn maps prepared by the hunter from his own observations and information received from his companions or guide based on their knowledge of the hunting area;

c) mental maps based upon the hunter's memory of the direction, approximate distances and turns he made during the hunt.

Maps tell you where you are in relation to your surroundings. Identify two or more landmarks such as lakes, mountains, ridges or high peaks, which can also be recognized and located on the map. You can then judge where you are in relation to these places.

Use of Maps and Compass

The latitude and longitude lines which form the grid framework of printed maps are aligned with true north. A printed map shows north at the top, with latitude lines forming the top and bottom edges of the map and longitude lines, running true north and south, forming the sides.

A compass points to magnetic north. For this reason, printed maps usually have a declination diagram, or state the degree of declination in the region, in the map margin. DECLINATION is simply the degree of angle formed by the intersection of a line running true north and south (longitude) and another line running toward magnetic north (meridian).

To follow a straight course by compass the hunter should carry the instrument in his hand and refer to it frequently to be sure he stays on course.

Sometimes the hunter prefers to pick out landmarks on the way to his destination, checking his course as each spot is reached. A landmark should be chosen that is on the course of the hunter's ultimate destination and one which will be visible until it is reached. On reaching the marker, he chooses another landmark in the distance and checks his bearings again with the map and compass.

In forest, a straight course can be maintained by lining up two trees and walking directly toward them. As the first tree is reached, another tree is lined up, behind and in a straight line with the second. This procedure is repeated each time another of the trees is reached.

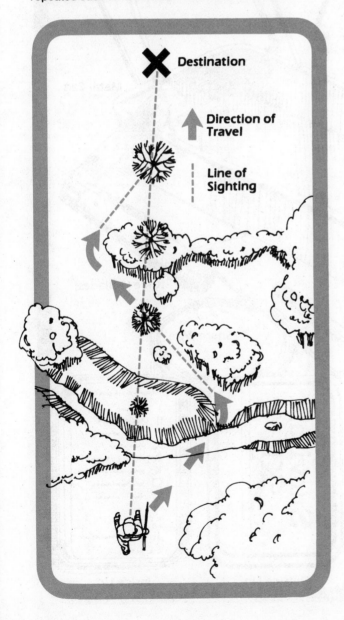

Survival Kit

Everyone who ventures into the woods, to hunt or fish, to hike or even just for a short walk, should take along a personal survival kit. (See chapter on survival). This kit should be small and light and should be carried with you at all times. The heavier you make this kit, the more unlikely you will be to take it along. The best survival kit is one that is small and compact enough to be carried in a pocket of your jacket.

Survival Kit Components

CONTAINER — an empty pipe tobacco can, approximately 3¼ × 4½ inches (8 cm × 11 cm) is a convenient size, which may also be used for cooking.
CONTAINER LID — painted a bright color so it can be found if lost with a ground to air signal card taped inside.
HANDLES — holes should be drilled in the container and handles attached for cooking.
MATCHES — long stemmed, wooden, strike anywhere matches or windproof matches with a striker.
FLINT AND STEEL
FIRE STARTER TABLET — burns for approximately 6 minutes.
ABSORBENT COTTON — excellent tinder, easily ignited with matches or flint and steel.
KNIFE — small pocket knife with 2 blades.
FISHING EQUIPMENT — 2 spoons (red and white Len Thompson #6), 2 dry flies (Royal Coachman), 2 wet flies (Black Gnat), 2 snelled hooks (size 8), 4 lead split shot, 15 yards (4 m) monofiliment line (10 lb./4 kilo) test.
SAFETY PINS — 4 assorted sizes
NEEDLE AND THREAD
NAILS — 4 assorted sizes
PENCIL AND PAPER
SNARE WIRE — 3 yards (2.7 m) of copper or brass wire
OXO CUBES — 2
TEA BAGS — 1 or 2 small packages
SIGNAL MIRROR — with signalling instructions
TAPE — tape lid to container with 18 inches (46 cm) of waterproof tape.

Items may be added to this list but do not include large amounts of food, cooking pots and other gear you would normally take camping.

Each time you go hunting, fishing or camping, practice using one or two items in your survival kit. This will give you confidence in your kit if you should ever need to use it. Replace any item that has been used.

Survival Kit

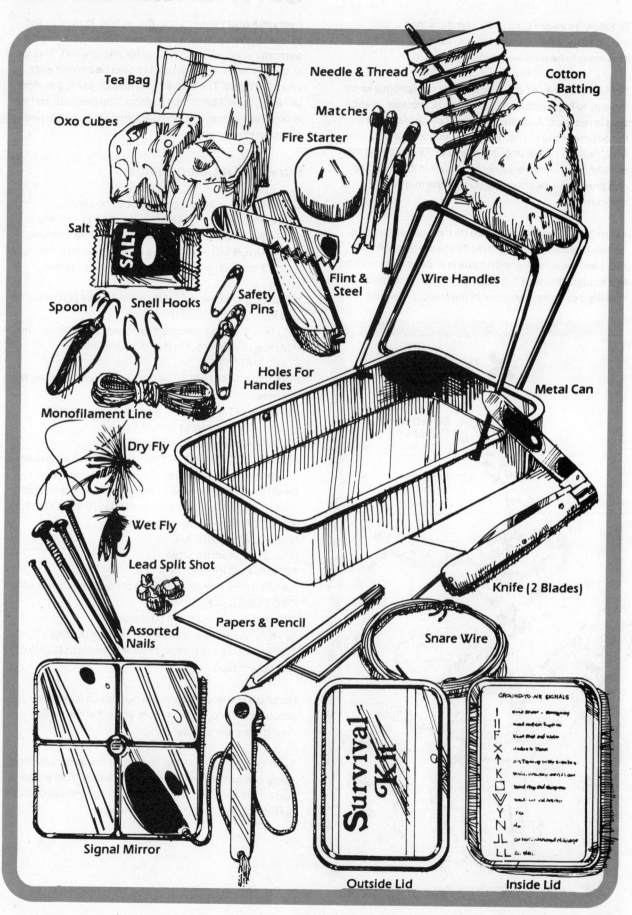

Tea Bag

Oxo Cubes

Salt

Spoon

Snell Hooks

Safety Pins

Monofilament Line

Dry Fly

Wet Fly

Lead Split Shot

Assorted Nails

Needle & Thread

Matches

Fire Starter

Flint & Steel

Holes For Handles

Papers & Pencil

Signal Mirror

Cotton Batting

Wire Handles

Metal Can

Knife (2 Blades)

Snare Wire

Survival Kit

Outside Lid

GROUND-TO-AIR SIGNALS

Inside Lid

First Aid Kit

With the knowledge of first aid, you will know what to do in emergencies. If someone is injured, you can provide aid until a doctor arrives—prevent injuries from becoming more serious—perhaps save a life. Every hunter's gear should include a first aid kit. First aid kits may be purchased in a variety of sizes. However, you may want to build one yourself. Know what is in your first aid kit and how to use it.

what is in your first aid kit and how to use it.

First Aid Kit Components

First aid handbook
Bandaids — approximately 6-12
4 × 4 inch (10 cm × 10 cm) sterile bandage
Roll of gauze bandage — 1 inch (2.5 cm)
Adhesive tape — ½ inch × 5 yards
(1 cm × 1.5 m)
Petroleum gel
Antiseptic
Razor blade
Small scissors
Tweezers
Eye snare
Small mirror

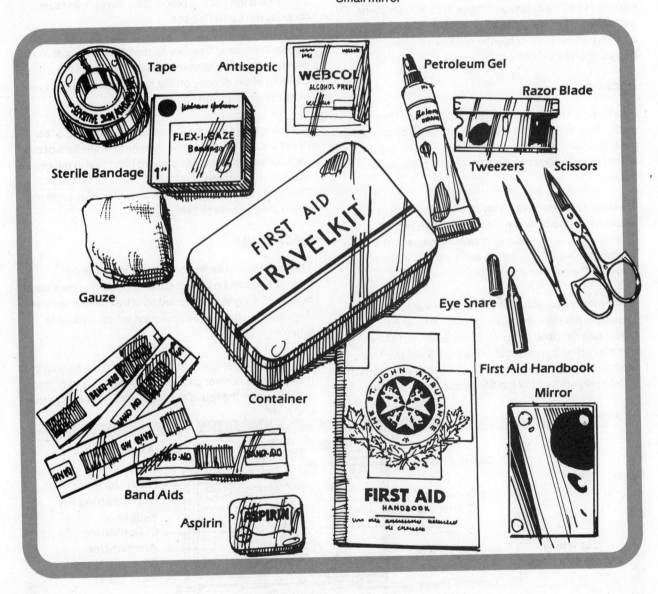

First aid kit designed for camp use.

Backpacking

For a hunting trip lasting several days in bush or rugged mountain country, backpacking may be the only satisfactory way to carry all your gear and equipment.

Backpack is a term describing the whole apparatus carried on your back. It usually includes a bag or sack to contain your gear and a frame to hold the bag in position on your back.

The hunter should choose a sturdy, heavy-duty frame to carry his gear. Some experienced backpackers say young people under 14 should carry a pack of 30 pounds (14 kilos) or less and those in their older teens can carry a pack weighing 40 to 45 pounds (18 kilos to 20 kilos). Other experts say the pack can weigh up to one-third of the carrier's body weight.

Packboards

Packboards are designed to rest easily against the back, allow freedom of movement and let air circulate freely between the pack and the back. Various loads or weight distributions can be arranged on packboard frames.

Most packboards have tightly stretched canvas or nylon webbing lashed between the vertical sides of the frame. The webbing serves as a sling to hold the pack. It cushions the load against the back and lets air in between the pack and your back to cool you.

Some modern packboards are made of welded aluminum or magnesium. These usually have an adjustable hip band attached to the lower part of the frame which supports most of the pack's weight. The hip band should be moved up or down to fit your body. It should ride above your hip bones and below your waist.

If it is too low, it restricts the thighs when you lift your legs while walking, and that is tiring. If it's too high, you use muscle instead of bone to support the weight, and that hurts. The hip band should be padded. Most manufacturers offer three lengths of frame. Be sure to buy the proper size.

To carry game and other heavy loads, many hunters use a "Trapper Nelson" frame, a simple packboard made of heavy canvas stretched between wooden sides with a detachable bag. The load is strapped to the wooden sides which are about one to two inches thick. Shoulder straps hold the pack in place. Only the canvas fabric touches the carrier's back.

Those who use a "Trapper Nelson" claim it holds loads closer to the body than other packs and puts the main carrying effort directly on the hips and legs rather than on the shoulders and spine.

Many backpackers use a tump line for carrying extra heavy packs. The tump line fastens to both sides of the packframe. It has a foam-padded head rest in the centre of the line which lays against the carrier's forehead. This takes some weight off the shoulder straps making heavy loads easier to carry.

Packsacks

The sack should be flexible in design so weight distribution can be varied. Gear to be carried for a short one-day hike and that carried for a trek lasting several days through heavy bush country, will be packed in different ways.

Generally, lighter items will be packed at the bottom of the sack with heavier gear near the top so most of the weight is near the top of the shoulders and close to the body.

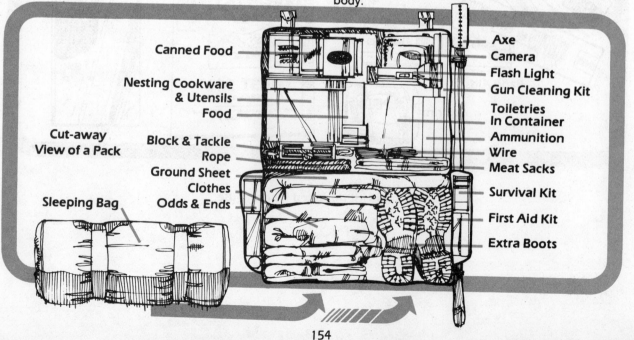

Cut-away View of a Pack

Canned Food
Nesting Cookware & Utensils
Food
Block & Tackle
Rope
Ground Sheet
Clothes
Odds & Ends
Sleeping Bag

Axe
Camera
Flash Light
Gun Cleaning Kit
Toiletries In Container
Ammunition
Wire
Meat Sacks
Survival Kit
First Aid Kit
Extra Boots

The pack should hang so it does not pull back on the shoulder straps. When the weight is properly distributed, there is an upward thrust from the hips and legs and a lift and pull from the shoulder harness while walking. The weight of the pack should be supported evenly by the back, shoulders and legs.

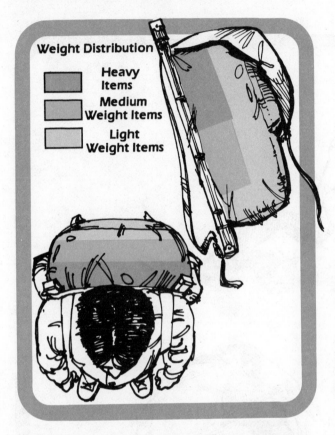

Weight Distribution

- ■ Heavy Items
- ▨ Medium Weight Items
- ▦ Light Weight Items

The support and shoulder straps should not restrict the movements of the back or arms. The straps should slide freely on the lift bars. This motion will act as a shock absorber if you slip or fall.

Correct weight distribution will also permit a constant flow of air between the pack and the carrier's back. Very heavy loads should be balanced so the center of gravity is high and close to the shoulders with the heaviest objects as close to the body as possible. This is the way to carry game or a heavy trophy head. When carrying game heads on a packboard, they should be flagged with blaze-orange ribbon..

Backpacking Trips

The hunter who plans to backpack should make up his pack ahead of time. Check the pack's weight and get the feel and balance of it. Then practice carrying it before starting out.

Know your weight limit. Know the weight you can carry under specific conditions such as rough ground and

hilly terrain, high altitude, hot or cold weather conditions, and your physical condition—and adjust your pack weight accordingly.

The only items a backpacker should carry in his pockets are those things required from time to time during the day such as a compass, pocket knife, waterproof match box, watch and handerchief, cigarettes or tobacco.

The beginning backpacker should plan to spend three or four days getting acquainted with his pack, his equipment and his ability to handle it.

To Put On a Pack:

a) Lift the frame onto your thigh.
b) Put the right arm through the shoulder strap and reach down to grasp the lower corner of the frame.
c) Lift the frame high and to the left with your right hand, then put your left arm through the left strap.

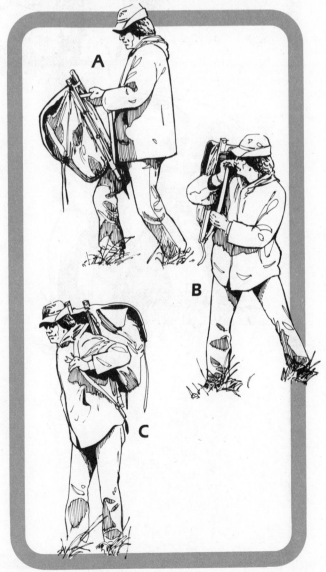

d) To get up with a very heavy load, lean the pack against something so it sits upright. Sit down and put shoulders in the straps. Tuck one foot under the other leg and fasten hip band loosely. Roll onto hands, knee and foot in the same motion, stand up. Once up, hunch the shoulders to raise load and tighten hip band.

To Take Off a Pack:

If you cannot readily swing out of the loaded pack frame harness, sit down and rest the frame on the ground or on a large rock and then slip out of the harness.

D

Sportsman's Check List

Big Game Hunt

Firearm Season

- [ ] Firearm
- [ ] Spare Firearm
- [ ] Rifle Cases
- [ ] Ammunition
- [ ] Rifle Cleaning Kit
- [ ] Hunting Regulations
- [ ] Hunting License
- [ ] Game Tags
- [ ] Spotting Scope

Archery Season

- [ ] Bow
- [ ] Extra Bow String
- [ ] Hunting Arrows
- [ ] Spare Broadheads
- [ ] Broadhead Cement
- [ ] Broadhead Sharpening File
- [ ] Field Arrows
- [ ] Bow Quiver
- [ ] Bow String Silencers
- [ ] Brush Deflectors
- [ ] Bow String Wax
- [ ] Bow Tip Protector
- [ ] Armguard
- [ ] Shooting Glove or Tab
- [ ] Camouflage Bow Cover
- [ ] Camouflage Outfit
- [ ] Archery Regulations
- [ ] Archery License

Include on Above Hunts

- [ ] Binoculars
- [ ] Compass
- [ ] Sheath Knife and Belt
- [ ] Pocket Knife
- [ ] Whetstone
- [ ] Map of Hunt Area
- [ ] Block and Tac
- [ ] Bone Saw
- [ ] Meat Sacks
- [ ] Bulk Salt
- [ ] Plastic Bags
- [ ] Rope and Wire
- [ ] Packboard

Upland Game and Water- fowl Hunt

- [ ] Shotgun
- [ ] Shotgun Case
- [ ] Shotshells
- [ ] Cleaning Kit
- [ ] Pocket Knife
- [ ] Hunting Regulations
- [ ] Hunting License
- [ ] Decoys
- [ ] Calls
- [ ] Waders or Hip Boots

Personal Gear

Clothing

- [ ] Duffle Bag
- [ ] Inner Socks
- [ ] Wool Socks
- [ ] Boots
- [ ] Camp Shoes
- [ ] Long Underwear
- [ ] Wool Shirt
- [ ] Sweater
- [ ] Trousers
- [ ] Hunting Jacket
- [ ] Vest
- [ ] Cap or Touque
- [ ] Gloves or Mitts
- [ ] Rain Gear
- [ ] Silicone Boot Dressing
- [ ] Spare Boot Laces

Toilet Articles

- [ ] Comb
- [ ] Hand Soap
- [ ] Razor
- [ ] Shaving Cream
- [ ] Toothbrush and Toothpaste
- [ ] Towel and Washcloth

Other

- [ ] Camera and Film
- [ ] Sunglasses
- [ ] Pencil and Notebook
- [ ] Tobacco
- [ ] Sewing Kit
- [ ] First Aid Kit
- [ ] Survival Kit

Camping Gear

Shelter

- [ ] Tent
- [ ] Tarp
- [ ] Sleeping Bag
- [ ] Foam Pad or Air Mattress

Cooking

- [ ] Camp Stove and Fuel
- [ ] Cooking Utensils
- [ ] Matches
- [ ] Cooler
- [ ] Water Cans
- [ ] Food

Lighting

- [ ] Lantern and Fuel
- [ ] Extra Mantles
- [ ] Flashlight
- [ ] Flare Gun and Flares

Tools

- [ ] Axe
- [ ] Buckets
- [ ] Hammer and Nails
- [ ] Rope and Wire
- [ ] Shovel
- [ ] Tool Kit

Notes

Firearms

Introduction

No one really knows who invented guns and gunpowder. History books credit the ancient Chinese with making the first explosive powder: a 13th century English doctor with discovering gunpowder ingredients in the Western World; and an Italian chemist with combining several different chemicals to produce powders which would ignite and explode.

In a very short time, man learned the possible uses of gunpowder. By putting this powder and pieces of metal together in a long tube and igniting the mixture, the metal was "shot" from the tube at great speed.

The development of guns and gunpowder grew with mankind's progress after the Middle Ages, evolving from this first "fire-stick" to the rifle and the handgun—the firearms which the pioneer used to feed and protect his family.

The pioneer learned to understand his gun, to know what it could do and what it could not do, and he learned the limits of his own ability. The man of that era was judged on his word, his way of life and his ability to shoot well.

Today, people are far less dependent upon shooting firearms to provide food and other necessities for survival. Shooting has become a form of recreation for many people.

History of Firearms

Matchlock

The matchlock was the principal firearm used by early explorers as they ventured into the wilderness. The matchlock was named after the manner in which the firearm was set off. A match ignited the powder to set of the charge.

The first "match" was a twisted rope of hemp which had been soaked in a solution of saltpetre and wine. It burned slowly and steadily.

Before "match" was invented, the shooter fired his gun by touching the powder with a red hot wire or a glowing coal. He could never stray far from a fire. However, a "match" would burn for hours allowing the hunter more freedom to pursue game at greater distances.

The matchlock had a simple S-shaped piece of metal called a "serpentine" fastened to it which held the smoldering match in one curve, away from the priming powder. When ready to fire, the shooter pressed the opposite end of the serpentine. This automatically moved the lighted match, bringing it into contact with the priming powder in the pan, thus setting off the charge. When the pressure was removed, the end of the serpentine holding the match moved back to its former position.

This serpentine mechanism was the first trigger. With it, the shooter was now able to hold the gun with both hands and aim more accurately.

Wheel-lock

The matchlock had many disadvantages. Weather was the worst problem. Rain or high wind would put out the match, making the gun useless.

The solution to this problem came in the form of a new kind of firearm—one that did not need a lighted fuse but produced its own fire for igniting the priming powder.

This device was called a wheel-lock and it worked much like the modern cigarette lighter. the wheel-lock mechanism was wound against the tension of a strong spring. When the trigger was pulled, a serrated wheel revolved against a piece of flint. This caused sparks to ignite the powder and discharge the bullet.

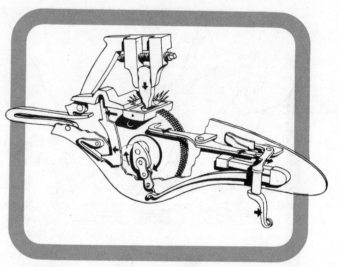

Flintlock

Although superior in many ways to the cumbersome and dangerous matchlock, the wheel-lock, too, had some serious disadvantages. Its lock was a complicated mechanism and therefore was expensive. It was slow because the wheel had to be rewound after each shot before the gun could be loaded and primed and ready to fire again.

A more practical ignition mechanism was needed. The answer came with the flintlock. The new lock was simplicity itself, producing its spark by striking flint against steel.

In the flintlock, the flint was clamped to the cock. The steel was directly opposite the cock. when the trigger was pulled, a strong spring snapped the cock down, striking the steel with the flint and producing sparks which fell into the flashpan below.

This new ignition system led to the development of today's modern ammunition.

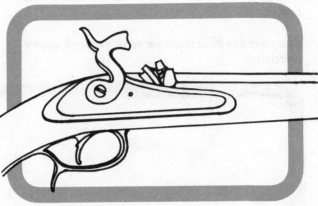

Modern Firearms

All early firearms were loaded from the muzzle. The major difference was the way in which the gun powder was ignited.

The next major advance in firearms design was the development of the cartridge. A cartridge is a container or case made of metal or cardboard which combines the ignition system, the propellant, and the projectile into a single unit. All modern firearms are based on the development of the cartridge.

Today's hunter has a wide and varied choice of firearms and ammunition designed to give excellent performance in specific situations. Before deciding which firearm is best for you, you should understand how each type of gun works and which is best suited to your needs for the kind of game you intend to hunt.

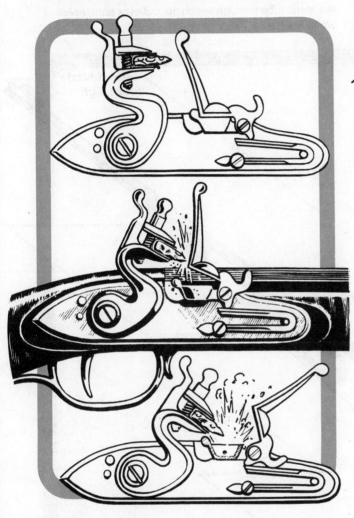

Percussion Cap

For almost 300 years, firearms were based on the principle of producing a spark by striking flint against steel. Then in the early 1800's, a powder which would explode when struck a hard blow was discovered and a new means of ignition was invented.

The percussion cap firearm used a separate self-contained primer called a "cap". The cap, which contained the new explosive powder was placed on a cone. When the hammer hit the percussion cap, the powder exploded, igniting another powder charge which propelled the bullet.

Firearms Characteristics

Before you can use a firearm safely, you must know the names of its parts and how they work. The mechanisms of most firearms are basically the same and so are their names.

Every gun has three major sections: the stock, action and barrel.

The stock assembly is the handle of the firearm. It is usually made of wood or synthetic material. The action assembly is the heart of the firearm. It contains the moving parts which load the gun, fire the ammunition and extract the empty shell case. The barrel assembly is the metal tube through which the bullet or shot travels when the gun is fired.

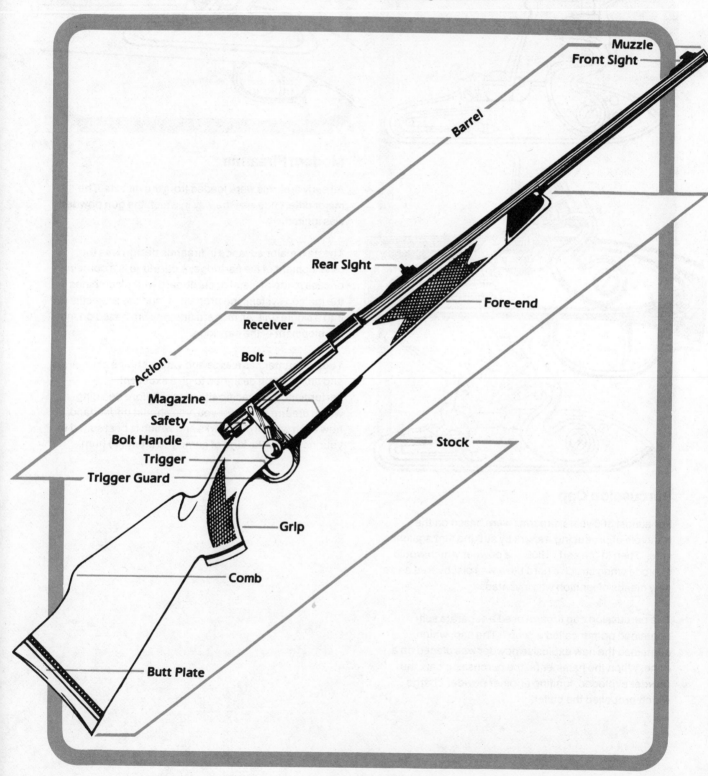

Muzzle
Front Sight
Barrel
Rear Sight
Fore-end
Receiver
Bolt
Action
Magazine
Safety
Bolt Handle
Trigger
Trigger Guard
Stock
Grip
Comb
Butt Plate

Rifling

Rifle and pistol barrels have a series of spiral grooves that twist through the "bore" or center of the barrel. The ridges of metal between the grooves are called "lands". The lands and grooves together make up the rifling.

Rifling makes the bullet spin as it leaves the gun so it will be more stable in flight. Rifling gives the bullet greater accuracy.

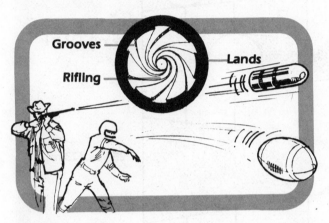

Caliber

The caliber of rifles and pistols is the inside diameter of the barrel before the rifling has been cut.

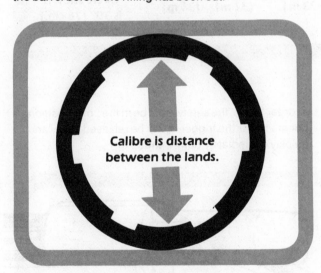

Caliber is usually expressed in hundredths of an inch or in millimetres. For example, a .22 caliber barrel measures $^{22}/_{100}$ of an inch in diameter. Calibers vary all the way from .17 to .600 caliber.

Shotgun Gauge

Shotgun barrels are classified by gauge instead of caliber. Gauge is determined by the number of lead balls (each having the same diameter as the bore) that weigh one pound. For example, find a lead ball that is the same diameter as a 12 gauge shotgun barrel. It will take 12 of these balls to make one pound. This is what we know today as a 12 gauge shotgun. One exception to this rule is the .410 shotgun which is actually measured in caliber.

The most common sizes of shotgun gauge are 12 gauge (the largest in practical use), 16 gauge, 20 gauge and .410 (the smallest).

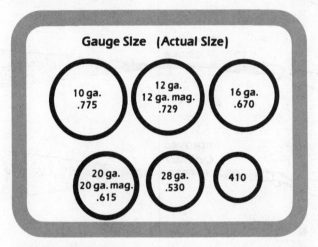

Shotgun Choke

The narrowing found at the muzzle end of most shotgun barrels is a choke. The choke controls the shot pattern and determines at what distance the shotgun will be most effective.

Just as the nozzle on a hose controls the spray of water, the choke of a shotgun barrel controls the spread of the shot. This shot spread is called the "pattern".

From the tightest to the widest spread, chokes are described as "full", "modified" and "improved cylinder". A gun barrel which has no choke is called a "cylinder bore".

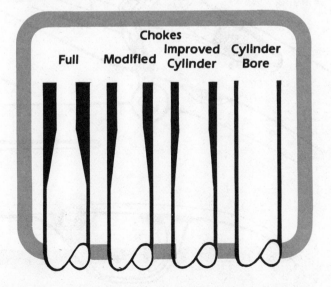

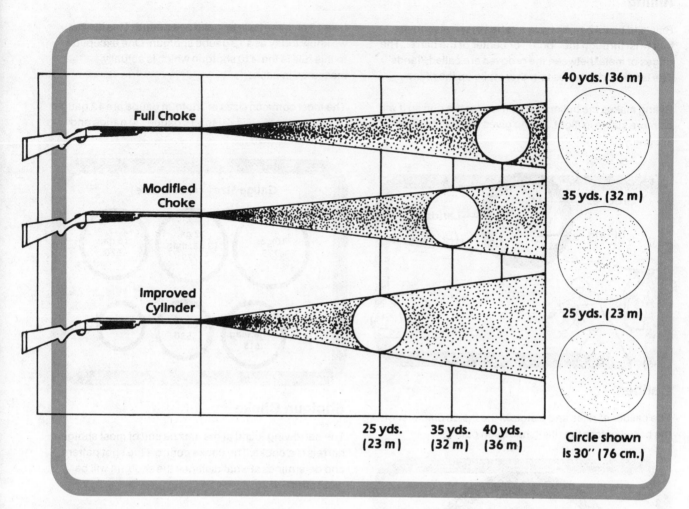

Full Choke

Modified Choke

Improved Cylinder

40 yds. (36 m)

35 yds. (32 m)

25 yds. (23 m)

| 25 yds. (23 m) | 35 yds. (32 m) | 40 yds. (36 m) |

Circle shown is 30" (76 cm.)

Safety

The safety on a firearm locks the trigger and blocks the gun's action so it cannot be fired.

In order to fire, the safety must be in the "off" position. Located near the trigger, it can be released easily and quickly immediately before shooting.

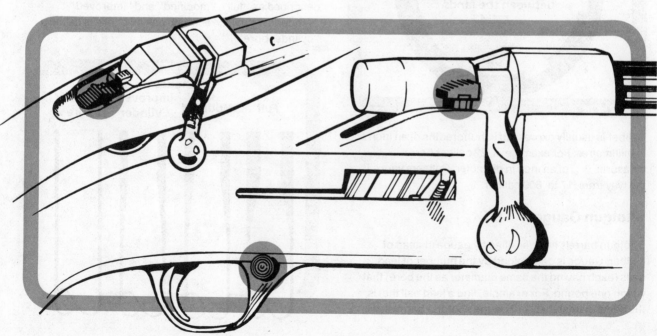

Sights

A sight is a device used to aim the firearm. There are three basic types of sights—open, aperture and scope.

Rifles may have any of these three types of sights. Handguns usually have open sights. Most shotguns have only a front sight called a bead although some may have open sights.

Open Sight

Most factory-issued rifles and handguns are equipped with an open rear sight and front bead sight. To aim, the shooter must line up the front bead with the rear open sight and with the target. This type of sight requires time to aim accurately and may be used with success when speed is not a factor.

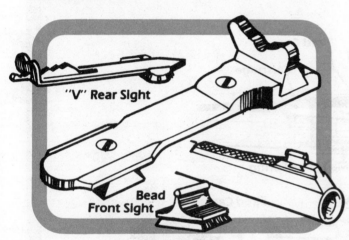

"V" Rear Sight

Bead Front Sight

Aperture Sight

The aperture is called a "peep" sight because it has a small hole that you peep through to aim at the target. All the shooter has to do is look through the peep hole at the front sight, then hold the front sight on the target.

Because the human eye, when it looks through an aperture or small opening, is naturally drawn to where the light is brightest (which is the exact centre of the peep), the peep sight is more accurate than the open sight.

Scope Sight

The scope sight is a mini-telescope mounted on the rifle. It simplifies sighting because the shooter needs to focus on only one object—the target. The scope sight helps the hunter see the target better because it magnifies, making the target appear larger and closer. It is designed to gather light so the shooter can identify a target even under dim light conditions.

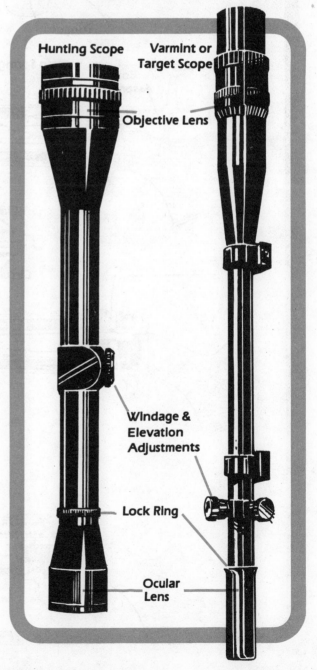

Hunting Scope

Varmint or Target Scope

Objective Lens

Windage & Elevation Adjustments

Lock Ring

Ocular Lens

Actions

Firearms are generally classified by their type of "action". The five basic types are: bolt action, pump action, lever action, hinge action and semi-automatic action.

Bolt Action

A bolt action firearm operates on a lift, pull and push sequence similar to a door bolt and even looks very similar.

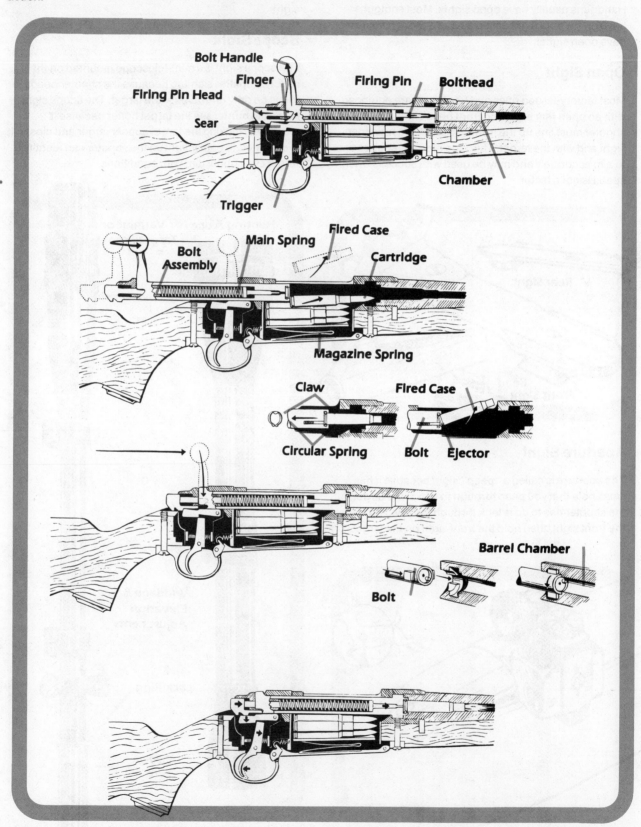

Pump Action

On a pump action firearm, the fore-end of the stock is pumped back and forth in order to open and close the action. The pump action firearm is sometimes called a "slide" or "trombone" action.

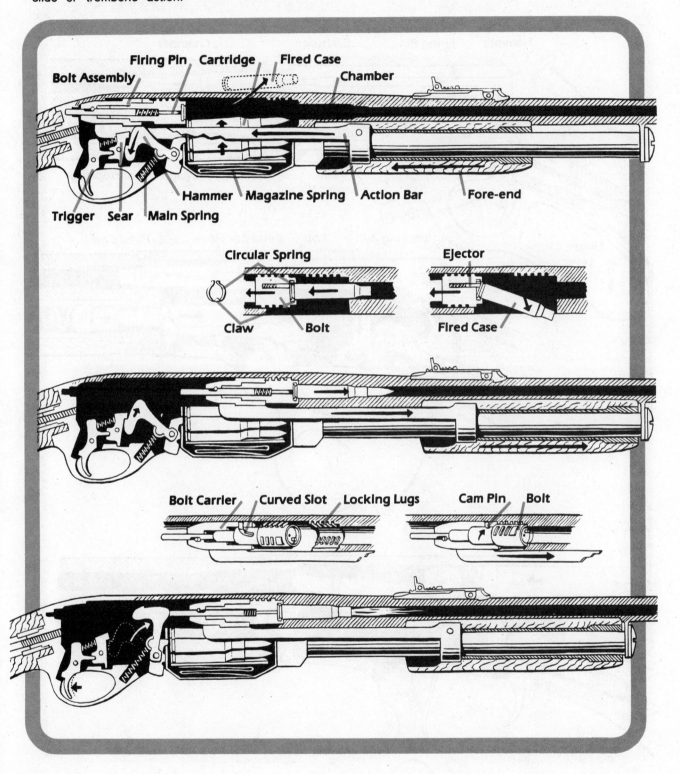

169

Lever Action

A lever action firearm has a metal handle which is located just behind the trigger. To open the action, the handle is pulled downward away from the stock.

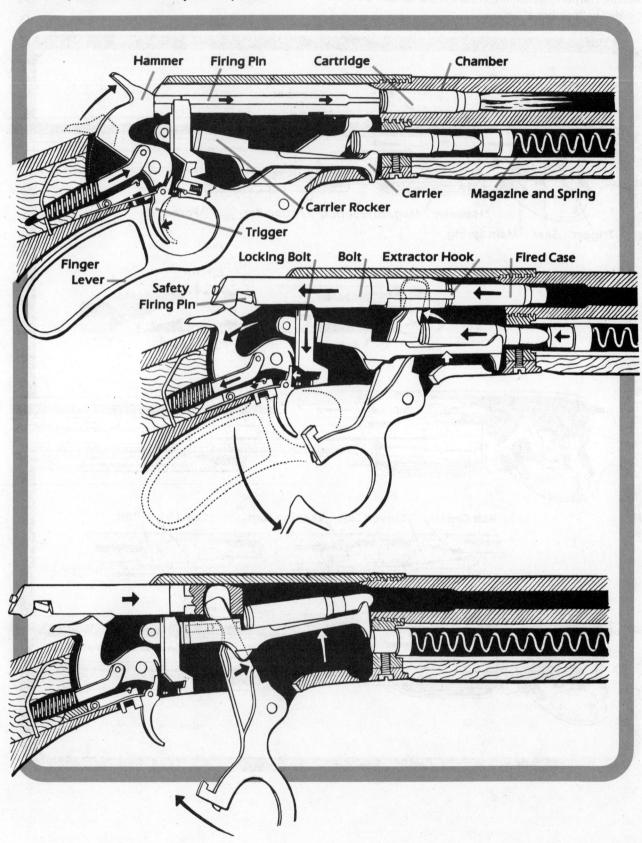

Hammer   Firing Pin   Cartridge   Chamber

Carrier   Magazine and Spring

Carrier Rocker

Trigger

Finger Lever

Safety Firing Pin

Locking Bolt   Bolt   Extractor Hook   Fired Case

Hinge Action

The hinge action firearm opens, or "breaks" in the center, similar to the movement of a door hinge. To open the action, the release handle is pushed to one side and the barrel or barrels are pressed downward.

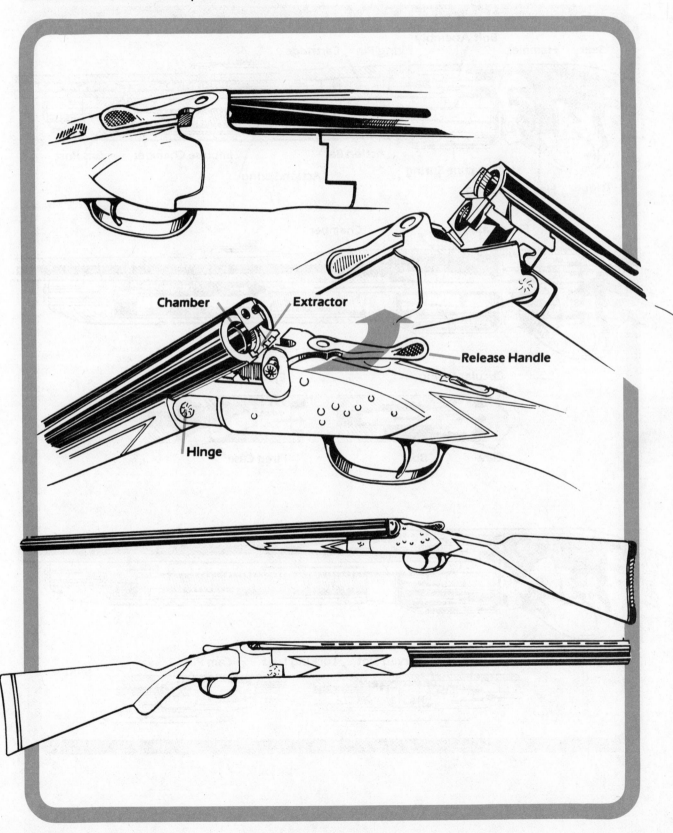

Chamber

Extractor

Release Handle

Hinge

Semi-automatic Action

The action of a semi-automatic firearm is opened by pulling back a handle. Most models of semi-automatics will stay open when empty. Others must be held open.

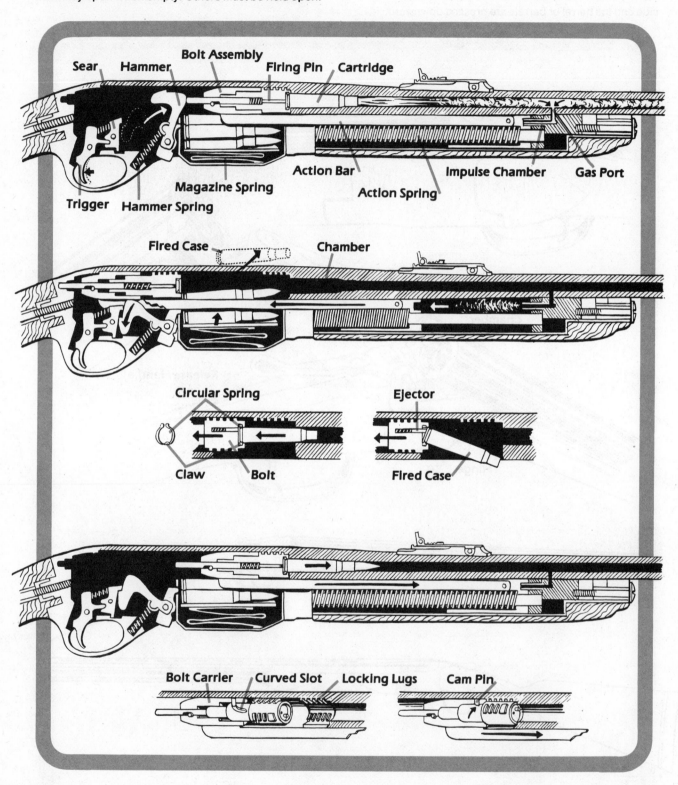

Other Action Types

Revolving Action

A revolving action is easy to identify because of its round cylinder. This cylinder is actually a magazine which acts as the chamber when properly aligned with the barrel.

The action release on a revolver is different on various models. Many revolvers have a latch type release on the side which allows the cylinder to swing out. Some revolvers have cylinders which cannot be swung out or lifted up and must be loaded and unloaded through a loading gate on the side.

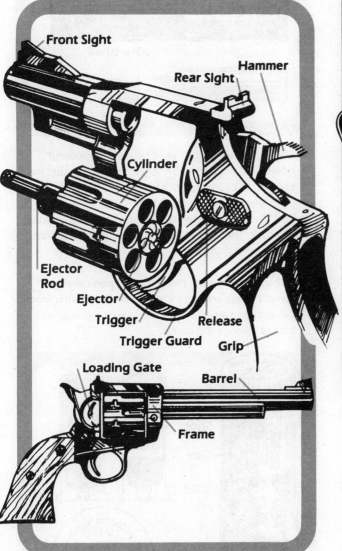

Front Sight
Rear Sight
Hammer
Cylinder
Ejector Rod
Ejector
Trigger
Trigger Guard
Release
Grip
Loading Gate
Barrel
Frame

Full Automatic Action

A firearm with full automatic action will insert, fire and eject all cartridges in its magazine with a single, continuous trigger pull.

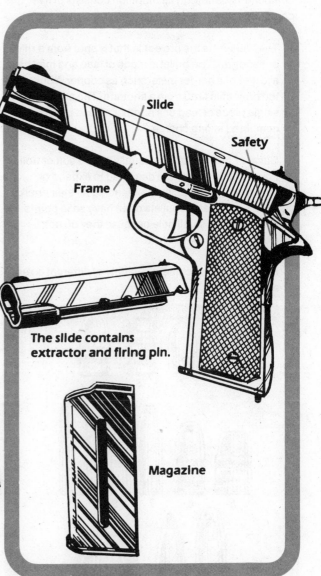

Slide
Safety
Frame

The slide contains extractor and firing pin.

Magazine

Action Release

Except for bolt action firearms, most guns have some type of action release mechanism. These mechanisms allow an action to be kept either opened or closed. The location of the action release mechanism depends on the make and model of the firearm.

Before handling any gun, know where its action release is located.

Ammunition

The ammunition used in rifles, shotguns and handguns varies in size, appearance and parts. Ammunition for rifles and handguns is made up of four basic components. Shotgun ammunition consists of five components.

1. The "bullet" is the projectile that is shot from a rifle or handgun. The bullet is made of lead and may have a jacket of a harder metal such as copper. "Shot" is the projectile fired from a shotgun. The shot may be a single piece of lead or a number of lead pellets combined in one charge.

   Game or hunting bullets usually have a soft or hollow point. These bullets are designed to expand or flatten upon impact, thus expending all their energy upon entry. Target bullets often have solid points which make a small hole because they do not expand.

   Bullets and shot come in a variety of different sizes and weights.

2. The "case" is a container in which all other ammunition parts are assembled. The case is commonly made of brass, steel, copper, paper or plastic.

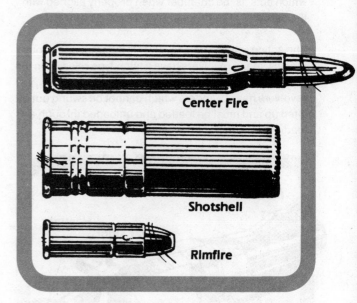

Center Fire

Shotshell

Rimfire

3. The "powder charge" is a chemical compound which, when burned, forms gases which propel the bullet or shot through the barrel.

4. The "primer" is a chemical mixture which explodes when hit. The flame of the primer explosion ignites the powder charge.

5. In the shotgun shell, there is a fifth part called a "wad". Wads are used to separate the powder from the shot and also hold the loose shot together as it travels through the barrel.

1. Semi-Jacketed Hollow Point
2. Metal Case
3. Wadcutter
4. Metal Point
5. Semi-Wadcutter Gas-Check
6. Standard Lead
7. "Power Lokt"
8. Pointed Soft Point
9. Hollow Point
10. Soft Point
11. Bronze Point Expanding
12. Shotgun Slug

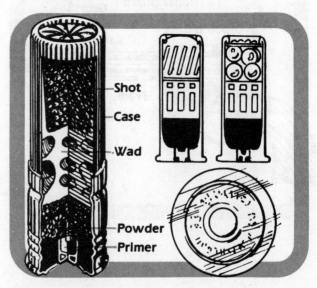

Shot
Case
Wad
Powder
Primer

There are two basic types of modern ammunition— "rimfire" and "center-fire".

In rimfire ammunition, the priming chemical is around the inside bottom rim of the cartridge case. The rim must be soft enough to allow the firing-pin of the gun to dent the rim when it strikes it. This crushes the priming compound, which then explodes, igniting the powder. Rimfire ammunition is used in low-pressure firearms.

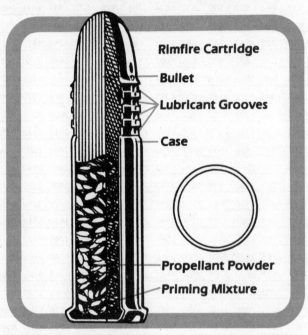

Rimfire Cartridge

- Bullet
- Lubricant Grooves
- Case
- Propellant Powder
- Priming Mixture

In center-fire ammunition, the primer is located in the center of the case bottom. The firing pin strikes the primer, exploding the priming compound and igniting the powder charge.

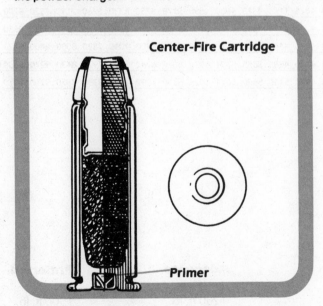

Center-Fire Cartridge

- Primer

Certain center-fire ammunition may also be classified as "belted" or "rimless". Belted ammunition is characterized by a raised ridge belt around the base of the cartridge.

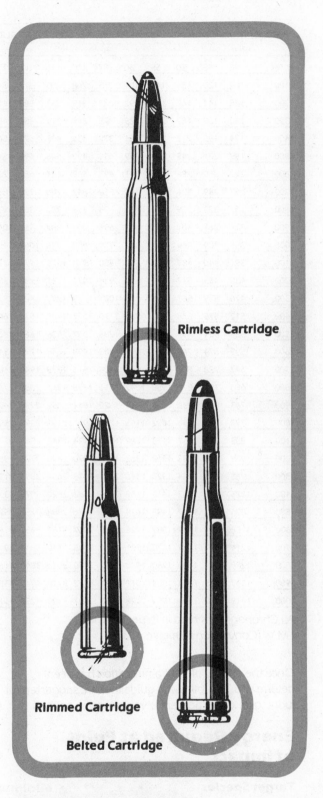

Rimless Cartridge

Rimmed Cartridge

Belted Cartridge

Impact Energy of Bullets

The potential killing power of various bullets is argued pro and con amongst hunters. One of the most important factors in determining the killing power of ammunition is its energy upon impact. This may be determined from the chart.

VELOCITY							BULLET WEIGHT — GRAINS															
Ft. Sec.	40	45	50	55	60	87	100	110	120	130	140	145	150	160	170	180	200	220	235	250	275	285
1100	107	120	134	147	161	233	268	295	322	349	376	389	402	429	457	483	537	591	630	671	738	765
1200	128	144	160	176	192	277	319	351	383	415	447	463	479	512	543	575	639	703	752	799	878	912
1300	150	168	187	206	225	325	375	412	450	487	524	543	562	599	637	674	750	825	881	937	1031	1068
1400	174	195	217	239	261	377	435	478	522	565	609	630	652	696	739	783	869	956	1021	1087	1195	1938
1500	199	224	249	274	299	434	498	548	598	648	698	722	747	797	847	897	997	1096	1170	1245	1372	1420
1600	227	255	284	312	341	493	568	624	682	738	795	823	852	908	965	1021	1133	1248	1330	1418	1558	1613
1700	257	289	321	353	385	558	642	706	770	834	898	930	962	1026	1090	1154	1282	1411	1511	1602	1763	1827
1800	287	323	359	395	432	625	718	792	863	934	1005	1041	1078	1149	1222	1293	1437	1580	1689	1796	1977	2048
1900	321	361	401	442	482	696	802	882	962	1042	1122	1162	1202	1282	1362	1443	1603	1763	1882	2004	2205	2283
2000	355	409	444	488	532	770	888	976	1064	1152	1242	1286	1330	1418	1508	1597	1774	1951	2082	2218	2440	2530
2100	391	440	489	538	587	850	978	1075	1173	1271	1369	1418	1468	1564	1662	1760	1956	2151	2298	2444	2688	2786
2200	430	483	537	590	644	934	1073	1181	1288	1396	1503	1556	1610	1718	1825	1933	2145	2362	2520	2686	2948	3058
2300	470	529	587	646	704	1021	1173	1292	1409	1526	1644	1703	1762	1878	1996	2112	2346	2585	2755	2935	3225	3313
2400	512	575	638	703	767	1110	1277	1405	1532	1660	1738	1853	1916	2045	2172	2298	2552	2812	3000	3195	3510	3635
2500	555	624	694	764	833	1206	1387	1526	1665	1803	1942	2012	2081	2220	2358	2496	2773	3053	3260	3470	3818	3950
2600	599	674	749	824	899	1302	1498	1648	1798	1948	2095	2187	2248	2396	2548	2697	2997	3296	3520	3749	4122	4270
2700	647	728	808	890	970	1405	1616	1778	1940	2102	2264	2345	2428	2588	2748	2910	3232	3558	3800	4040	4450	4605
2800	696	786	870	958	1042	1511	1738	1913	2088	2262	2434	2521	2600	2784	2957	3131	3479	3829	4085	4349	4785	4958
2900	747	840	933	1028	1119	1620	1864	2052	2238	2426	2612	2702	2797	2986	3170	3358	3732	4101	4380	4665	5130	5315
3000	797	897	996	1092	1195	1730	1991	2191	2390	2590	2788	2878	2988	3188	3386	3586	3985	4380	4680	4978	5480	5680
3100	853	960	1067	1173	1280	1856	2134	2347	2561	2774	2988	3094	3202	3415	3628	3841	4268	4695	5015	5336	5869	6083
3200	909	1023	1135	1248	1362	1973	2270	2498	2728	2952	3180	3292	3410	3634	3861	4085	4545	5000	5332	5680	6250	6475
3300	965	1085	1204	1323	1446	2107	2413	2654	2893	3135	3375	3495	3616	3858	4100	4340	4820	5308	5660	6030	6635	6870
3400	1025	1153	1282	1410	1538	2224	2562	2820	3078	3332	3590	3718	3848	4105	4360	4618	5130	5642	6025	6410	7062	7304
3500	1086	1221	1357	1493	1629	2360	2716	2988	3258	3528	3800	3938	4070	4345	4618	4884	5430	5975	6380	6785	7475	7735
3600	1150	1294	1437	1583	1726	2500	2877	3164	3452	3740	4025	1165	4315	4600	4890	5178	5752	6330	6760	7190	7920	8200
3700	1214	1367	1517	1670	1821	2640	3035	3340	3644	3948	4250	4401	4555	4860	5165	5470	6074	6680	7144	7592	8350	8650
3800	1280	1440	1600	1760	1920	2782	3200	3520	3840	4160	4480	4645	4800	5120	5440	5760	6400	7040	7520	8000	8800	9120
3900	1347	1517	1684	1853	2011	2931	3372	3710	4045	4380	4720	4885	5055	5394	5730	6070	6742	7420	7925	8430	9270	9600
4000	1418	1592	1773	1950	2128	3086	3547	3900	4255	4610	4970	5150	5320	5674	6025	6380	7092	7800	8338	8870	9750	10010

All Chronographs read in ft. per second
I.M.V. (Conversion to meters x .305)

Once the energy of your ammunition has been determined, the following guidelines are suggested for judging its killing power for various game animals.

Energy Required at Point of Impact

Target Species	Minimum	Adequate	Preferred
Deer, antelope, sheep, goat	900 ft. lb.	1200 ft. lb.	1500 ft. lb.
Elk, bear up to 600 lbs.	1500 ft. lb.	2000 ft. lb.	2500 ft. lb.
Large bear, moose	2100 ft. lb.	2800 ft. lb.	3500 ft. lb.

Safety and Firearms Care Introduction

Almost every young person is interested in firearms. There is something about a gun, old or new, that makes us want to pick it up, see how it feels, and try to work its mechanism. When this interest is properly guided, young people can benefit in many ways. From old guns they can learn history and an understanding of some of the hardships faced by men who relied on such firearms for their lives. They can learn mechanical principles from studying gun actions. And from target practice with modern arms, they can develop physical skills that will help them in many other activities.

But guns are not toys. They must be treated with respect. If you want to learn how to shoot a gun, be sure to learn from qualified instructors. They will show you how to do it properly and safely.

For the beginning shooter, a rifle or shotgun that is loaded with a single shell or cartridge is the best and safest choice. The most common rifle of this type is the bolt action. The most common shotgun of this type is the hinge action.

General Rules of Firearms Safety

The responsible shooter lessens the chance of an accident by following some basic rules of firearms safety. And these rules must be followed whenever and wherever firearms are being handled.

1. Always keep the muzzle pointed in a safe direction.

2. Treat every firearm as if it were loaded—even when you think it's not.

3. Keep the action of the firearm open except when actually shooting or when storing an unloaded gun.

4. Use the right ammunition for your firearm. Carry only one type of ammunition to be sure you will not mix different types.

5. Be sure of your target—and beyond. Identify the target, then look past it to be sure it is safe to shoot. Do not shoot where your bullet will ricochet. Bullets can ricochet off rocks, trees, metal, water and other surfaces.

6. Alcohol, drugs and shooting do not mix. Drugs and alcohol may impair your judgment. Keen judgment is essential to safe shooting.

7. Beware of fatigue. When you are so tired, hunting isn't fun any more, go back to camp. Fatigue can cause carelessness and clumsiness which can cause accidents. Fatigue can cause you to see things that aren't really there.

8. When you have finished hunting, unload your gun before returning to your vehicle or camp.

PRACTICE SAFE GUN HANDLING ALL THE TIME.

Firearms Safety when Hunting

As well as the general rules of firearms safety, there are additional rules which must be followed when hunting.

Before Leaving Home

The responsible hunter learns before the hunt how to shoot safely and accurately. He practices regularly so he is familiar with his firearms and checks his equipment to see it is operating properly. He knows the range and effectiveness of his ammunition and ensures he has the right ammunition for the gun being used and the game to be hunted. His gun is accurately sighted-in.

Firearms Safety while Travelling

Whether your gun is being carried in a car, boat, on a horse, motorcycle, or in any other vehicle, these rules of safe gun handling must be followed:

1. Be sure the gun is unloaded.

2. Place it in a protective case.

3. Position the firearm securely so it will not move about during travel.

4. To transport a gun on a public transportation vehicle such as a bus, train or plane, check first with the carrier's agent concerning the regulations.

Firearms Safety in the Field

There are several ways to carry a gun safely and at the same time have your gun ready for quick use in the field.

Whichever carrying method you use, these basic rules apply:

1. Keep the muzzle pointed away from yourself and others.

2. Keep the safety in the "ON" position when carrying a firearm.

3. Keep your finger outside the trigger guard.

Two-Hand or Ready Carry

The "two-hand" or "ready carry" is the safest carry for hunters.

This carry gives you good control of the muzzle and allows you to raise your gun quickly for a shot.

Cradle Carry

The "cradle carry" is another safe carry. However, because the muzzle points to one side, this method should not be used when walking beside anyone.

Trail Carry

The "trail carry" is safe when several people are walking abreast. It is also safe for the leader when people are walking single file but others in the line should not carry their guns this way.

Elbow or Side Carry

The "elbow or side carry" is safe when walking in open terrain. It should not be used when walking through bush because branches can get tangled around the gun and push the barrel downward. Do not use the side carry when others are ahead of you.

Shoulder Carry

The "shoulder carry" is safe when walking beside or behind someone. Special care must be taken to keep the muzzle pointed upward. Do not use this carry when others are behind you.

Sling Carry

The "sling carry" is often used by hunters who must walk a long way before taking a shot. The sling carry leaves both of the hunter's hands free. However, when walking in dense bush, it should not be used because the gun may get caught in brush and be pulled off the hunter's shoulder.

The carry you use will depend on where your companions are and the kind of terrain.

When hunters are positioned in a line abreast, the hunters at either end should use the cradle or side carry. The hunters in the middle should use either the side or two-hand carry.

When walking single file, the leader may choose any of the carries except the shoulder carry. Center of the line hunters should use the two-hand or cradle carry. The last person in line may use the two-hand, cradle, sling or shoulder carry.

Zones of Fire

When hunting with others, "zones of fire" must be established so each hunter will not endanger others when he shoots.

If three hunters in pursuit of game birds were to walk across an open field, the middle hunter's zone of fire would be birds flying in the center of the field. the zone of fire for the hunter on the right would be birds flying in the area to the right side. The third hunter's zone of fire would be birds flying in the area to the left. The same zones of fire apply when hunters are walking abreast in pursuit of small game like rabbits.

After zones of fire are determined, each hunter must shoot only within his specific zone. If a hunter shoots out of his zone of fire, he could hit one of his companions.

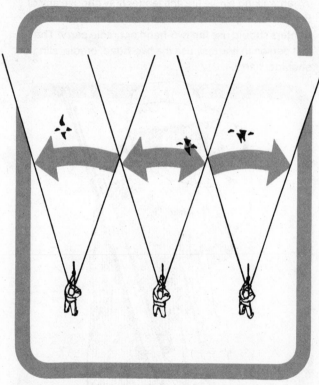

Because a flock of waterfowl usually flies in one direction, hunters shooting from a boat or duck blind must determine zones of fire for each person in the group. Each person shoots only when birds are flying within his particular zone of fire.

Big game hunters often separate while hunting and unless zones of fire are established, a hunter could be mistaken for game by one of his companions. Before separating from the group, each hunter determines his planned location and the direction he will travel and this is established as his particular zone of fire. Every member of the hunting party must be informed of each hunter's zone of fire.

Firearms Safety in Boats, Pits and Blinds

When hunting from a boat, the firearm to be carried in the bow should be placed in first. It should be unloaded and pointed forward. After the first hunter is in the bow of the boat, the second unloaded firearm should be placed in the stern, pointing backwards. The second hunter can then shove-off and take his position in the stern. While the boat is moving, do not permit the front firearm to protrude past the bow or gunwales because it could catch on reeds or brush.

Before shooting, anchor the boat firmly. Both hunters should remain in the center of the boat with their firearms always pointing away from each other.

When hunting from a pit or blind, lay your unloaded firearm on the ground near the entrance to the pit. When you are in the pit, bring in the unloaded gun. Check your firearm carefully to be sure the muzzle has not become clogged with dirt or snow. Unload the gun before leaving the pit or blind. Lay it on the ground outside before you come out.

Other Rules of Field Safety

1. Be positive of your target's identity before shooting.

2. Take time to fire a safe shot. If unsure, if you must move too quickly, pass up the shot. When in doubt—don't! When you wonder whether you should shoot—don't.

3. If you fall, try to control where the muzzle points. After a fall, check your gun for dirt and damage and make sure the barrel is free of obstructions.

4. Unload your gun before attempting to climb a steep bank or travel across slippery ground.

5. When you are alone and must cross a fence, unload your firearm and place it under the fence with the muzzle pointed away from where you are crossing. When hunting with others and you must cross a fence, unload the gun and keep the action open. Have one of your companions hold the gun while you cross. When over the fence, take your gun and your companion's unloaded gun, so that he may cross safely.

6. Never use a scope sight as a substitute for binoculars.

7. When finished hunting, unload your firearm before returning to camp.

Rules are safe only when they are obeyed. If a companion doesn't follow the rules of safe firearms handling, you should refuse to hunt with him unless he is prepared to correct his behavior.

Care and Maintenance of Firearms

Regular cleaning will help keep your gun in good working order and will prevent it from rusting. Any firearm which has been stored uncovered for a long time or has been exposed to moisture or dirt, must be cleaned thoroughly before use.

To clean a firearm you will need:

1. cleaning rod

2. patches

3. powder solvent

4. light gun oil

Before cleaning any firearm, check to be sure it is unloaded.

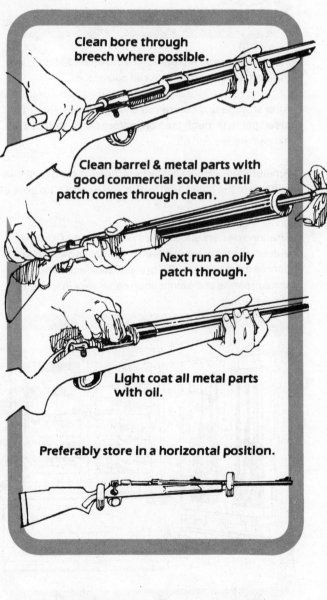

Clean bore through breech where possible.

Clean barrel & metal parts with good commercial solvent until patch comes through clean.

Next run an oily patch through.

Light coat all metal parts with oil.

Preferably store in a horizontal position.

After cleaning the gun with rod and patches, apply a light coat of oil to the metal parts of the gun. Make sure to use the oil sparingly. Too much oil can clog the gun and prevent the firearm action from working smoothly.

Before firing remove excess grease and oil.

When the firearm is clean, store the unloaded gun, in a horizontal position, in a locked cabinet.

After storage and before you use the gun again, run a clean patch through the bore before firing. Remove all excess grease and oil.

Ammunition should also be kept clean. If sand or dirt collects in the bullet lubricant, it can damage the bore of the gun.

Firearms owners should always assume that anyone untrained in the use of firearms will not know how to handle them properly. To prevent accidents, always store firearms and ammunition separately in locked storage units.

Firearms are precision instruments. Guns which are not operating properly should be examined by a gunsmith or returned to the manufacturer. Even minor repairs should be made by an expert. Beginning and inexperienced shooters should never attempt to repair any firearm.

Fundamentals of Rifle Shooting

Marksmanship

Marksmanship is the ability to hit your mark or target. It is important that a hunter be a good marksman for two major reasons.

The first reason is safety. If you have the ability to hit your target, you will be self-confident. When you know you can shoot accurately, you will not need to spend time thinking about how to shoot, but can concentrate instead on where to aim. You will have time to think—Is this shot safe? Is the path to and beyond the target clear?

The second reason is to make a clean kill. An accurate shot will kill quickly, cleanly and humanely. A good hunter practices marksmanship skills until his shots are consistently accurate and studies animal anatomy to know where vital organs are located.

Shooting excellence depends on several fundamental techniques which must be learned and practiced. They are aiming, trigger squeeze, breath control, follow through and shooting position.

Aiming

Master Eye

The "master eye" is the eye you use for sighting purposes. The master eye is the stronger of your two eyes. This eye will judge speed and range, and focus more accurately than your other eye.

Even though you are right-handed, you may have a left master eye. To determine which is your master eye, point your finger at an object with both eyes open. Then alternately close one eye and then the other. Your finger will remain "lined up" with the object when your master eye is open.

Sight Alignment and Sight Picture

The correct use of gun sights is essential if your aim is to be accurate. Of the three types of sights, only the open sight requires you to physically line-up the sights. This process is called "sight alignment."

The advantage of aperture and scope sights is they do not require conscious alignment.

The aiming of any sight at a target creates a "sight picture."

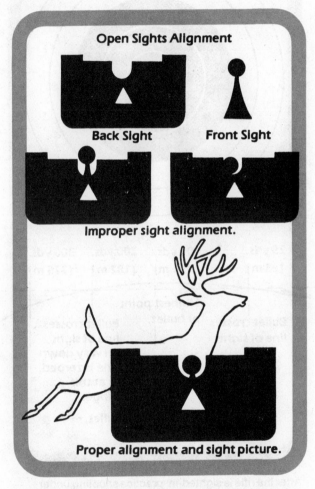

Open Sights Alignment

Back Sight　　　**Front Sight**

Improper sight alignment.

Proper alignment and sight picture.

The scope sight simplifies aiming. It magnifies, which enables you to see your target better. You don't have to line up a pair of sights. You simply look through the scope and hold the cross hairs on the target to aim accurately.

There are disadvantages to scope sights, however. Because they are precision instruments, they must be handled with extreme care to prevent damage to the delicate mechanism. Scope sights have a very narrow field of view which can make sighting on a moving target potentially dangerous. Because of the scope's viewing limitations, you might not see a person or object coming into the path of your shot.

Trigger Control

Correct trigger control is essential for an accurate shot. When the sights are aligned on your target, squeeze the trigger slowly and steadily. Do not yank. Do not pull. Anything other than a smooth squeeze will cause the sight picture to waver and will send the shot off target.

Do not tense before the rifle fires. You should be relaxed, allowing each shot to happen as a surprise.

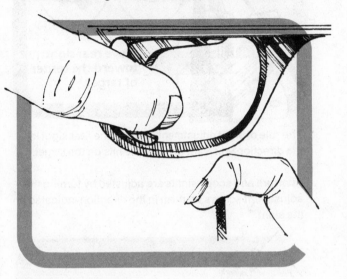

Breath Control

Controlled breathing is necessary to shoot accurately. As you breathe in and out, it is normal for your chest to rise and fall and your arm to waver. So will your gun barrel unless you control your breathing at the exact moment you fire.

When you are in shooting position, with your cheek hard against the stock, take a deep breath, exhale a portion of it, and hold your breath while you aim and squeeze the trigger. This should allow you to hold the barrel and sights in perfect alignment on the target at the final instant when the gun fires.

If you hold your breath too long, you may lose control and your shot will be off the mark. If you run out of breath before firing, relax, take a deep breath and do it again.

Follow Through

Follow through, which simply means continuing to hold still until after the bullet has been fired, is important to accurate shooting. If the rifle is moved a split second too soon, your aim will be off target. Follow through will ensure the rifle isn't moved until the bullet is well on its way to the target.

Sight Adjustment

When using iron sights on the practice range, if your shots are consistently hitting the target in small groups, but are off-centre, then you must adjust the rear sight.

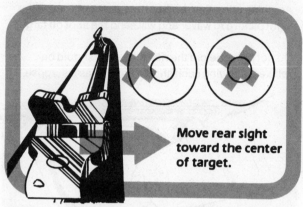

Move rear sight toward the center of target.

The rule of sight adjustment is, move the rear sight in the direction you want to move the hits on the target.

Aperture and scope sights are adjusted by turning the adjustment screws on them in the direction indicated on the sight.

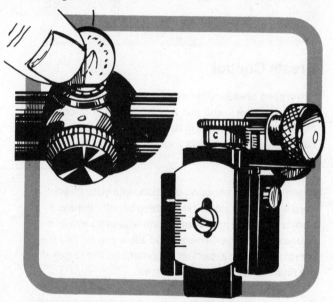

Sighting-in

Before hunting, your rifle must be "sighted-in", which means the rifle's sights must be adjusted so that the bullet will hit the target at a specific range.

Set up a target with a safe back-stop at 25 metres and fire at least three test shots. Be sure to use the same type of ammunition you will use when hunting. Check the target. If the group of hits is not at the point of aim, correct the sight. If the shots are not together, it could be due to your technique or some other mechanical factor.

If your shots are on the point of aim at 25 metres, they will be on the point of aim again at approximately 200 metres due to the bullet's trajectory.

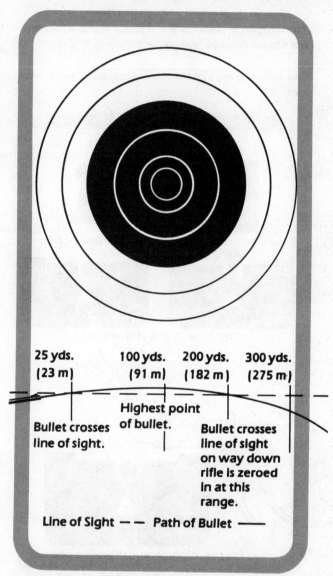

| 25 yds. (23 m) | 100 yds. (91 m) | 200 yds. (182 m) | 300 yds. (275 m) |

Highest point of bullet.

Bullet crosses line of sight.

Bullet crosses line of sight on way down rifle is zeroed in at this range.

Line of Sight – – Path of Bullet ——

After the rifle is sighted-in, practice shooting under various light and weather conditions and at various distances.

Normally you sight-in your rifle for a specific distance by shooting across level ground. However, when shooting in the field, you must make some allowance for differences in elevation between you and your target. When standing on a ridge or in a gulley, you will need to aim slightly below the spot you would hold on if you were standing on level ground. This is due to the effect of gravity on the bullet.

If your rifle is sighted-in correctly and you squeeze the trigger with steady even pressure and remain relaxed, you will score a hit.

Shooting Positions

Prone Position

The prone position is the steadiest shooting position and the one from which the fundamentals of rifle shooting are best learned. It is a good position for firing accurate long distance shots. But it is usually not suitable when hunting in tall grass or dense brush which can obscure the line of sight to the target.

If you are right-handed, lie on your stomach with your body slightly to the left of the line of aim. If you are left-handed, reverse this position. Keep your back straight and legs in a relaxed position. Both elbows should be bent and your shoulders curved slightly forward to form a solid upper body position. The upper body and arms support the rifle weight.

When shooting, a sling should be used for extra support. Hold the rifle grip with the trigger hand. Place your opposite arm through the sling as far as it will go. Swing your arm in an outward circular motion ending with your hand under the fore-end of the rifle and the sling across the back of your hand.

With practice the shooter will learn to bring the rifle butt in to his shoulder correctly and quickly. The shooter should adjust the sling and practice using it before the hunt.

Sitting Position

The sitting position is the next steadiest shooting position. Both short and long range shots can be fired accurately from this position.

Sit solidly on the ground. The legs may be crossed or open and the body should be positioned about 30 degrees to the right of the line of aim.

Place the left elbow near but not on the bony part of the left knee. As in the prone position, tuck the elbow as far

under the rifle as possible. Place the right elbow on or near the right knee. You have now formed two triangles which make a firm support for the rifle. Reverse the procedure if you are a left-handed shooter.

Hold the rifle firmly but do not grip it tightly. Bracing your body against something stable such as a tree or rock will help steady your aim for a more accurate shot.

Kneeling Position

Because the shooting arm is free, this position leaves the shooting arm and elbow unsupported and is not as steady as either the prone or sitting positions. But with practice, the shooter can maintain control and shoot accurately.

Turn so you are approximately at a 45 degree angle to the target. Lower your body so the right knee touches the ground and place your left foot forward to steady you. Sit comfortably on the heel or the side of the right foot. Place the left elbow near but not on the bony part of the left knee, as far under the rifle as you can.

If you are a left-handed shooter, kneel on the left knee with the right foot forward and the right elbow on the bent knee.

Standing Position

The standing position is the most unstable shooting position. It is also the most difficult position from which to fire an accurate shot.

It requires excellent control. The shooter must be skilled in all of the rifle shooting fundamentals—sighting, breath control, trigger squeeze and follow through.

Turn your body approximately 90 degrees to the right of the target. Place your feet shoulder width apart.

Support the rifle with your left arm. Hold the left arm against your body for extra support. Hold the rifle firmly against your shoulder with the right hand. Do not grip the rifle tightly. Reverse the procedure if you are a left-handed shooter.

If there is too much waver, do not shoot. Resting or supporting the rifle on a stable object such as a tree or large rock, or using a carrying strap as a sling, will help steady your shot.

Fundamentals of Shotgun Shooting

Shooting a shotgun is different from shooting a rifle. With the rifle you must aim precisely. With a shotgun you "point" at the target. Because of this, the fundamentals of shotgun shooting are different.

Accurate shotgun shooting requires a fast sequence of movements involving the body, gun and eyes. These movements need to be performed in one smooth, co-ordinated movement for accuracy.

There are some shotguns which are equipped with adjustable sights and some models that fire slugs. These types use the same shooting techniques required for accurate rifle shooting.

Shotgun Shooting Stance

The shotgun shooting position, or "stance", resembles that of a boxer in the ring—feet spread apart, well balanced, arms and trunk free to swing to the right and the left of the target. This position must be comfortable and natural to allow quick movement in any direction.

When shooting, the body weight shifts to the leading leg (left leg if you shoot right-handed, right leg if you shoot left-handed). The leading hand holds the shotgun fore-end and points naturally to the target area.

You don't aim the shotgun—you "point" it at your target.

Mounting the Shotgun

The action of placing the shotgun to your shoulder is called "mounting the gun". You must place the stock against your cheek first, then against your shoulder. This makes sure the gun is in exactly the same position each time you shoot.

Do not make the error of raising the gun to the shoulder first and dropping your head so the cheek rests against the stock. When this happens, you may make several shooting errors, which will likely cause you to miss the target.

Eyes on the Target

Keep both eyes wide open and focussed on the moving target—not on the gun barrel or the bead sight. While watching the target, mount the gun correctly and point it toward the target area.

Remember, you do not aim a shotgun, you simply point it.

Slap the Trigger

You do not fire a shotgun with slow, steady trigger pressure as you do a rifle. The shotgun trigger is consciously "slapped". The trigger slap is similar to the action of striking a typewriter key. Slap the trigger quickly, but not hard.

Leading

"Leading" means shooting ahead of the moving target. Leading is necessary when shooting at any moving target. If you shoot directly at a moving target, by the time the shot reaches that spot, the target will have already passed by. With correct lead, the shot and the moving target will reach the same spot at the same time.

With practice, this leading will soon become automatic, requiring no conscious thought on your part.

There are three commonly used methods of leading—"swing through", "sustained lead" and "snap shooting".

Swing Through Lead

For the beginning shooter, the swing through method is easiest to learn.

Swing the muzzle of the shotgun so it points at the flying bird. Follow its flight path, increasing the speed of your swing until the gun muzzle has passed through the bird to a spot just ahead—then fire. Continue your swing during the shot and after.

It is extremely important to continue swinging your shotgun after the shot. This is called "follow through". It ensures against shooting behind your target.

Sustained Lead

A shooter using the sustained lead technique must estimate the speed, range and angle at which his quarry is flying. Having decided on the amount of lead necessary, he swings the muzzle that distance ahead of the target. He then maintains this distance, or lead, in front of the bird up to and after the shot is fired.

Snap Shooting

Anticipating the amount of time he thinks it will take a flying bird to get there, a hunter, using the snap shot method, picks a spot in front of his target and fires at that spot. He hopes that the shot and the target will meet at the same place.

191

Fundamentals of Handgun Shooting

The use of handguns for hunting is legal in many states, however regulations vary from state to state. You should check the appropriate state laws before going to field with a handgun.

The person who masters the fundamentals of good rifle shooting (grip, position, sight alignment, trigger squeeze and breath control) will find them adaptable to handgun shooting.

Shooting Position

Stand with body turned approximately 45 degrees from the target. Spread your feet about shoulder width apart with weight distributed evenly on both feet to give you solid balance. Keep your knees straight but not locked.

Stretch out your firing arm and lock your elbow and wrist. Keep your head erect.

This position will give you stability when firing and keep body movement to a minimum.

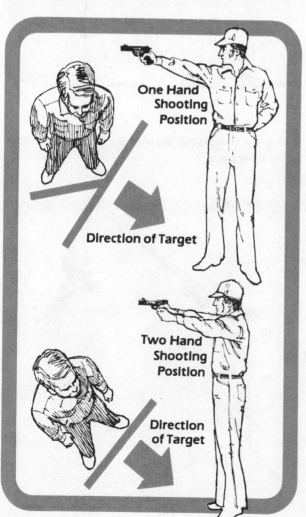

One Hand Shooting Position

Direction of Target

Two Hand Shooting Position

Direction of Target

Grip

Good marksmanship requires that the grip remain firm for each shot. Change in the grip will affect the ability to maintain sight alignment and accurate bullet placement.

The correct hold gives the shooter complete control of the handgun when it fires.

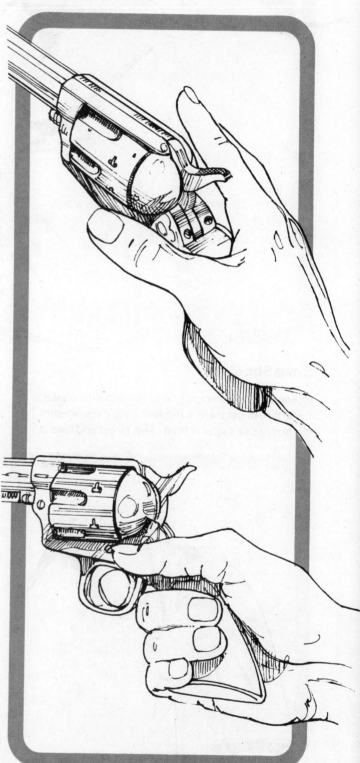

Sighting and Aiming

You sight and aim a handgun the same way as you would a rifle with open sights.

Because the sights of a handgun are close to each other—much closer than rear and front rifle sights—sight alignment of a handgun must be exact for accurate aiming.

Proper Sight Alignment

Trigger Control

Squeeze the handgun trigger as you would squeeze the trigger of a rifle.

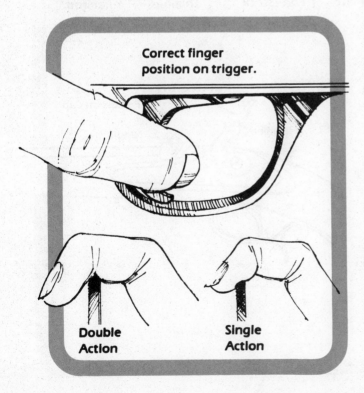

Correct finger position on trigger.

Double Action

Single Action

Breath Control

Control your breathing in the same manner as when shooting a rifle.

Follow Through

As in rifle shooting, when shooting a handgun it is necessary to follow through by continuing to hold still until after the bullet has been fired.

Loading a Handgun

WHEN LOADING A HANDGUN, BE SURE IT IS ALWAYS POINTED IN A SAFE DIRECTION.

Be sure handgun is always pointing in a safe direction when loading.

193

Black Powder and Muzzleloading

Black powder hasn't been used to fire guns since early in this century. In recent years hunting with black powder firearms or muzzle-loaders has been revived.

Selecting Black Powder Firearms

Black powder enthusiasts will find a wide choice of firearms available today. There are muskets, pistols, muzzleloading rifles and shotguns. Black powder shooting need not be expensive. A black powder gun costs about the same as a standard shotgun. Muzzleloaders can also be made from inexpensive do-it-yourself kits. If you do have an antique gun, before using it, have it inspected by a firearms expert to be sure it can be fired safely.

With percussion cap models, the breech plug should be removed and the nipple, drum and threads checked for rust and deterioration.

Special attention must be given to antique black powder shotguns. If they are corroded, they are not safe to fire.

Antique shotguns, especially those with Damascus barrels, are particularly susceptible to corrosion.

Today, the safest guns for black powder use are reproductions of muzzle-loaders.

Before buying a black powder gun, the newcomer to the sport should first attend several black powder shoots as a spectator. Talk with the participants and learn why they like a particular model. A gun which is good for target shooting is not necessarily the best model for hunting. Know the gun's capabilities and those functions which it can perform before purchasing a black powder firearm.

If you intend to hunt big game with your black powder gun, give consideration to the size of caliber you choose.

The caliber of gun used to hunt big game is prescribed by regulations in many states which permit the use of black powder guns. You should check the hunting regulations for any restrictions on the use of muzzle-loaders in hunting.

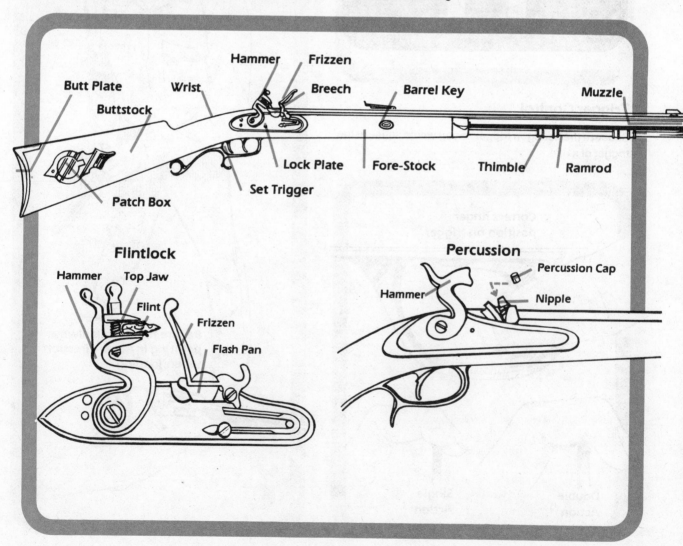

Selecting Powder and Ball

Muzzleloaders require different loads for hunting and for target shooting. There are four types of black powder, Fg, FFg, FFFg, and FFFFg. Each type has a different burning rate depending on the coarseness or size of the powder granules.

Fg is very coarse and is the ammunition used to fire muskets with large bores.

Most muzzleloading shotguns, big bore rifles and pistols between .54 and .69 caliber fire FFg, the second coarsest powder available.

A faster burning black powder is FFFg. It is the powder used with most cap and ball revolvers, single shot pistols and rifles ranging from .36 to .54 caliber.

FFFFg is very fine powder and is seldom used except when priming flash pans of flintlocks. It is extremely fast burning and creates pressures too great for most black powder guns.

Most muzzleloading rifles fire round lead balls or conical shaped bullets called mini-balls.

Tables showing the correct bullet diameter, powder type and charge in grains for various black powder guns are listed in most publications about black powder shooting.

Selecting Accessories

The black powder shooter must have certain shooting accessories close at hand.

a) PATCHING MATERIAL—linen or cotton fabric (not synthetic) cut into individual patches or one inch wide strips, Vaseline or shortening to lubricate the bullet and a knife to trim the patches.

b) POWDER HORN OR FLASK—a container for powder made of material such as horn, brass or copper that will not generate sparks or static electricity.

c) POWDER MEASURE—a brass measuring scoop to ensure the correct powder charge is loaded.

d) STARTER—a short and long starter are usually combined in one tool. The short starter fixes the ball firmly in the muzzle and the long starter is used to move the ball down the barrel.

e) RAMROD—the ramrod is used to push the tight-fitting bullet down the length of the barrel.

f) RAMROD ACCESSORIES
(i) Worm—a corkscrew tip on the ramrod used to remove cleaning patches which have stuck in the bore.
(ii) Ball screw—a tip on the ramrod used to remove the lead ball without discharging the firearm.

g) NIPPLE PRICK OR VENT PRICK—a length of wire slender enough to be inserted through the vent hole in a caplock or the flashhole in a flintlock to clear any fouling or obstruction. A nipple wrench should also be carried to replace a broken nipple.

h) CAP HOLDER AND LOADING BLOCK—The cap holder is a small strip or disc of leather punched with holes which will hold extra caps securely. The loading block holds pre-patched and lubricated balls.

i) POSSIBLES BAG—A shoulder bag or pouch in which the necessary accessories are carried.

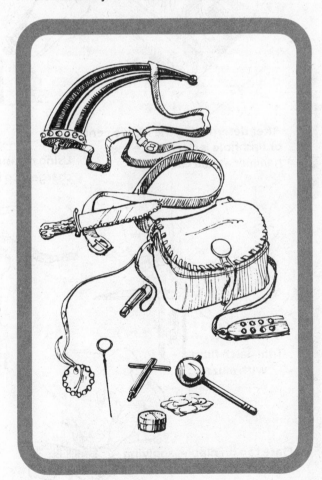

Loading

Before loading, the barrel of the muzzleloader should be wiped with a cleaning patch to remove any fouling or oil residue. The patching cloth is moistened with Vaseline, shortening or saliva, then wrapped around the ball forming a tight seal. With a sharp knife or razor, trim excess patching from around the ball after sealing.

To test a percussion cap firearm, fire a cap in the unloaded gun. If the gun is in good working condition, a small curl of smoke will come out through the barrel. Or, if the muzzle is held near a leaf or blade of grass, the puff of air which comes out of the barrel will move it.

To test a flintlock, prime the flash pan and flashhole with powder and touch it off with the muzzle pointing in a safe direction. Smoke should show from the muzzle.

If the nipple vent on the percussion cap gun or the flashhole on the flintlock appear to be closed, work the hole clear with a nipple prick.

For convenience when on a hunting trip, pre-measured powder loads may be carried in small plastic pill containers, or in individual paper tubes twisted tightly at each end.

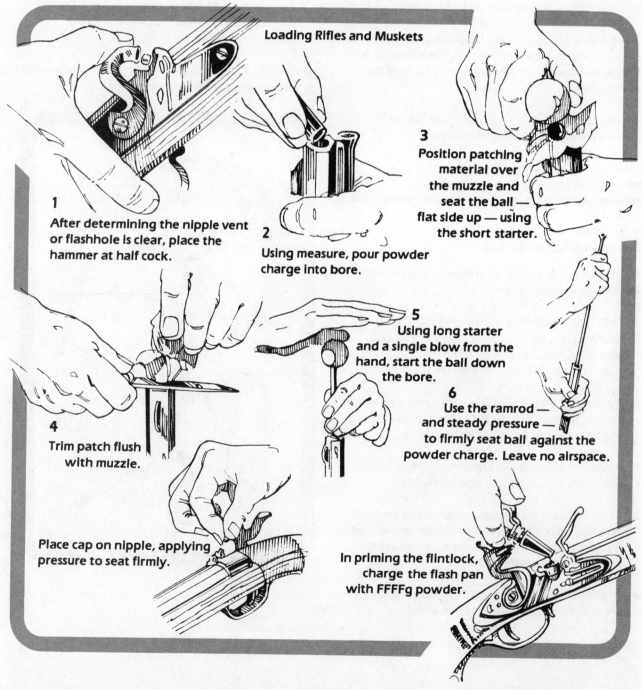

Loading Rifles and Muskets

1
After determining the nipple vent or flashhole is clear, place the hammer at half cock.

2
Using measure, pour powder charge into bore.

3
Position patching material over the muzzle and seat the ball — flat side up — using the short starter.

4
Trim patch flush with muzzle.

5
Using long starter and a single blow from the hand, start the ball down the bore.

6
Use the ramrod — and steady pressure — to firmly seat ball against the powder charge. Leave no airspace.

Place cap on nipple, applying pressure to seat firmly.

In priming the flintlock, charge the flash pan with FFFFg powder.

Safety Considerations

1. Muzzleloaders must be handled with the same care afforded other firearms.

2. Muzzleloaders are to be used with black powder only. Never use a smokeless powder. Black powder is highly combustible and can be ignited by a small spark. Never smoke near black powder and be sure to store black powder far from any open flame such as a campfire.

3. Never pour powder from the horn or flask directly into the muzzle. After a shot has been fired, smouldering residue often remains in the barrel, which could cause an explosion or backfire into the powder container.

4. Hold the muzzle away from the body when loading. This will protect you from burns if the powder is accidentally ignited.

5. Be certain the ball is seated firmly in place. To shoot with a ball lodged midway down the barrel will damage the gun and could severely injure the shooter.

6. Wipe the bore with a damp patch after each firing.

7. It is important to know when a gun is loaded. Experienced muzzleloaders mark the gun's ramrod at levels which show the bore depth when the bore is empty, when charged with a light target load and when charged with a heavy hunting load. When the ramrod is inserted in the barrel, it is immediately apparent whether or not the gun is loaded and if loaded, with how heavy a charge. This safety precaution is especially important.

Other Recreational Shooting Activities
Introduction

It is important that a beginning hunter have a high level of shooting proficiency before he goes hunting. It is also important that he know his firearm is sighted in accurately and that he know how to handle and operate it safely. It is too late to find these things out when in the field hunting. They must be determined beforehand. The best way a hunter can accomplish this is to participate in other forms of recreational shooting activity before the hunting season. These activities can be done year round. Some activities may be done during the years before a person is legally old enough to hunt. By doing a lot of supervised shooting at this time, hopefully he will have overcome the urge to do a lot of indiscriminate shooting when he first goes into the field hunting.

Plinking

Some people enjoy shooting just for the fun of it. They spend many hours "plinking" at tin cans, targets or pest species of wildlife such as gophers. But just like hunters, people who go plinking have certain responsibilities. They must ask permission to shoot on private property, they must pick up and remove targets when the shooting is finished, and they must be concerned about safety. Thoughtless, inconsiderate plinkers are not welcome anywhere. One problem that greatly concerns landowners is plinkers who shoot glass bottles and leave the broken pieces lying around where they may injure livestock or damage tires.

Empty

Target Load

Hunting Load

Before going plinking:

1. Find out if plinking is lawful in the area.

2. Obtain permission from the landowner.

3. Know what wildlife are classified as pest species which may be shot while plinking and which species of wildlife are protected.

4. Check first with the state conservation agency, state police or local police department to determine local laws governing the carrying and discharge of firearms.

Before You Shoot:

1. Be sure there is a safe backstop behind your target.

2. Be sure the noise from your shooting will not annoy neighbors or passersby!

After You Shoot:

1. Be sure you have cleaned up your shells, targets and other trash.

2. Leave all gates as you find them and report any open gates to the landowner when leaving.

3. Thank the landowner.

Guns for Plinking

The .22 rimfire rifle is the most popular choice for plinking. Although this firearm has many features which make it suitable for this purpose, there are several factors which should be considered.

Positive Features

a) inexpensive to shoot

b) makes little noise

c) does not recoil when fired

Negative Features

a) because it has no recoil and it's quiet, shooters tend to forget that a loaded .22 rimfire can be a dangerous and lethal firearm in the hands of the inexperienced and careless.

b) the low velocity, all lead bullet has a tendency to ricochet after impact.

A better and safer choice for plinking is a .22 center-fire such as the .22 Remington. It has a louder noise. However, this high speed bullet will disintegrate on impact, thereby eliminating the possibility of a ricochet.

Air rifles and pellet guns are sometimes used for plinking. Some air rifles and pellet guns are classified as firearms, and are subject to laws governing firearm use.

Novelty Shooting Sports

Novelty shoots are shooting activities that, unlike plinking, are organized and supervised by an experienced range officer and conducted on a range or area designated as a safe shooting area.

Turkey Shoot

One of the most popular of all novelty shoots is the "turkey shoot". Often held at Thanksgiving or Christmas, the local turkey shoot draws sportsmen of all ages to the target range to test their skill and try their luck at bringing home a prize. Contestants win prizes either for their marksmanship or their luck in winning a draw.

Turkey shoots may be held indoors on short ranges or outdoors on longer target ranges.

.22 Sporting Rifle Match

These matches are held either indoors or outdoors and may be held on a target range of any distance. Contests are judged on either 10 or 20 shots with a .22 caliber rimfire sporting rifle fired from the standing (offhand) shooting position.

The .22 sporting rifle used must not weigh more than seven pounds including sights. The trigger pull must not be less than three pounds and only iron sights are permitted.

All other shooting aids and accessories are prohibited.

The shooter with the highest marksmanship score wins.

Air Gun Match

Air gun matches are usually held indoors on short ranges where space is limited and sturdy backstops are not available.

Contestants use air guns (spring, pneumatic or CO_2 powered).

Bingo Target Match

Bingo matches can be held on any firearms range using .22 rimfire rifles or air guns.

Bingo cards are used as targets for this novelty match. Each competitor attempts to score a "bingo" by firing five shots in a straight line across the bingo card. The shooter who does so wins.

Miss and Out Match

The Miss and Out match is fired using shotguns on a standard 16 yard trap range. Contestants may shoot with their own shotgun but are required to use ammunition provided by the organizers in charge of the match. For the match, each contestant is issued one box of shotshells and 25 clay birds.

The match is played much like a trap shoot except when a shooter misses a bird he is eliminated. The last man to drop out is the winner.

Regulation Shooting Sports

Shotgun Sports

a)   Trap

Trap is a shotgun shooting sport which requires the gunner to try to hit targets thrown from a machine. Each shooter fires at five targets from each of five different shooting stations. A trapshooting round is made up of 25 birds (or 25 pairs when shooting doubles). The targets are thrown from a trap house at various angles anywhere within the 94 degree field. The shooter does not know what the target's angle of flight will be. In doubles, two birds are thrown at the same time.

b)   Skeet

In skeet, the shooter fires at a target thrown from a high trap house and then one from the low trap house.

A round of skeet consists of 25 birds. The birds always fly in the same path. The field layout consists of eight shooting stations.

A skeet round consists of:

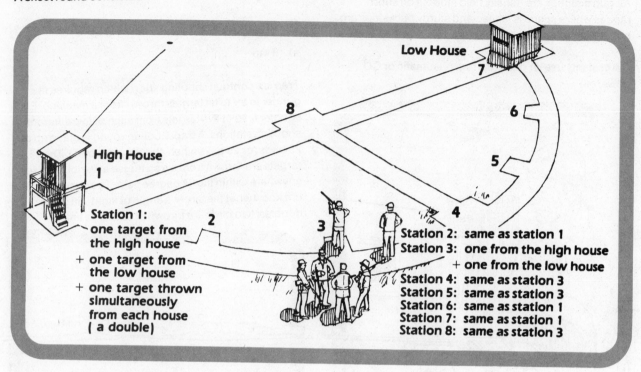

Station 1:
one target from
the high house
+ one target from
the low house
+ one target thrown
simultaneously
from each house
(a double)

Station 2: same as station 1
Station 3: one from the high house
         + one from the low house
Station 4: same as station 3
Station 5: same as station 3
Station 6: same as station 1
Station 7: same as station 1
Station 8: same as station 3

This accounts for 24 shots. One other shot is a repeat of the first miss or, if no miss has occurred, the 25th shot must be made from station 8 at a target from the low house.

Rifle Sports

a)   Metallic Silhouette Match

This sport requires the shooter to hit target silhouettes of various game species using a hunting rifle. All shooting is done from a single station and from a standing position.

Targets are positioned as follows:

(i)   Mountain sheep at 500 meters

(ii) Turkey at 385 meters

(iii) Javelina at 300 meters

(iv) Chicken at 200 meters

As indicated by the target species, this sport was developed in Mexico where wild pigs and wild turkeys are game animals.

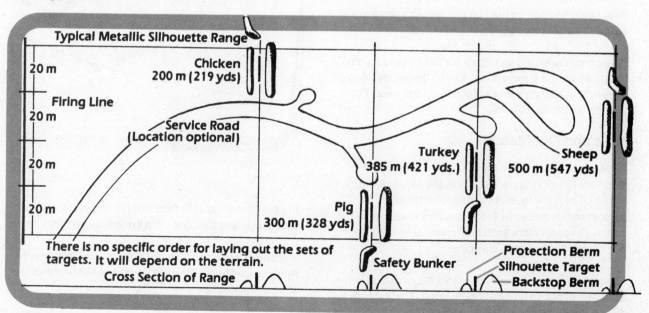

Range Procedure

Regardless of whether you use a range to sight in your gun or participate in a shooting sport, you must first understand and obey the following procedure used on all firearm ranges:

1
On the command "FIRST RELAY — ON THE FIRING LINE" the shooters assigned to the first relay (each group of shooters using a rifle range is known as a relay) take their positions on the line and prepare to shoot.

2
When everyone appears ready the Range Officer will inquire "IS THE LINE READY?" Anyone not ready should call out "NOT READY" and the Range Officer will state "THE LINE IS NOT READY."

3
When the difficulty has been corrected, the Range Officer is informed.

4
He will then say, "THE LINE IS READY."

5
The next command in order is "LOAD."

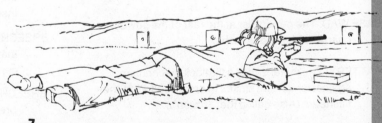

6
The final preparatory command is "READY ON THE FIRING LINE."
This is followed by the command "COMMENCE FIRING."

7
When the time limit expires or everyone is finished with that target, the Range Officer commands "CEASE FIRING." Immediately everyone stops, opens the action and makes sure the rifle is unloaded.
Any situation which is unfamiliar or which cannot be readily cleared, CALL THE RANGE OFFICER.
The Range Officer must maintain control over the firing line and the entire range at all times.

Glossary of Firearms Terminology

ACTION: The mechanism of a firearm located directly behind the barrel, by which a gun is loaded, locked, fired, unlocked, extracted and ejected.

ANVIL: That part of the cartridge primer which is a solid surface, against which the firing pin strikes to set off the priming powder.

AUTOLOADING: See SEMI-AUTOMATIC.

AUTOMATIC: A firearm that will insert, fire and eject continuously all cartridges in its magazine with a single, continuous trigger pull.

BALL: The round lead missile fired by smoothbore firearms. (The term is used today when referring to some types of bullets fired from rifled barrels).

BALLISTIC COEFFICIENT: A number which indicates how a bullet's shape, length, weight, diameter and nose design affect its stability, velocity and range against air resistance.

BALLISTICS: The study of what happens to moving projectiles in the barrel and in flight—their trajectory, force, impact and penetration. "Internal ballistics" refers to what happens inside the barrel before the bullet or shot leaves the muzzle; "external ballistics" is what happens after the bullet or shot leaves the barrel and travels to its final point of impact and "terminal ballistics" is what happens to the bullet at the final point of impact.

BARREL: The metal tube of a firearm made from iron or steel, through which the bullet or shot charge passes when the firearm is fired.

BASE WAD: The paper filler at the rear of the powder charge of the shotgun shell.

BATTERY: The metal arm of a flintlock mechanism, against which flint strikes to create sparks in the flashpan. (Also called the "frizzen").

BEAVERTAIL: A wide, flat fore-end of a rifle or shotgun.

BEDDING: That part of the stock into which the barrel fits.

BELT: The narrow band around the rear section of a cartridge case just forward of the extractor groove. (The belt arrests the progress of the case into the chamber and controls headspace).

BERDAN PRIMER: See PRIMER.

BLACK POWDER: A finely ground mixture of three basic ingredients—saltpeter (potassium nitrate), charcoal (carbon) and sulfur.

BLOWN PATTERN: A shotgun pattern with erratic shot distribution, generally caused by gas escaping past the wads and getting into the shot.

BLUING: A process of treating metal gun parts in a bath of metallic salts and water, which colors them blue to prevent rust.

BOATTAIL: The tapered rear end of a bullet. (Also called "taper heel", this design is used to increase ballistic efficiency at long range).

BOLT: A steel rod-like assembly which moves back and forth in a bolt action, sealing the cartridge in the chamber during firing.

BOLT FACE: The forward end of the bolt which supports the base of the cartridge and contains the firing pin.

BORE: The tunnel down the barrel of a firearm through which the projectiles travel.

BORE DIAMETER: The measurement from one side of the bore to the other. In a rifled barrel this means measurement of the bore before the rifling grooves are cut.

BOXER PRIMER: See PRIMER.

BREECH: The rear end of the barrel (In modern arms, the portion of the barrel into which the cartridge is inserted. See CHAMBER).

BREECHBLOCK: The part in the breech mechanism that locks the action against the firing of the cartridge.

BREECHLOADER: A firearm loaded through the breech.

BUCKSHOT: Large lead pellets used in shotshells.

BULLET: A single projectile fired from a firearm.

BUTT: The rear end of a rifle or shotgun stock. (The portion that rests against the shoulder).

BUTTPLATE: A plate which covers the butt. (Some steel buttplates have trap doors covering a recess for storage of cleaning equipment).

CALIBER: The diameter of the bore of a rifle before the rifling grooves are cut.

CANNELURE: A groove around the circumference of a bullet or case. (For example, the lubrication grooves of lead bullets, or the grooves into which the mouth of the cartridge case is crimped, or the extractor grooves of the rimless or belted case).

CANT: To tilt or lean a gun to one side when aiming.

CAP: See PERCUSSION CAP.

CARBINE: A light short-barreled rifle.

CARTRIDGE: A case, usually made of brass or copper, containing the powder charge, the primer and the bullet. (Before development of the metallic cartridge, the term was used to mean a roll or case of paper containing powder and shot. Modern cartridges are generally classified in three categories—"centerfire metallics", "rimfires" and "shotshells". Centerfire metallics include all metal cartridges that have primers in the center of the base. Rimfires include all cartridges in which the priming powder is sealed in the soft rim around the base. Shotshells include all cartridges that contain shot, or small pellets, instead of a single bullet).

CENTER-FIRE: See CARTRIDGE.

CHAMBER: The enlarged portion of the barrel at the breech in which the cartridge is placed ready for firing.

CHECKERING: A diamond-like pattern on fore-ends and grips of firearms. (The diamonds are made by cutting crossing lines into the material with special tools).

CHOKE: The constriction at the muzzle of a shotgun barrel by which the spread of the shot pattern is controlled.

CLIP: A detachable metal case designed to hold a number of cartridges for loading into the firearm.

COCK: To set the action into position for firing. (On some firearms the action has an intermediate position called half cock. On early weapons such as the flintlock and percussion cap, the hammer was called a cock).

COMB: The upper edge of a rifle or shotgun stock where the cheek rests.

CONE: The sloping portion at the front end of a shotgun chamber in which the chamber diameter is decreased to the diameter of the muzzle. Also, the rear portion of the choke at the muzzle of a shotgun.

CONICAL BULLET: A cone-shaped bullet.

CORDITE: A double-base smokeless powder made of nitroglycerine and guncotton which is used in the form of long, stringy cords.

CORE: The part of a bullet that is covered by a jacket.

CORROSION: The gradual eating away of the metal parts of a firearm caused by rust.

CREEP: The movement of the trigger before it releases. (Also called drag or crawl).

CRIMP: The portion of a cartridge case that is bent inward to hold the bullet in place, or in the case of a shotshell, to hold the shot charge in place.

CROSS HAIRS: The sighting lines in a telescopic sight.

DAMASCUS BARRELS: Barrels made of strips of iron and steel welded together in a spiral fashion. (Modern ammunition should not be used in such firearms).

DETERRENT: A material added to an explosive to slow its burning rate.

DOUBLE-BASE POWDER: A rapidly burning powder made by absorbing nitroglycerine into nitrocellulose (guncotton). (Cordite is a double-base powder).

DOUGHNUT PATTERN: A shotgun pattern with a hole in the middle generally caused by the interference of the top wad.

DOWN RANGE: The direction from the shooting position to the target on a range. See RANGE.

DRIFT: The departure of a bullet or shot charge from the normal line of flight. (This can be caused by wind or the unbalanced spinning of the bullet.)

DRILLING: A three-barrel gun with a rifle barrel beneath two shotgun barrels. (Generally of German manufacture).

EJECTOR: The mechanism which throws the cartridge case free from the gun.

ELEVATION: The degree of adjustment of a rear sight or scope reticule necessary to cause the bullet to strike higher on the target.

ENERGY: The amount of work done by a bullet, expressed in foot pounds.

EROSION: The wearing away of a barrel's metal surface by a bullet or shot charge or by the heat of powder gases.

EXTRACTOR: A hook device which pulls the case out of a chamber as the breech mechanism is opened. (The extractor generally brings the case within reach of the ejector, which then flips it out of the gun).

FEED: The action of moving live cartridges from the magazine of a firearm into the chamber.

FIRING PIN: The part of the breech mechanism which strikes the primer of the cartridge. (In most firearms, the firing pin is part of the bolt assembly).

FLINCH: To move or jerk a firearm involuntarily while shooting.

FLINT: A piece of stone held in the cock of a firearm. (When it strikes the steel battery, or "frizzen", this causes a shower of sparks to fall into the flashpan and ignite the powder).

FLINTLOCK: The gunlock of early firearms in which flint is thrown against steel, causing sparks to ignite the powder charge.

FLOOR PLATE: The detachable metal plate at the bottom of the cartridge magazine of a bolt action rifle. (The floor plate is usually hinged at the front and held by a release spring located just ahead of the trigger guard).

FORE-END: The forward portion of a shoulder-arm stock. (Located under the barrel, the fore-end serves as a hand-hold).

f.p.s.: Abbreviation for feet per second. A term used in expressing the velocity of a bullet.

FRIZZEN: See BATTERY.

FULMINATE OF MERCURY: A highly sensitive explosive used as a primer compound.

GAIN TWIST: Barrel rifling which increases in pitch from the breech to the muzzle to accelerate the spin of a bullet.

GAS CHECK: A metal cup placed on the end of a lead bullet to protect the lead against the hot gases of the burning powder charge.

GAS PORT: A small hole in the barrel of a gas-operated firearm through which expanding gases escape to power the autoloading system.

GAUGE: Measurement of shotgun bores derived from the number of bore-sized balls of lead to the pound. For example, 12 balls which fit the bore of a 12-gauge shotgun weigh one pound.

GRIP: The small portion of the stock gripped by the trigger hand.

GRIP CAP: A cap fastened over the end of a pistol grip on a rifle or shotgun stock.

GROOVES: See RIFLING.

GROUP: A series of shots fired with the same sight setting and the same aim.

HALF COCK: See COCK.

HAMMER: The part of the action that drives the firing pin forward.

HAMMERLESS: Refers to a firearm whose hammer and striker are concealed within the metal frame.

HAND CANNON: One of a variety of small, crude cannons used in the early 15th century.

HANGFIRE: Delay in firing a cartridge after the firing pin has struck the primer.

HEADSPACE: The distance between the base of the cartridge and the face of the bolt or breechlock. (This is determined by the rim of rimmed cartridges, the belt of belted cartridges and the shoulder or rimless cartridges).

HEEL: The rear end of the upper edge of a gunstock. Also the base of a bullet.

HIGH INTENSITY: Refers to cartridges having velocities of 2,700 feet per second (822.96 meters per second) or more.

HIGH POWER: A term applied to the first smokeless powder cartridges with velocities of approximately 2,000 feet per second (609.6 meters per second).

HOLDING: The action of keeping the sights on the target while applying pressure to the trigger.

HOLLOW POINT: A bullet with a nose cavity designed to increase its expansion on impact.

IGNITING CHARGE: The charge used to ignite the propelling charge. (See PRIMER).

INERTIA FIRING PIN: A firing pin which moves freely forward and backward in the breechblock. (The striker impels it forward while the explosion of the primer impels it backward).

INTERNAL BALLISTICS: See BALLISTICS.

IRON PYRITES: See PYRITES, FLINT.

JACKET: The outer covering over the inner metal core of a bullet.

JAWS: The vise-like device on a flintlock hammer used to hold the flint.

JUMP: The amount of change in the bore axis, measured both vertically and horizontally, while the projectile moves from the chamber to the muzzle when it is fired.

KENTUCKY RIFLE: A flintlock rifle with a long barrel and short, crooked stock.

KEYHOLING: The failure of a bullet to remain balanced in flight so that it enters the target sideways, leaving an elongated opening.

KICK: The backward movement of a firearm generated by the discharge of the projectile. See RECOIL.

KNURLED SURFACE: A metal surface which contains a pattern of ridges or beads. (This rough surface aids grasping a metal part to move it).

LANDS: In the rifling of a bore, the uncut portions of the barrel's inner surface left after the rifling grooves have been cut into the metal. See RIFLING.

LEADING: Fouling of a firearm bore by metal particles from bullets adhering to the metal surface caused by heat or friction.

LEDE: The bevelled portion of the rifling at the rear end of the barrel (and the forward portion of the chamber) where the bullet first engages the lands.

LENGTH OF PULL: The distance from the front trigger of a shotgun to the center of the butt.

LEVER ACTION: An action operated by a lever located underneath it. (A secondary purpose of the lever is to serve as a trigger guard).

LINE OF BORE: An imaginary straight line through the center of the bore of a firearm extending to infinity.

LINE OF SIGHT: An imaginary straight line from the eye through the sights of a firearm to the target.

LOAD: A charge of powder, a projectile or a cartridge. Also, to prepare a gun for firing by inserting ammunition into it.

LOADING GATE: The hinged cover over the opening through which cartridges are inserted into the magazine.

LOCK: The firing mechanism of a muzzle-loading weapon. In breech-loading firearms, the lock is the firing mechanism and breech-sealing assembly.

LOCKING LUGS: A series of projections on the bolt of a firearm designed to fit into corresponding slots in the receiver to lock the action in closed position for firing.

LOCKPLATE: A metal plate on which the firing mechanism is mounted on percussion and earlier firearms.

LOCK TIME: The interval of time between trigger release and the detonation of the primer. (Also called lock speed).

L.R.: Abbreviation for long rifle.

MACHINE GUN: A firearm which continuously fires ammunition at a high rate of fire when the trigger is pulled only once. See AUTOMATIC.

MAGAZINE: The part of a repeating firearm which holds the cartridges or shells in position ready to be loaded one at a time into the chamber. (The magazine may be an integral part of a firearm or a separate device attached to the action.)

MAGNUM: A cartridge or shell with greater power than normal, (i.e. .300 magnum rifle, 3 inch magnum shotshell).

MAINSPRING: A strong spring which activates the striker or hammer of a firearm.

MATCH: A long cord of hemp, flax or cotton, saturated in saltpeter, which burns slowly without a flame. (It was used to ignite powder in early firearms).

MATCHLOCK: A firearm action which relies upon a serpentine or S-shaped piece of metal to hold a smoldering match. By pressing the lower end of the serpentine, the upper end holding the burning match contacts the priming powder in the pan.

METAL CASED: A bullet with a lead core and a solid metal jacket.

METALLIC CARTRIDGE: A cartridge with a metallic case. (Early cartridge cases were made of linen, paper, etc.)

METALLIC SIGHT: A non-telescopic firearm sight.

MID-RANGE: The point in the trajectory halfway between the muzzle and the target.

MILLIMETER: A metric measurement equalling .03907 inches. (Its abbreviation is mm.)

MINI-BALL: An elongated lead bullet with a pointed head and a cup-shaped hollow in its base which spreads as it is fired, forcing the metal into the rifle grooves.

MISFIRE: Failure of a cartridge to discharge after the firearm's firing pin has struck the primer. See HANGFIRE.

MOUTH: The open end of a cartridge case into which the bullet is inserted.

MUSHROOM: The shape many bullets assume when the tip expands upon striking. (Sometimes called mushroom bullets).

MUSKET: A smoothbore shoulder gun (commonly used by military in the 17th, 18th and 19th centuries).

MUSKETOON: A musket shortened for cavalry use.

MUZZLE: The forward end of a barrel.

MUZZLE BLAST: The violent disturbance in the atmosphere after discharge of a firearm, caused by release of powder gases into the air.

MUZZLE BRAKE: A slotted device attached to the muzzle which softens the kick of the firearm.

MUZZLE ENERGY: The energy of a bullet as it emerges from the muzzle. (Usually expressed in foot pounds.)

MUZZLE FLASH: The bright flash at the muzzle of a firearm resulting from burning of gases.

MUZZLELOADER: A firearm that is loaded through the muzzle.

MUZZLE VELOCITY: See VELOCITY.

NAKED BULLET: A bullet not covered by a metal jacket or patch.

NECK: The forward portion of a bottlenecked cartridge case. Also the portion of a rifle chamber in which the neck of the cartridge case rests.

NEEDLE GUN: The first rifle known to use a bolt action.

NIPPLE: A small metal tube extending through the breech of a percussion firearm through which the flame passes from the percussion cap to fire the powder charge.

NOSE: The point of a projectile.

OBTURATION: The expansion of the cartridge case which seals the chamber preventing gases from escaping.

OPEN SIGHT: A non-telescopic firearm sight. See SIGHT.

OPTICAL SIGHT: Usually a telescopic firearm sight. See SIGHT.

OVER-AND-UNDER GUN: A firearm with two or more barrels placed one over the other.

PAN: The small dished container located on the side or top of a matchlock, wheel-lock or flintlock firearm used to hold the priming powder charge.

PARALLAX: The displacement of an object viewed from two different positions. (For example, when using a telescopic sight, the apparent movement of the reticule in relation to the target when the eye is shifted to a different position).

PARKERIZING: A non-reflecting rust-preventive finish used on the metal of firearms.

PATCH: A piece of leather or cloth. The patch is greased and placed around a bullet before ramming it down the barrel of a muzzleloader.

PATCH BOX: Covered compartment in the buttstock of a muzzle-loading rifle used to carry patches or other small items.

PATTERN: Distribution of shotgun pellets. This is measured at a standard distance of 40 yards (37 m) using a 30 inch circle (762 mm). (A full choke charge should throw a pattern of at least 70 per cent of the shot into the 30 inch circle at a distance of 40 yards).

PENETRATION: The distance travelled by a projectile from the point where it strikes the target to the point where it stops.

PENNSYLVANIA RIFLE: See KENTUCKY RIFLE.

PERCUSSION CAP: A small metal explosive-filled cup which is placed over the nipple of a percussion firearm. (As the cap is struck by the hammer, it explodes and sends a flame through the flashhole in the nipple to the main powder charge.

PISTOL GRIP: See GRIP.

PITCH: The angle of the barrel of a rifle or shotgun away from the angle of the stock. (It is measured by placing the butt of the stock on the floor and measuring the angle of the muzzle away from a line perpendicular to the floor).

POWDER: The general term for any propellant used in firearms which burns upon ignition. (The two major types are black powder, which is a physical mixture of charcoal, sulfur and saltpeter, and smokeless powder, which is a nitrated chemical compound in granular form).

PRESSURE: The force exerted by burning gases against the cartridge case, base of the bullet, chamber and bolt face of the rifle.

PRIME: To prepare or charge a muzzle loader for firing.

PRIMER: The collective term for the chemical primer compound, cup and anvil which, when struck, ignites the powder charge.

PRIMER CUP: The housing in a shotgun cartridge base which holds a primer.

PRIMER POCKET: The depression in the base of a centerfire cartridge which contains the primer.

PRIMING PAN: See PAN.

PROJECTILE: A bullet or shot in flight after discharge from a firearm.

PROPELLANT: The chemical substance which imparts movement to the projectile in a firearm.

PUMPKIN BALL: A large round ball of lead used in shotguns. (These projectiles are the same size as the shotgun bore).

PYRITES: A mineral used to produce sparks in primitive firearms. (It was replaced by flint.)

RAMROD: A wood or metal rod used to force the wad and bullet down the barrel of a muzzle-loading firearm.

RANGE: The distance travelled by a projectile from the firearm to the target. "Pointblank range" is the distance a projectile will travel before it drops to the extent that sight adjustment is required. "Effective range" is the greatest distance a projectile will travel with accuracy. "Extreme range" is the maximum distance a projectile will travel. Also, a facility designed for the safe shooting of firearms.

RECEIVER: The metal frame of a rifle or shotgun which contains the breech, locking mechanism and reloading mechanism.

RECEIVER RING: The portion of the receiver which is threaded so the barrel can be attached to it.

RECEIVER SIGHT: A sight attached to the receiver.

RECOIL: The backward force of a firearm caused by expansion of powder gases which also impels the bullet out of the barrel. Recoil is measured in foot pounds. See KICK.

R.F.: Abbreviation for RIMFIRE.

RIFLE: A shoulder firearm with a rifled barrel designed to fire one projectile at a time. See RIFLING.

RIFLED SLUG: A large, single projectile used in shotguns.

RIFLING: Spiral grooves cut into the inside barrel surface to cause a bullet to spin, thereby stabilizing it. The cut-away portions of the rifling are called GROOVES and the uncut portions are called LANDS. See LANDS and GROOVES.

RIM: The edge on the base of a cartridge case which stops the progress of the case into the chamber. (It's also the part of the case the extractor grips to remove it from the chamber.)

RIMFIRE: A cartridge in which the priming compound is contained in the rim at the base of the cartridge. (See also CARTRIDGE.)

SAFETY: A device that blocks the firing mechanism of a firearm.

SEAR: The part of a firearm which links the trigger and the firing pin and releases it when the trigger is pulled.

SECTIONAL DENSITY: The relationship between the weight of the bullet and the cross-sectional area.

SEMI-AUTOMATIC: An action which fires, extracts, ejects, reloads and cocks with each separate pull of the trigger and is powered by the propellant gases. (Also called autoloading.)

SERPENTINE: See MATCHLOCK.

SETSCREW: A screw that regulates the amount of pressure needed to release the sear.

SHOTGUN: A firearm with a smoothbore designed to fire small pellets called shot or rifled slugs.

SHOTSHELL: See CARTRIDGE.

SHOULDER: The sharply sloping portion of the cartridge case joining the body and neck. (Found only on bottleneck shaped cartridge cases.)

SIGHT: The device on a firearm designed to help the shooter aim accurately.

SLACK: The amount of movement in a trigger mechanism before it engages the sear.

SLING: A strap used to carry and aid in shooting a rifle.

SLING SWIVEL: A metal loop, sometimes detachable, by which the sling is attached to the firearm.

SMALL BORE: Generally refers to a .22 caliber firearm.

SMALL-OF-THE-STOCK: The narrow portion of the stock between the comb and the receiver of a shoulder firearm.

SMOKELESS POWDER: See POWDER.

SMOOTH BORE: A firearm with a bore that is not rifled.

SNAP SHOT: A quick shot taken without deliberate aim.

SPANNER: A small metal wrench used to wind the mechanism of a wheel-lock.

SPENT BULLET: A projectile which has lost nearly all its energy and lacks the force needed to penetrate the target.

SPITZER: A bullet with a sharp point for better stability during flight.

STOCK: The part of a shoulder firearm by which it is held for firing and into which the metal parts are fitted.

STRAIGHT-PULL ACTION: A bolt action in which the bolt is pulled and pushed straight backward and forward.

STRIKER: The front part of a firing pin which strikes the cartridge.

SWIVEL: See SLING SWIVEL.

TANG: A metal strip extending rearward from a rifle or shotgun receiver to attach the action to the stock.

THROAT: The forward portion of the chamber where it is tapered to meet the bore.

TOE: The bottom part of the butt of a rifle or shotgun.

TRAJECTORY: The path a bullet travels from muzzle to impact.

TRIGGER: The part of a firearm mechanism which releases the firing pin.

TRIGGER GUARD: A metal loop around the trigger designed to protect it.

TRIGGER PLATE: The metal part under the receiver of a rifle or shotgun through which the trigger projects.

TROMBONE ACTION: A pump or slide action.

TURN-BOLT ACTION: A bolt action which is locked by pressing the bolt handle in and down, thereby turning its locking lugs into the receiver.

TWIST: The angle of rifling grooves relative to the bore axis. (Expressed as the distance in inches over which a turn or twist is completed i.e. 1-10, 1-22.)

VELOCITY: The speed at which a projectile travels. (Usually measured in feet per second or meters per second.)

WAD: A disc used to separate powder from shot; or to seal propellant gases behind the shot; or to hold shot together in the barrel.

WHEEL-LOCK: An early firearm mechanism in which a wheel with serrated edges is wound against the tension of a strong spring and spins against a piece of iron pyrite, sending a shower of sparks into the pan to ignite the charge.

WILDCAT CARTRIDGE: A non-standard cartridge usually made by modifying the shape of a standard cartridge.

WINDAGE: The lateral drift of a bullet in flight caused by wind.

ZERO: Sight adjustment so the bullet will strike the target at the point of aim.

Notes

Bow Hunting

History

Archery is one of man's oldest skills. Archaeologists say that some tribes of Neanderthal man used a crude form of bow many thousands of years ago. Pictures etched on walls of ancient caves show prehistoric man used bows for hunting and survival.

Historians claim it is almost certain primitive man roamed North America thousands of years ago, and with his bow and arrow, killed the plentiful bison for its meat and hide. In later years, nomadic Indians roamed the prairie, parklands and northern forests, using the bow to hunt for food and defend their families against enemies.

In time settlers, fur traders and explorers came to North America. They brought firearms, which had replaced bows and arrows as the weapons of hunters and soldiers in other parts of the world. Guns were the tools with which pioneers hunted for food, clothing and shelter. Guns were the pioneers' protection against enemies.

For many years, the gun remained the hunter's choice; but in recent years, the bow and arrow has again become popular. Archery, one of man's earliest skills, is now a sport in many countries and is an olympic sport. Each new hunting season, more and more sportsmen join the ranks of bow hunters.

Introduction

Archery is defined as the art, practice or skill of shooting with a bow and arrow. Shooting a bow and arrow does not require great strength. Archery fundamentals, co-ordination and control are more important than muscle power. However, these skills can only be acquired through practice.

The equipment required for bowhunting need not be expensive. While learning how to shoot a bow is easy, it is best to have a qualified archer teach you the fundamentals.

(Bowhunting is the sport of hunting game using archery equipment.)

To become a bow hunter, it is important to learn what the bow can do and what it cannot do. Learning the habits of game animals you expect to hunt and the ways to hunt them are equally important.

The bow hunter should not hunt game until he learns the fundamentals of archery and is capable of making clean kills in the field.

Bows

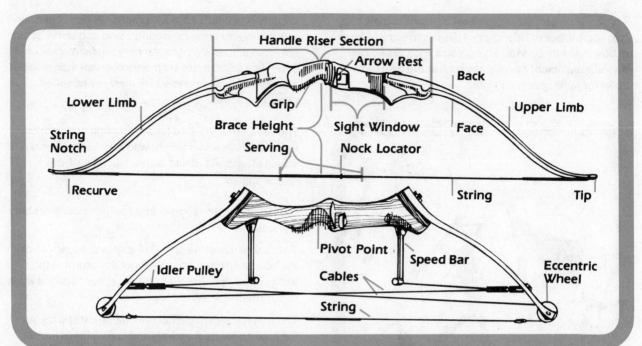

Handle Riser Section
Arrow Rest
Back
Lower Limb
Grip
Upper Limb
String Notch
Brace Height
Sight Window
Face
Serving
Nock Locator
Recurve
String
Tip

Pivot Point
Speed Bar
Idler Pulley
Cables
Eccentric Wheel
String

Bow Parts

The bow's handle is the middle portion called the RISER. It includes the grip, arrow rest and sight window.

The upper and lower sections of the bow are the LIMBS. They are light, very flexible and strong.

The outside surface of the limbs is the BACK and the inside is the FACE. An easy way to remember this: you are face to face when you draw a bow. The back is to the outside.

The bow TIPS are the extreme ends of the limbs. The distance between the grip and the bowstring, before the bowstring is pulled back to shooting position, is called the BRACE HEIGHT.

Bow Design

There are three basic designs of modern bows: straight limb, recurve and compound.

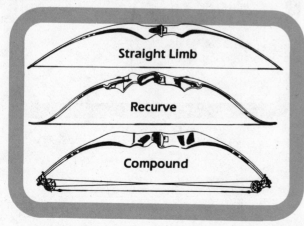

Straight Limb

Recurve

Compound

Bow Construction

Bows may be made of a single material or a combination of several materials bonded together. If more than one material is combined to form the bow it is referred to as a LAMINATED bow. Most bows limbs today are laminated from wood and fiberglass. Bow handle or riser may be made of wood, metal or wood and fiberglass.

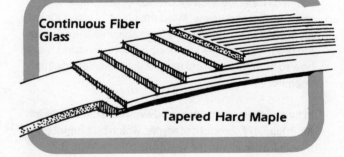

Continuous Fiber Glass

Tapered Hard Maple

Bow Weight

Bows also vary in their length and draw weight. DRAW WEIGHT, means the number of pounds of energy required to pull the bowstring to a distance of 28 inches (71 cm) from the back of the bow. For example, a 40-pound (18 kg) bow is one that requires a pull of 40 pounds (18 kg) to draw a 28 inch (71 cm) arrow to the arrowhead.

The draw weight of a hunting bow may vary from 40 pounds (18 kg) upwards. Some states require a minimum draw weight for bows used for hunting. Check your state hunting laws or contact your local conservation officer to obtain this information.

Hunting bows are usually shorter than those used for target shooting because a short bow is easier to handle.

Arrows

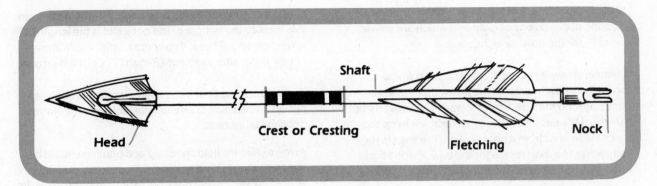

Shaft

Crest or Cresting

Head

Fletching

Nock

Arrow Parts and Construction

The basic parts of an arrow are the shaft, head, fletching and nock.

Arrow SHAFTS are commonly made from wood, fiberglass, graphite or aluminum. Although many types of wood can be used, most wooden shafts are cedar. Cedar is light in weight, straight-grained and less susceptible to warpage than most woods. Wooden shafts are inexpensive.

Both fiberglass, graphite and aluminum shafts are more expensive than wood but they have several advantages. Because they are machine made under rigid production controls, they are straighter and more uniform in diameter and weight. Shafts made of these materials are strong and will not warp.

Arrow HEADS, or points, come in a variety of shapes; target point, field point, hunting point and blunt.

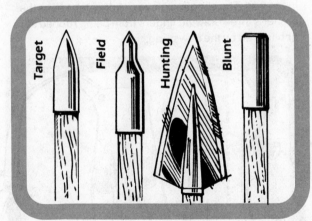

Target

Field

Hunting

Blunt

Bow hunting requires specialized heads. When upland game birds or other small game are the quarry, a blunt should be used. Blunts are also used in field practice.

To hunt big game, broadheads are necessary. Broadheads are made of steel and come in several

different shapes with a number of blades, all designed for maximum penetration of the animal. Some states prescribe minimum specifications for broadheads to be used in hunting big game. Beginning bow hunters should learn the safe, correct way to sharpen broadheads.

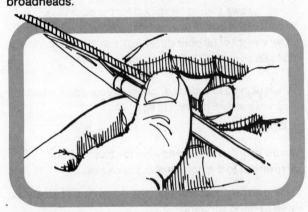

The Nock and Fletching are at the opposite end of the arrow from the head. The NOCK is the notch or small slit into which the bowstring fits when the arrow is drawn. It is usually made of plastic or nylon.

The FLETCHING is made of turkey-wing feathers or plastic vanes. Its purpose is to guide and stabilize the arrow's flight. Increased stability can be obtained by increasing the number of feathers on the shaft from the normal three.

One feather in the fletching is a different color than the others. It is called the COCK FEATHER. The other two are called hen feathers. When the arrow is nocked, the cock feather is at a right angle to the bowstring.

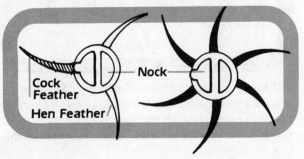

Nock

Cock Feather

Hen Feather

Spine

SPINE is the stiffness of the arrow's shaft. Accurate shooting depends on using arrows which are spined correctly for the bow's weight.

When an arrow is released, the bowstring whips forward with such force on the arrow that the shaft bends around the bow handle before it straightens out in flight. If the shaft has a weak spine, it will bend too much when shot from a heavy bow. If the shaft is too stiff, or has too much spine for the bow, it won't bend enough. In either case, the arrow will veer off course.

Arrows are graded according to their spines. Bows having up to five pounds (2 kg) difference in draw weight will use arrows with the same spine. For example, arrows graded as 40 to 45 pounds (18 to 20 kg) spine are suitable for bows having any draw weight between 40 and 45 pounds (18 to 20 kg). For compound bows, arrows should be spined for the peak draw weight of the bow. For example, in bows having a peak draw weight of 60 pounds (27 kg), use arrows graded as 60 to 65 pounds (27 to 29 kg) spine.

When using a broadhead, increase your spine weight approximately 5 pounds (2 kg).

Length

Arrow length is measured from the base of the arrowhead to the bottom of the nock slot.

Using arrows of correct length is important to safety as well as good shooting.

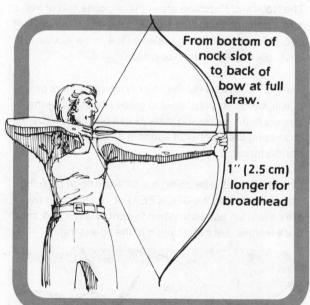

From bottom of nock slot to back of bow at full draw.

1" (2.5 cm) longer for broadhead

A practical method of determining the right length of arrow for you is to draw an extra long arrow on a very light bow until the length of draw is consistent and feels comfortable. While at full draw, have someone mark the

shaft where it crosses the bow back. The distance from this mark to the bottom of the nock slot is the length of arrow you should use. If your draw length is 28 inches (71 cm), you should select 28-inch (71 cm) field arrows.

To avoid cutting your hand when drawing broadhead tipped arrows, select arrows one inch longer than your draw measurement.

Arrows used for field shooting and hunting should be the same length. The field arrow is used for practice and should be as close as possible to your hunting arrow in weight, length and spine.

Arrow Selection

MATCHED ARROWS are a set of arrows having the same weight, shafts of equal stiffness and diameter, the same fletching and the same length. An arrow which differs from others in a set will fly differently than the others. Matched arrows are important for consistent shooting.

Bowhunting Accessories

In addition to a good bow and arrows, a bowhunter needs an ARMGUARD and a three-fingered SHOOTING GLOVE or FINGER TAB to protect his forearm and fingers from the pressure of the bowstring. The armguard is made of leather or vinyl and protects the arm against the lash of the bowstring when the arrow is released. It also keeps the archer's sleeve from getting in the way. The shooting glove or finger tab keeps the archer's three drawing fingers from being rubbed sore or blistered by the bowstring.

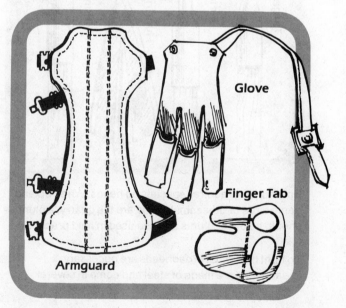

Glove

Finger Tab

Armguard

Bow Sights

The QUIVER or arrow carrier is another essential accessory. Quivers come in three basic designs; back, hip, or bow quiver. The back or shoulder quiver is slung across the archer's back so the opening is just under the shoulder, putting the arrow's nock and fletching end within convenient reach.

Although many bow hunters prefer to use the point-of-aim technique, many others use a bow sight. Bow sights come in many different designs. They can be simple and inexpensive, consisting of a single fixed or moveable pin, or they can be complicated and expensive, utilizing precision optical devices.

Most bow sights consist of a slotted bar fixed to the bow handle and an adjustable pin, bead or post, which can be moved up or down and from side to side. Some types use a prism or crosshairs and others have a series of pins which can be pre-set for various distances.

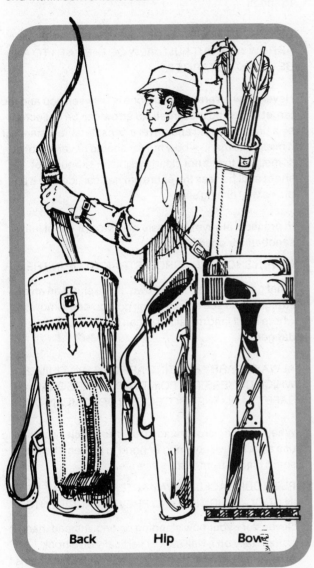

Back   **Hip**   **Bow**

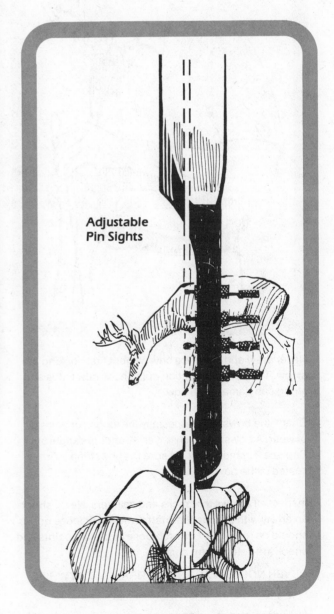

Adjustable Pin Sights

The hip quiver, sometimes called the belt or pocket quiver, is usually used to hold field arrows.

Most bowhunters prefer the bow quiver which is clipped or screwed to the bow handle. This type is less likely to become entangled in brush, is fast and quiet in the woods.

Other practical accessories are an extra bowstring, spare rest and tube of bowstring wax, a flat file and honing stone for sharpening broadheads, Allen wrenches, pliers for retrieving arrow points from trees and stumps, a bowstringer, string silencers and brush buttons, bowtip protectors and some type of bow camouflage.

Bow Handling

Primary Safety Rules

ALWAYS CHECK THE CONDITION OF YOUR EQUIPMENT BEFORE USING IT.

Check your bow for cracks, twisted limbs and broken or splintered bow tips.

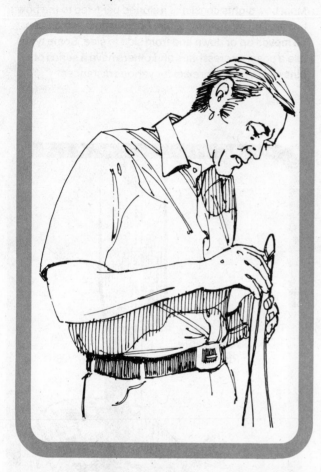

Never draw and release a bow without first nocking an arrow. The strain this action puts on the bow limbs and string can damage the bow.

Check the bowstring, especially the loops, for any sign of wear. A bowstring with frayed strands is dangerous. Replace it immediately. Be sure the bowstring is firmly seated in the bow nocks.

Inspect all arrows for cracks and splinters. Never shoot an arrow with a damaged shaft. Cracked or loose nocks should be replaced. Look for loose or broken points and check the fletching for damage.

NEVER NOCK AN ARROW OR DRAW A BOW WHILE FACING SOMEONE.

Never draw an arrow and aim it at anything you don't intend to shoot, even in fun. Never aim a drawn bow at another person.

Never carry an arrow nocked in the bowstring. Sometimes bowstrings snap and plastic nocks break, accidentally causing the arrow to fly off. A stumble or fall might release the arrow, injuring one of your companions. Nock the arrow only when you are ready to shoot.

BE SURE OF YOUR TARGET. NEVER RELEASE AN ARROW WITHOUT FULL VIEW OF THE PATH TO AND BEYOND THE TARGET.

Never draw an arrow if someone is between you and the target or behind the target. An arrow can be deflected by a branch or twig and travel a considerable distance if it misses its mark. A bow hunter should never shoot at something that is not clearly visible. He should not shoot until he sees the entire animal, can identify it and pick a vital aiming spot.

In practice, always use a safe backstop or shoot into a sandbank or open hillside.

NEVER SHOOT AN ARROW STRAIGHT UP IN THE AIR.

What goes up must come down. If you shoot an arrow straight up to see how far it will go, you don't know where it will land. In falling, it can be extremely dangerous.

ALWAYS CARRY HUNTING ARROWS IN A QUIVER WHICH COVERS THE POINTS—FOR PERSONAL SAFETY AND THE PROTECTION OF COMPANIONS.

When carrying broadhead arrows be specially careful to use a protective covering or hood to prevent the razor sharp blades from cutting anyone.

PUT YOUR TACKLE AWAY AFTER USE—TO KEEP IT IN GOOD CONDITION AND PREVENT ACCIDENTS.

Never store your bow standing on end. Instead, hang it horizontally on a wall rack or vertically on a hook. Arrows should be stored in an arrow rack which helps keep them straight and prevents warping. Arrows should be stored in an upright position.

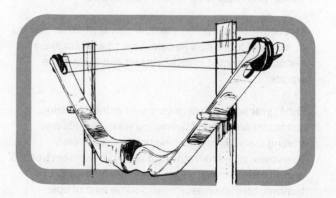

Safe Handling in the Field

When carrying broadheads in the field be especially on guard when climbing. If you are hunting from an elevated blind or tree stand, pull the bow and quiver up with a length of cord. Secure yourself to the tree stand with a safety line.

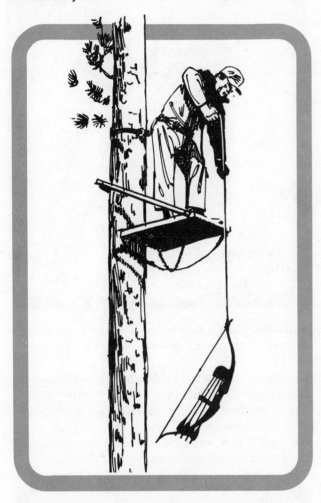

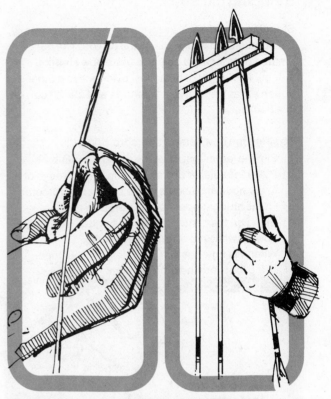

Always take an arrow out of your bow and place it in the quiver when not hunting. Never go into a camp, dwelling or group of people with your bow and arrow in shooting position.

Never use your equipment without having the basic rules of bow hunting safety uppermost in your mind.

Equipment Care

Care and Maintenance

A bow and arrows will give many years of service and enjoyment to the owner who gives them thoughtful care.

Fiberglass arrows are rugged and will not bend. Wooden arrows may warp. Aluminum arrows may bend if they hit a rock or tree stump. Check your wood or aluminum arrows to be sure they are straight. A light coat of furniture polish will protect wooden shafts and help prevent warping.

When an arrow hits a hard object, its point may be bent. Check to be sure the nock and head are properly aligned.

If an arrow's fletching is damaged, your shot will not be accurate. Make sure the feathers have not loosened or come unglued.

Keep your arrows clean. A little dirt on the head will change the weight of the point and cause a bad shot. Glass and aluminum arrows can be cleaned with a little soap and water.

Protect the bow's finish and keep out moisture by occasionally giving it a light coat of furniture polish.

Compound bows should be checked regularly to be sure all the bolts are tight. The idler wheels and cams should be oiled often and the cables checked for wear and replaced when necessary.

The bowstring should be waxed every time the bow is used. Wax will prolong the bowstring's life. Rub the wax well into the strands and remove any excess wax with a soft cloth.

Stringing the Bow

Stringing must be done with care. If braced incorrectly, the bow limbs may snap back and hit you. The best method of stringing a bow is to use a bow stringer. The stringer is a length of heavy test nylon with a leather pouch at each end. It is inexpensive and can be carried in a pocket.

To string the bow using a bow cord stringer;
a) Slip the larger loop over the upper bow limb.
b) Place the smaller bowstring loop in the groove of the lower nock and secure with a rubber tip protector.
c) Fit the stringer pouches over the bow tips.
d) Stand on the center of the bowstringer, pulling the bow up while holding it by the handle.
e) When the bow has sufficient flex, slip the upper string loop into the grooved nock.

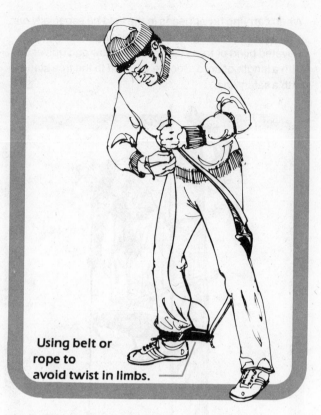

Using belt or rope to avoid twist in limbs.

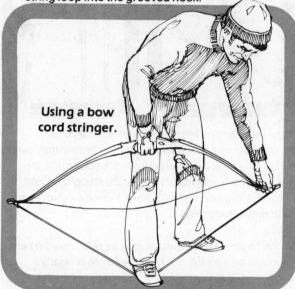

Using a bow cord stringer.

Another way to string a bow is called the "step-through" method:

a) Place the bottom bowstring loop in the groove of the lower nock and secure with a rubber tip protector.
b) With the right leg, step through or between the string and bow and hook the lower recurve on the outside of the left foot and over the instep.
c) Place thigh against the bow handle and apply pressure backward. At the same time, bend the bow by leaning forward from the waist and applying pressure with the right hand. The string loop can then be slipped into place in the upper nock. Before pressure is released, check to make sure the string loops are firmly seated in the bow nocks.

After you string your bow, check the brace height. This is the distance between the face of the bow at the handle and the string. Most manufacturers specify the proper brace height for each bow. Buying a bowstring specified for your particular bow is made easier by taking your old bowstring with you when purchasing a new one.

If your bowstring is slightly long, you can twist the bowstring until you obtain the proper brace height.

Compound bows must be strung by using a compound bow stringer. Compound bows are not unstrung after use, as are other types of bows, so you will need to use the bow stringer only when a worn string must be replaced. Follow the instructions provided with the compound bow stringer carefully.

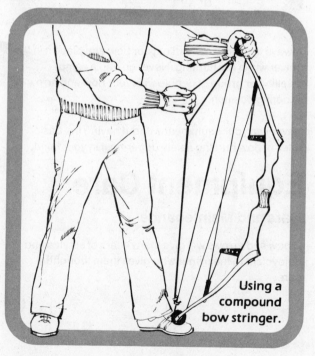

Using a compound bow stringer.

Marking the Nocking Point

You must have a specified point on your bowstring to place the arrow for every shot. The point where the arrow rests on the bowstring is called the nocking point. Every time you place an arrow on the string, or nock it, you should use the same nocking point.

To find the nocking point, place an arrow on the bow with the shaft lying on the arrow rest on the handle and the nock fitted onto the bow string.

Adjust the arrow so it makes a 90 degree angle with the bowstring. The nocking point is ⅛ to ³⁄₁₆ of an inch (3 mm to 5 mm) higher than the place where the bowstring and arrow are at right angles. You can buy a tiny nocking bead to attach to the bowstring to mark this point. Some archers use a double nocking point, and the arrow nock is positioned in the center of the two markers.

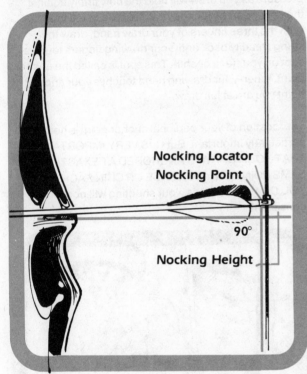

Nocking Locator
Nocking Point

90°

Nocking Height

Fundamentals of Bow Shooting

Master Eye

As in rifle, pistol and shotgun shooting, it is necessary for an archer to determine which of his eyes is the more important one. Although both eyes should be used when shooting the bow, the archer should shoot from the right side if his right eye is his master eye—from the left if he has a master left eye. Otherwise, he will not be shooting where he is looking.

Archery Fundamentals

To shoot a bow properly and effectively, an archer must learn the fundamentals of archery thoroughly before putting them into practice. Every beginning bow hunter should learn to shoot under the guidance of a competent coach or experienced bowman.

There are six basic steps in correct shooting techniques:

1. Stance
2. Gripping the bow
3. Nocking
4. Draw, anchor and aim
5. Releasing
6. Follow-through

Stance

The correct stance will give your body a solid foundation from which to shoot. Stand at approximately a right angle to your target. Your weight should be evenly distributed on both feet which should be spread apart far enough to give you a steady balance and a comfortable relaxed position. Keep your body erect but not stiff. Once you have turned your head towards the target, keep very still. Any movement will affect the accuracy of the shot.

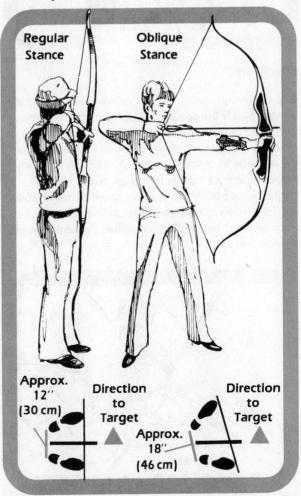

Regular Stance

Oblique Stance

Approx. 12" (30 cm)

Direction to Target

Approx. 18" (46 cm)

Direction to Target

Gripping the Bow

The correct grip on the bow is essential to good shooting. Hold the bow in your left hand if you are right-handed; in your right hand if you are left-handed. The thumb and forefinger should form a "V" at the inside of the bow handle. The bow handle should press against the base of the thumb and not against the heel of the hand. Your grip should be firm but relaxed. Do not clench the bow tightly. Keep your wrist straight, but not rigid. If your wrist bends inward it will be stung by the bowstring when it is released; if it bends outward, your grip will be weak and awkward and the bow may waver. In either case, your aim will be poor and you are likely to miss your target.

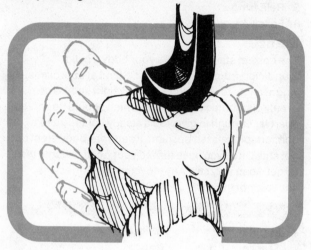

Nocking

Grip the bow properly with your gripping hand. Hold the bow parallel to the ground, about waist high, with the bowstring toward your body. Reach for an arrow with the other hand. Using your thumb and forefinger, grasp the arrow by the nock. Place the shaft across the arrow rest with the cock feather facing up, that is, at right angles to the bowstring. Slide the arrow nock towards you so the bowstring enters the slot. Then slide the nock on the string until it is positioned just underneath the nocking point.

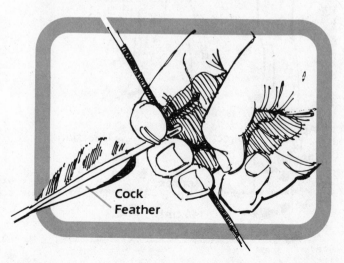

Cock
Feather

When the arrow is nocked, hook the first three fingers of your right hand (left if you are left-handed) around the bowstring. Your forefinger goes above the nock, and your other two fingers go under the nock. The string should lie in the creases of your fingers' knuckle joints.

Draw, Anchor and Aim

After you have nocked the arrow and while the bow is still in horizontal position, extend the arm which holds the bow toward the target. With your outstretched arm parallel to the ground, turn the bow to the upright position. Keep your bow-hand and forearm level with your shoulder but bend your elbow slightly to allow for clearance of the bowstring.

Hold the bow lightly, just tightly enough to prevent it from jumping away when the string is released. The pressure as you draw will hold the bow firmly against the fleshy part of your palm at the base of the thumb. With the three fingers of your draw hand, draw the string steadily back until your drawing fingers touch a spot on your face or chin. This spot is called the anchor point. When your drawing hand touches your anchor point you are at full draw.

The location of your personal anchor point is not particularly important. But IT IS VERY IMPORTANT THAT YOUR DRAW IS ANCHORED AT EXACTLY THE SAME POINT ON YOUR FACE OR CHIN EACH TIME YOU DRAW. If it varies, your shooting will not be consistent.

Drawing a bow is a dual action. You pull back on the bowstring, and at the same time you press the bow itself forward. Be sure to use your back and shoulder muscles to do the pulling and not the arm or hand. As you draw the bowstring steadily back, breathe in deeply. Drawing, from the time you begin to pull the string to your face until the arrow is released, should always be one smooth, continuous action.

When your drawing hand reaches the anchor position, hold it tightly against your anchor point for a few seconds to steady your aim. While holding the full draw, tighten your back muscles. If you attempt to keep the bow at full draw without increasing the pressure, your back and shoulder muscles will quickly tire and the arrow will creep forward. Even a little lessening of full draw will make your shot less powerful and not as accurate.

There are many aiming techniques but two very reliable methods to use a BOW SIGHT or to shoot using the POINT-OF-AIM technique.

For consistent accuracy in shooting, a BOW SIGHT has several advantages. Use of a bow sight is the surest of all methods of aiming. It is the quickest way for a novice to become expert at hitting the target.

The sighting mechanism of most basic sights is usually a movable pin, bead or post. More sophisticated models and telescopic sights use cross hair optical devices as the sighting instrument. The sight mechanism can be moved up and down or sideways to correspond with various distances marked on the panel of the bow sight.

To set the bow sight, line up the head of the pin or other device with the target. Then shoot. If the arrow hits low, adjust the sight by moving the pin down. If the arrow hits high, move the sight up. To adjust the shot to the left or right, move the sight pin sideways. When the arrow is left of the centre, move the sight pin left. When the arrow is right of centre, move the sight pin right. Continue this trial and error adjustment until the arrows hit the target exactly.

When the sight is properly set for a given distance, the archer lines up the pin or other sighting device with the target and shoots, usually with remarkable accuracy.

Using the POINT-OF-AIM technique, the archer focuses on the point of the arrow instead of the target and lines up the arrow's tip with some point either above or below the actual target.

The point of aim can be almost anything—a rock, a post, a tree in the distance or specific spot of ground. On long shots, the arrow tip should be focused on some point above the true target. When distances are short, focus below the target.

By trial and error and experience, the archer will learn where the point of aim should be for various distances.

Release

A crisp, straight, even release is very important to accuracy. The release must be smooth and consistent. If it varies each time you shoot, so will the accuracy of your shot.

Hold the full draw just long enough to be sure your aim is correct. Then, simply relax the three fingers holding the bowstring, letting the string slip away smoothly. Don't jerk your fingers off the string. This will cause the shot to veer off its mark. There should be no movement except for the easy relaxing of the draw fingers.

Follow-Through

The follow-through in archery means, hold your shooting position until the arrow hits the target. If you don't follow-through, keeping the bow-arm and hand perfectly still and remaining in the same position as at full draw, your shot will not be accurate and on target.

CONSISTENT ACCURACY AND SAFE SHOOTING DEPENDS ON DOING THE SAME THING THE SAME WAY EVERY TIME YOU SHOOT. If you practice the fundamental techniques of archery regularly, safe and accurate shooting will soon become a habit.

The practiced archer and bow hunter doesn't need time to think about how to shoot. He concentrates on the target and thinks "Is it a safe shot? Is it legal game? Should I take it?"

Common Errors

When you have learned the fundamentals of archery from a book or in the classroom, you should practice on the target range. At first, the shot will probably be erratic but the archer should not be discouraged. With practice and concentration, the arrows will soon begin to group on the target.

If your arrows are not hitting the bull's-eye, the following may explain why you are missing the target.

a.) HIGH—Overdrawing the bow; pulling bowstring back beyond anchor point; nocking point may be too low.

b.) LOW—Insufficient draw; not pulling back to anchor point; string hand may be creeping forward at the instant of release.

c.) RIGHT—Arrows of insufficient spine for bow weight; having fingers bent too far around bowstring; improper stance.

d.) LEFT—Arrows have too much spine; gripping the bow handle too tightly; moving string hand away from anchor point.

e.) HIGH AND RIGHT—Jerking the drawing hand back and inward as arrow is released; too much of the fingers around bowstring.

f.) LOW AND LEFT—Dropping bow arm as arrow is released.

Bow Hunting

Just as bow hunting requires special equipment, the bow hunter must have special knowledge—a thorough knowledge of bow hunting equipment, its use and its limitations; knowledge of the game to be hunted, its habits and habitat; knowledge of the challenge; and knowledge of self.

The prospective bow hunter should learn by reading as much as possible about the sport and learn the special techniques required under the guidance of an experienced bow hunter.

A bow hunter should keep these following thoughts in mind:

1. He must get close to his quarry to be able to aim with a reasonable chance for success. He must therefore become familiar with the species of game to be hunted; know when and where these animals travel; where they feed and what they eat; and learn their particular habits.

2. He must accept the limitations of his equipment. An arrow, if well placed and shot from a reasonable distance, will kill an animal quickly, but the shot must be accurate and hit a vital spot. The bow hunter must master the skills of the marksman before attempting to take game in the field. The first shot is most often the only shot the hunter will have.

3. He must know the vital areas of the game species being hunted. As well as being accurate, the bow hunter must know where to aim in order to kill the animal quickly and cleanly. The bow hunter must know where the animal's arteries, heart, lungs, spine, shoulders and pelvis are located. These locations differ in various species of game.

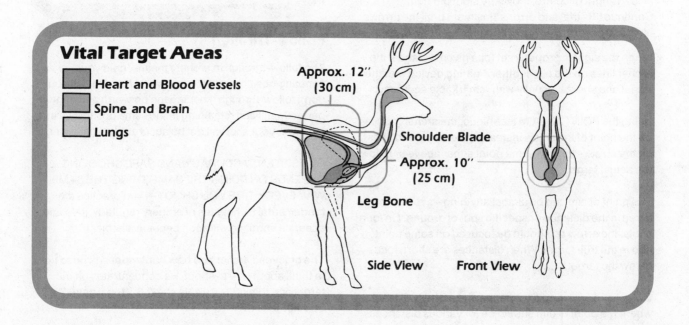

Vital Target Areas

■ Heart and Blood Vessels
■ Spine and Brain
□ Lungs

Approx. 12" (30 cm)

Shoulder Blade

Approx. 10" (25 cm)

Leg Bone

Side View   Front View

4. When game has been wounded, it must not be lost. The hunter should know the kind of wound and the extent of the injury, based on color, thickness and amount of blood trail. He must pursue the wounded animal until it is found, or until he is sure the wound is slight and the animal will recover.

5. The bow hunter must be committed to the sport. If he needs to know game—he learns about it; if he must shoot well—he practices until he can; if the requirements for success are high—he must choose to meet them and succeed.

To the sportsman bow hunter who examines these points and accepts the challenge, the rewards are many and the satisfaction complete.

Bow Hunting Regulations

Bow hunting regulations vary from state to state and may also change from year to year. Bow hunters should become familiar with the appropriate regulations for those areas in which they bow hunt. When in doubt, consult with your local conservation officer or your state conservation agency about bow hunting laws.

Notes

Field Techniques

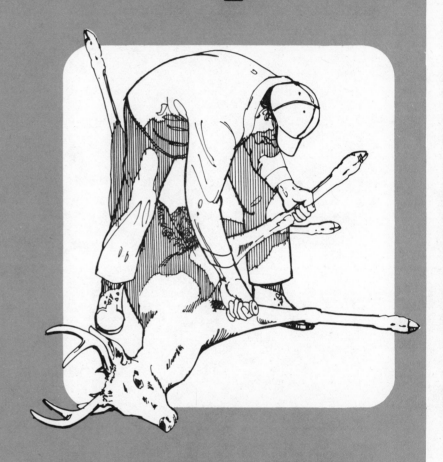

Introduction

Even though the purpose of hunting has changed considerably in modern times, many of the field techniques and skills remain similar to those used decades ago. Early man hunted for survival. Hunting provided meat for food, hides for clothing, feathers for ornamentation and bones for tools and implements. Hunting skills also served as a means of self-defense against man-eating animals. Today, hunting is done for recreational purposes but the field techniques associated with it have their roots in earlier times.

Vital Target Areas on Game

To ensure game is killed quickly and humanely, every hunter must know the vital areas of his quarry. He must develop the skills necessary to ensure his shot hits one of these areas.

Big game

The best means of insuring a clean kill on a big-game animal is to stalk it so you are within close range before you shoot. This will enable you to place your shot in a vital area such as the neck or immediately behind the front shoulder of the animal.

If your quarry disappears following your shot, carefully inspect the immediate area for blood or other signs which indicate the animal was hit. If such evidence is found, resist the urge to immediately pursue the animal. Wait approximately one-half hour, then follow the animal's tracks and other signs until you find it. A wounded animal will usually lie down after running a short distance if it is not being pursued.

If your quarry is still alive, carefully place your shot to dispatch it quickly. If it is a trophy animal, shoot at a vital area on its body other than the head or neck, such as the spinal column or chest cavity.

Be sure the animal is dead before getting too close to it. Always approach a big-game animal from the rear. Poke its hind leg with a stick—not your rifle—to see if it moves.

Most states' game laws require that you tag the animal as soon as it is killed and retain evidence of the animal's sex.

Vital Target Areas

Approx. 18" (46 cm)
Shoulder Blade

Approx. 16" (41 cm)
Leg Bone

Side View

Approx. 16" (41 cm)

Heart and Blood Vessels

Spine and Brain

Lungs

Front View

Game birds

When shooting game birds with a shotgun, the vital areas to aim at are generally in the air in front of your quarry. To hit a flying target, you must shoot ahead of it so the shot and target will run into each other. This is called "leading" the target. It requires good coordination of legs, arms, feet and hands and proper control of your eyes, brain and trigger finger to be successful.

"Sustained lead" is a method of leading a target which is used successfully by many waterfowl hunters. The gunner points the shotgun at his game and swings past it, keeping his gun on the same line as the bird's flight-path. While maintaining a lead in front of the bird, the gunner pulls the trigger and continues to swing his shotgun ahead of the bird. When the motion is smooth, the shot is usually accurate. If hurried or poorly controlled, the shot will either miss or wound the bird.

Judging the speed and distance of the target, the timing of your own responses and the amount of lead necessary, require a great deal of practice and experience.

In contrast to big-game, you should try to recover all game birds you shoot as quickly as possible. If wounded, they may escape by hiding in dense cover or swimming away out of shotgun range. Using a hunting dog is the best way to ensure all downed game birds are retrieved. When downed birds are in water and out of reach, a fishing rod with floating lures is useful to retrieve them. Wounded birds on land should be dispatched quickly by wringing the bird's neck or using a dispatching club.

Do not use your gun as a club to kill a wounded game bird. It may discharge, causing serious injury or death to you or someone nearby. At the very least, such thoughtless abuse of your gun will likely damage it.

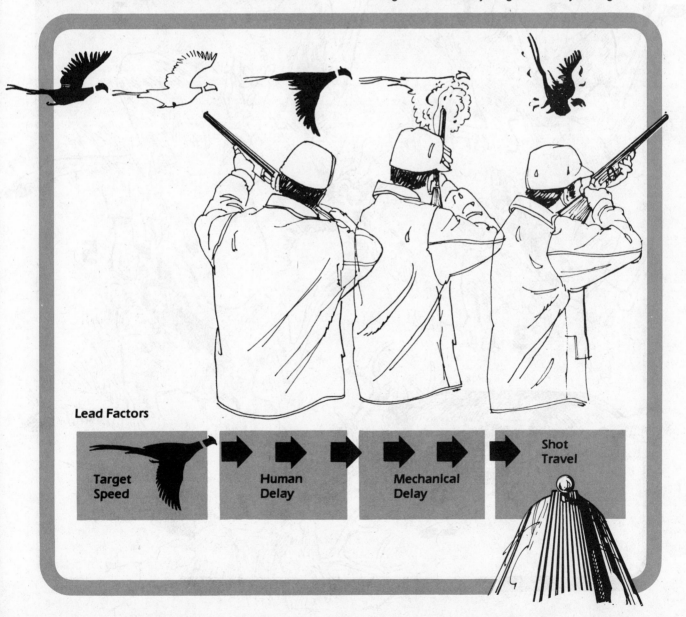

Lead Factors

Target Speed → Human Delay → Mechanical Delay → Shot Travel

Field Dressing

Field dressing is the procedure performed by a hunter to remove the entrails and skin from his game to prevent the meat and hide from spoiling.

Big Game

Equipment

Initially, you will require a hunting knife and sharpening stone to dress a big-game animal. In addition, an axe or small meat saw, nylon rope (30 ft.—9m), cheesecloth, twine and some hunter orange flagging material will be useful. Black pepper will help keep flies away from the meat after dressing and salt will help preserve the hide from spoilage.

Dressing

First, you must decide whether the cape of the animal is to be used for mounting. If it is, follow the procedure outlined on page 234 of this chapter. If the cape is not required, the following method of field dressing is recommended.

Lay the animal on its side or, if possible, on its back. It is not necessary to bleed the animal as sufficient bleeding will occur from the bullet wound and the cuts made to dress the animal.

With a sharp hunting knife, cut through the skin and abdominal wall from the crotch to throat. Be careful not to puncture the intestines or the stomach and avoid getting hair in the body cavity. Split the breastbone with

your knife or axe. Loosen the organs in the body cavity by cutting all connecting tissue including the diaphragm. Cut carefully around the vent in the rump—be careful not to puncture the intestine. Loosen the intestine enough to pull it out after tying the vent closed with a piece of string. This will prevent body wastes in the intestine from spilling onto the meat when you remove the entrails.

Now with the carcass on its side, turn its head uphill. Cut the windpipe free at the throat. Hold the windpipe in one hand and pull backward. With the other hand, free any internal organs by cutting through the tissue attaching them to the animal. Strip all the entrails from the body cavity. Recover the liver and heart if desired. Prop the chest cavity open by spreading the ribcage apart with a stick. With a dry clean cloth, wipe blood and other waste matter from the inside of the carcass. Trim away all damaged parts. If possible, wash the body cavity with water. Be sure to thoroughly dry the body cavity after washing as a dry surface will help check spoilage of the meat.

Skinning

Antlered or Horned Animals

Game should be skinned as soon as possible after the animal is dead. Skinning is easiest when the carcass is warm.

First, decide if you want to have the head mounted as a trophy. If so, follow the skinning procedure outlined for trophy specimens on page 234. Otherwise, the following skinning procedure is recommended.

Non-Trophy Animals

The steps in skinning most big game animals which have antlers or horns are the same.

If possible, hang the animal off the ground upside down; otherwise skin it where it lies. If possible, move it to an area of level ground or to your hunting camp before removing the skin. This will prevent dirt and other debris from getting on the meat while it is being transported.

Cut along the inside of each leg from above the knee joints to the belly incision. Next cut around each leg at the knee. Then cut completely around the neck to join the cut made along the throat when the windpipe was removed.

Cut the meat and tissue around the knee joints to remove the lower legs. Now use your knife carefully to free the skin from the body by cutting the connecting tissue in between. Once the hide has been peeled back from the hind legs, cut through the tail. This will enable you to remove the hide in one piece.

Trim away excess fat and tissue from the hide and salt it to prevent spoilage. The hide can be tanned later to make leather for gloves, jackets and other clothing or it can be donated to others for such use.

Trophy Animals

When skinning an antlered or horned animal for mounting, do not cut the skin of the throat because this will ruin the cape. Start by circling the shoulders. Begin at a point on the back between the shoulder blades and cut down each side to a point behind the front legs. Next, cut a curve over the two front legs to connect with the breast incision. Then make a cut along the back of the neck to a point between the ears and the base of the antlers or horns. Cut from this point to the base of each antler or horn to form a "T" shaped cut on the top of the head.

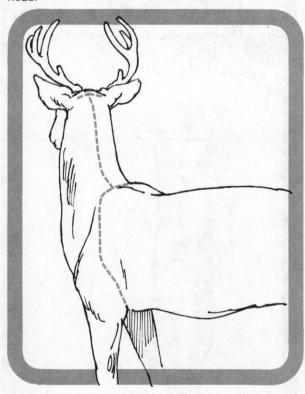

Now free the hide around the neck and shoulders by pulling the hide away from the body while cutting all the connecting tissue with a knife. At this point, the remaining steps necessary to skin out the head can be greatly simplified by cutting off the animal's head.

To remove the head, cut through the muscle covering the large neck joint immediately behind the skull. Bend the head back to expose the first vertebrae where it joins the skull. Cut as much tissue free around this joint as you can. Then twist the head off.

Once the skull is free, work carefully toward the base of the ears. Skin over the muscle at the base of each ear until yellow cartilage is visible. Cut down and forward through this cartilage to the skull to free the ears. Continue skinning along the head to the base of the antlers or horns. With the point of your knife, cut upward, close to the skull and around the base of the antlers or horns, freeing the skin attached to them as you proceed. Once the skin has been freed and pulled forward, insert the forefinger of your left hand under the rear edge of the eyelid from the outside. Pull taut and cut the tissue between the eyelid and bone until the tear duct is reached. Continue skinning close to the bone until you reach the corners of the mouth. Insert your forefingers in the mouth and lift the lips. Sever the

cheek muscles about three-quarters of an inch (2 cm) from the corner of the mouth. Skin close to the bone until the lower lip is free, being very careful not to split the lip. Leave the upper lip attached for the time being.

Skin out the muzzle up to the nostrils. Then insert your finger in the nostrils to guide you as you cut through nose cartilage to the bone. Skin close to the bone until the nose and upper lip are free.

Skin out the remainder of the carcass as described for non-trophy animals.

Use a bone saw to cut the top off the skull with the antlers or horns attached. Leave a fairly large portion of skull attached to the antlers for use in mounting your trophy.

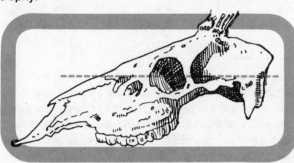

Once the hide is back in camp, finish skinning it out as soon as possible. Open the lips and nose by slitting the fleshy parts from the inside. Remove excess fat and flesh from the hide. Cut away the flesh from the base of the ear cartilage. Separate the skin from the cartilage only at the back of the ear. To do this, cut the tissue connecting the skin to the cartilage, cutting with the knife as necessary and turning the ear inside out as you skin. A long, blunt pointed stick is helpful in turning the ear. Extreme care is necessary while separating the skin from the cartilage or the ear will tear.

Salt your cape thoroughly as described elsewhere in this chapter.

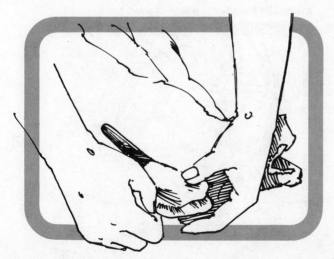

Two Important Points to Remember:

a) If you're unsure about your ability to skin out a trophy head properly, you can leave the cape intact on the head and neck and have a taxidermist skin it out for a nominal fee.

b) If you skin a trophy head, be extra careful when cutting around the lips, eyes, ears and nose to avoid cutting through the skin.

Bears, Wolves, Coyotes, Cougars

To skin a bear, cut from the tip of the tail along the center of the abdomen to within about three inches of the lower lip. Cut the hind legs starting from the inside edge of the pad near the heel, along the center of the leg until the cut meets the incision in the abdomen.

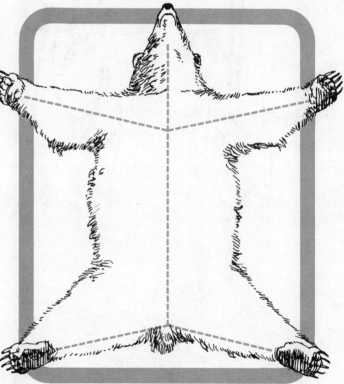

Sever the foot from the carcass, leaving it attached to the hide. Repeat this procedure for the front legs. Now peel the skin off the carcass working from the hind end forward. Remove the skin around the head in the same fashion as for antlered animals except avoid cutting the hide on the top of the neck, shoulder and head.

Cougars, coyotes, wolves and similar large animals are skinned like a bear. Open the long tail along the center line on the underside with the tip of a sharp knife. Be careful to cut in a straight line—do not zig-zag from side to side. Leave the feet and claws on the pelt, especially if the skin will be used as a rug.

Hanging and Cooling

It is not always possible to skin out big game animals immediately. However, all big game should be kept off the ground after field dressing. The meat on an animal's back is insulated from cool air by its hide and by the ground on which it is lying. Unless it is cooled, it will spoil. The best way to cool the meat is to hang the carcass in a shady, cool place. A block and tackle is the easiest way to hoist a large animal. If this is not available, improvise a winch using nylon rope.

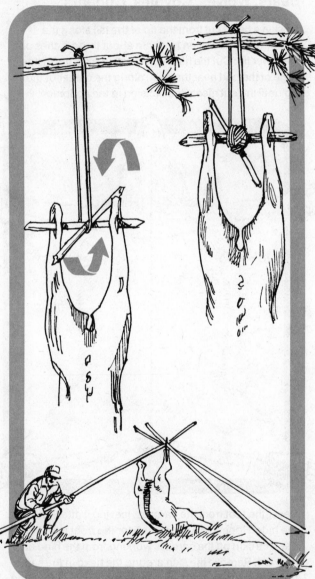

If the animal cannot be hung until later, prop the body cavity open with sticks. Place it belly down over some logs or rocks and cover it with spruce boughs to keep flies and birds away.

In warm weather, black pepper can be sprinkled over the carcass to keep flies off. Once the animal has been skinned, it should be covered with cheese cloth to keep it clean while it cools.

Preserving the Hide

It is essential to salt a hide thoroughly soon after its removal to preserve it for taxidermy purposes. Use common table salt or pickling salt in the amounts indicated in the following table:

Game species	Amount of salt required	
	Cape only	Whole hide
Antelope	1 lb. (.4 kg)	3 lbs. (1.2 kg)
Mountain sheep	2 lbs. (.9 kg)	4 lbs. (1.8 kg)
Deer	2 lbs. (.9 kg)	5 lbs. (2.2 kg)
Caribou	3 lbs. (1.3 kg)	8 lbs. (3.6 kg)
Elk	4 lbs. (1.8 kg)	15 lbs. (6.6 kg)
Moose	5 lbs. (2.2 kg)	20 lbs. (9.0 kg)
Black bear		5 lbs. (2.2 kg)
Grizzly bear		10 lbs. (4.5 kg)

Lay the hide flat on the ground, fur side down and stretch it to its fullest extent. Sprinkle salt freely and evenly over the entire hide. Rub the salt vigorously into the skin with the flat of your hand. Be certain the edges of the skin are thoroughly salted. Work salt into the lips, ears, nose and other difficult areas to ensure it covers them completely.

Salt draws the moisture out of the hide. After leaving the salted hide exposed to the air for 24 hours or more, sprinkle salt lightly over the hide once more. Then fold it up towards the skin side. Keep it cool until it is delivered to the taxidermist. Don't place it in a plastic bag or closed container while transporting it.

Bear skins require a little extra care when salting. As much excess fat as possible should be removed from the skin before salting. Open the ears, nose and lips and cut away as much fat as you can. Be careful not to cut the hair which is rooted to the inner surface of the bear skin.

The feet should be skinned out to the last joint of the toes and the bones disconnected. Cut away all fatty tissue. Use plenty of salt and rub it in well. If there appears to be an excessive amount of grease, rub wood ashes into the greasy areas to absorb it.

Salting a skin is always preferable to stretching and air drying it. Only when salt is not available should you cure a skin by stretching it in a frame or pegging it on the ground. Pegging will leave holes in a skin's edges which must be trimmed away, wasting part of the skin.

Even though a skin may be stretched larger than its original size, it will revert to its normal size when tanned. After curing, treating and tanning is complete, a skin that has been stretched and air dried will probably be smaller than if it had been salt cured.

Transporting

If you are backpacking game from field to camp, tie hunter orange flagging on your packsack. If the animal has antlers or horns, tie hunter orange flagging around them as well so you will not be mistaken for an animal by other hunters. A bell tied to your pack-frame will also help others recognize you as a hunter returning from the field.

To prevent damaging the hide, do not drag game along the ground or roll it downhill. If a animal must be dragged, lay it on a blanket or coat, or put a layer of

brush or boughs underneath the animal. Pull the animal along by its head.

When carrying an animal or hide on horseback, be careful that ropes used to hold it in place do not rub the skin and damage the hide. A blanket, cloth or layers of grass placed between the ropes and hide will prevent damage.

A burlap bag is useful for carrying a hide or meat from field to camp.

When transporting game by vehicle, be sure to keep the carcass away from engine heat, gasoline, sunlight and road dust to prevent its spoilage.

Butchering

The most effective way to cut up your game is to have it done commercially at a butcher shop. For a reasonable charge, they will cut, wrap and freeze your meat with minimum waste. If you choose to butcher your game yourself, meat cutting guides are available at many bookstores.

Game Birds

Game birds should be field dressed as soon as possible. Be sure to retain evidence of the bird's sex and species—one wing with feathers intact must be attached to each migratory or upland game bird in your bag.

Skinning, Plucking and Cleaning

Some hunters prefer to pluck game birds rather than skin them. If you plan to pluck your birds, do it at a place which is acceptable to the landowner. Upland game birds should be plucked as quickly as possible. Ten minutes after they are dead, their feathers will be set firmly and they will be difficult to remove without tearing the skin. Waterfowl should be rough plucked in the field as well. This makes the final plucking at home much easier. Then clean them immediately.

The easiest way to clean a grouse is, with the bird held breast upward, cut through the belly skin at the base of the breast and cut around the bottom margin of the breast. Then bend the bird backwards. This will open the incision. The innards can now be removed easily.

If the weather is cool, you may use a different method of field dressing game birds. Cut behind the breast to one side of the vent. Insert your fingers and draw out the innards. In warm weather, the opening may have to be enlarged to cool the bird enough to avoid spoiling.

Be certain to dry game birds well after cleaning. A roll of paper towels is useful for cleaning out and drying the body cavity after innards have been removed.

Once home, one technique to simplify the removal of down and pin feathers from waterfowl is scalding the birds in hot paraffin wax. First melt three cakes of paraffin wax in six quarts (5.7l) of hot water (185° F, 67° C). After removing the wings, dunk the birds, one at a time, into the hot wax mixture. When cooled, the wax can be peeled off, removing pin feathers and down and any feathers remaining after rough plucking.

After plucking, some long hair like feathers may remain on the bird. These may be burned off with a lighted match. Do not use burning newspaper because the ink from the newsprint could taint the meat. A butane torch is useful for this job.

Skinning a game bird is easier than plucking and it need not be done immediately. When you have returned home, you can skin the bird with less chance of dirt contaminating the meat.

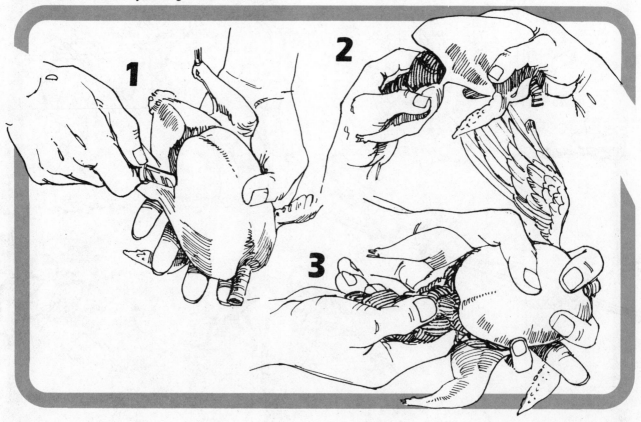

Cooling and Transportation

Birds must be quickly cooled or their meat will spoil. Do not pile birds together in a bag or box. Spread the birds out so air can circulate between them. They are best carried on a wire rack or game carrier which allows good air circulation around them.

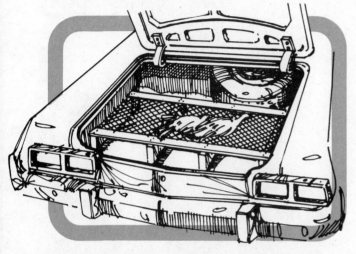

Some hunters prefer hanging their birds two to three days to cure them before freezing. Others freeze their birds immediately after cleaning and washing them. If birds are heavily shot up, soak them overnight in a salt solution to remove blood clotted around the wounds before freezing them for storage.

Care of Trophy Game Birds

If you plan to have a taxidermist mount a trophy bird for display, follow this procedure.

Immediately after retrieving your game bird, wipe any blood off its feathers using a clean cloth. Dab the cloth lightly in water if necessary to remove stubborn stains. Do not rough up the feathers but wipe in the direction they lie. Stuff cotton batting in the bird's mouth and nostrils to prevent further bleeding.

If your car is nearby, lay the bird on clean paper in a place where it will not be disturbed. Be sure to smooth out the feathers before laying it down. If the car is not accessible, the bird can be rolled in a cone of newspapers or a paper bag and carried with its head down. If it is not carried head down, blood could drain through the nostrils and beak and stain the feathers.

Do not dress any bird you intend to take to a taxidermist.

Do not wrap your trophy bird in a plastic bag when taking it home as it will retain its body heat and spoil. Once home, double check to ensure all feathers are correctly positioned and smooth. Wrap it in paper or a plastic bag and freeze it solidly. Keep it frozen for delivery to the taxidermist as he will likely have to store it for several weeks before mounting it.

Rabbits

To field dress a rabbit, cut off its head and remove its feet at the ankle joint. Pinch the loose skin on its back between your fingers and insert your knife through the skin, cutting across the back. Now grasp the hide on both sides of the cut and pull it away in opposite directions. Peel the hide completely off and remove the tail. Cut the abdomen open and remove the entrails. Trim away any shot-damaged meat, wash the carcass and wipe it dry to prevent spoilage. Keep it cool while transporting it home.

Notes

Survival

Introduction

Survival is the ability to cope with emergency conditions that occur when in the outdoors. Knowing how to cope with emergencies is essential to hunters. Basic survival techniques should be learned and practiced by every hunter before going into the field.

Fire drills are a regular practice, even though a real fire seldom happens. But should there ever be a fire, you'll know what to do. Similarly, practicing survival techniques makes good sense. If an emergency happens while hunting, you'll know what to do. You'll be able to cope with the situation if you become lost or disabled.

A survival situation usually lasts less than 72 hours and seldom longer than five days. Searches can take time, however, and you'll need to rely on your own resources to survive until help comes.

If you're in trouble, stay calm. Accept the fact that immediate help may not be available. Resist the urge to travel further seeking safety if you're lost. Stay put! Collect your thoughts and put the survival procedure outlined in this manual into practice. This procedure is designed to sustain life with as little discomfort as possible until help arrives.

Factors Affecting Survival

Pain, cold, thirst, hunger, fatigue, boredom, loneliness and fear are feelings we've all had before, but never so strongly as when we must survive a serious emergency situation. No matter how severe these feelings are, they can be overcome when you know how to deal with them.

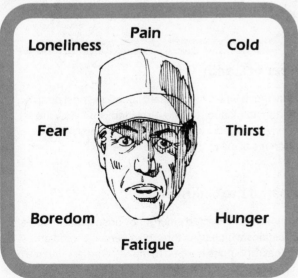

Pain

Pain is nature's way of telling a person that something is wrong. Attend to any injuries immediately, using appropriate first aid treatment (see First Aid chapter).

If your mind is busy making plans to cope with your situation, you'll feel less pain and may even forget about it for a while. If you give in to the pain, you might stop trying to survive.

Cold

Cold is a serious threat to survival. The victim of cold often loses the ability to function normally. When you are very cold, it's hard to think about anything other than becoming warm.

Exposure to cold, wetness and wind—even in temperatures that are not considered severe—can lead to hypothermia (see Hypothermia chapter).

To survive in the outdoors, the hunter must find ways to maintain his body temperature by staying dry, building a fire and constructing a shelter to protect himself from the weather.

Thirst

Don't think about how thirsty you are. A person can survive for several days without water if he's in normal health.

Instead, keep your mind active and busy with plans for coping with the situation at hand. Such activity may even make you forget for a while about how thirsty you are. Later, you can easily locate water near your survival camp or collect it when it rains or snows.

Hunger

Though hunger will make you feel uncomfortable, it is not a serious factor in most survival situations. Your body fat will supply energy to enable you to survive 30 days or more if your health is normal.

Fatigue

When you are tired you do not think clearly and can become careless. Extreme fatigue can even destroy a person's desire to survive.

Though overexertion is the usual cause of fatigue, lack of sleep and boredom may contribute to it. Try to rest as much as possible and avoid over-exertion. By making a comfortable shelter, you will be able to sleep soundly and avoid fatigue.

Boredom and Loneliness

Boredom and loneliness creep up on you when nothing happens and nobody comes to rescue you. You may act irrationally and your actions could make matters worse.

Your reaction to boredom and loneliness can often be more of a problem to your survival than any physical factors such as pain, cold, thirst or hunger.

Boredom and loneliness can be overcome by:

1. Making decisions and acting on them.

2. Adapting to your situation and improvising solutions to problems.

3. Tolerating solitude.

4. Avoiding panic and keeping calm.

5. Thinking positively and planning ways to overcome problems.

6. Being patient.

7. Keeping your hands busy—even by whittling a stick.

Fear

Fear is a normal reaction. Everyone is afraid. Fear affects the way you behave and, if not overcome, it can become your greatest obstacle to survival. In a survival situation, you may experience.

1. Fear of death

2. Fear of the unknown

3. Fear of animals

4. Fear of being alone

5. Fear of darkness

6. Fear of weakness

7. Fear of punishment

8. Fear of ridicule

9. Fear of discomfort

10. Fear of personal guilt

The best way to deal with these ten basic fears is to prepare yourself mentally to:

(a) identify which fears you are feeling; and

(b) try to understand why you are afraid and use common sense to deal with and overcome each particular fear.

Fear of Death

Until faced with a life or death situation, most people seldom think about death. Provided you follow the survival procedure outlined in this chapter, your chances of staying alive are excellent.

Fear of the Unknown

When an unexpected emergency arises, the immediate questions which flash through a person's mind are: "What is going to happen to me?" "Will they find me?"

This is normal. Fear of the unknown is by far the most common fear of any we experience. Practicing survival skills and thinking about how to cope with new and unusual situations should they arise will prepare you to handle most "unknowns". Reading other people's accounts of their survival experiences and trying to place yourself in their shoes will help to prepare you to deal with this fear.

Fear of Animals

Most animals are wary of humans and will stay out of their way. Learning about wildlife and their habits will help you overcome this fear. Don't let your imagination conjure up dangers from wildlife that are not real.

Realize, for example that wolves are curious animals but they will not attack you. Despite all kinds of stories about wolves, no person has ever been attacked and killed by a wolf in North America. Making noise around your camp and keeping a fire going at night will make other animals such as bears shy away from you.

You should learn to view wildlife positively. They can be a potential source of food to you and they also provide interesting company.

Fear of Being Alone

We are seldom alone in our daily lives. Being alone is almost an unknown experience for many. Solitude and solving problems for ourselves is something every outdoorsman must learn to cope with through solitary outdoor experiences. Spend time on your hunting and fishing trips getting away from your companions to learn what it's like to be alone in the outdoors.

Fear of Darkness

When it is dark, we depend more on hearing than seeing things around us. We often hear sounds in the darkness and imagine all sorts of threats to us. Most of us have experienced this fear at some time. Practicing being alone in the dark will help overcome this fear.

Fear of Weakness

People are stronger than they realize. Countless experiences have proven that people acting under stress can accomplish superhuman tasks. Be confident that you can cope with any physical or mental problem if you think about it logically. Plan a step-by-step approach towards solving the problem and then act.

Fear of Punishment

Because most of us are used to meeting time commitments, such as being home for supper, we get concerned about being late. When you're lost and alone, don't worry about missing appointments. Being late will alert your friends to the fact that you are lost and they will begin to search for you.

Fear of Ridicule

Normally, you'll be embarrassed by getting yourself lost and you'll worry about what your companions will think about you. You're afraid they'll think you are dumb for getting into such a predicament. Don't worry—each and every one of them will likely have been in a similar situation at one time and they'll understand how it can happen to you.

Fear of Discomfort

If you follow the basic steps of survival outlined in this chapter, there is no reason why you should experience severe discomfort. You may actually find that a survival experience can be exciting and pleasurable.

Fear of Personal Guilt

In a survival situation, blaming yourself for your predicament will accomplish nothing. It is not what you did wrong to get into trouble that counts. It's what you do right from now on that will make the difference. Think positively at all times.

Helplessness and hopelessness are two factors which increase fear. Through training and putting into practice the knowledge of survival in this guide, your fears will be overcome by confidence in your ability to handle a survival situation.

In summary:

1. Recognize that fear is a very normal reaction.

2. Be alert to physical dangers, recognize potentially dangerous situations, then plan to avoid them.

3. Subdue fears by simply keeping mentally and physically busy.

4. Be realistic, think positively and do not let your imagination get carried away.

5. Pray—prayer has proved to be a very effective tool to survival. Under stress conditions, you are at the mercy of your mind.

Survival Procedure Preparation

There are some basic rules to follow before hunting to ensure you're prepared for a survival situation:

1) Tell someone where and when you are going, and when you plan to return. If you change your plans, or move from one area to another, let someone know.

2) Choose clothing which is suitable for the expected weather conditions but will also be comfortable and protect you should the weather change.

3) Take a compass and a detailed map of your hunting area. Know how to use them.

4) Carry a personal survival kit and basic first aid kit (see Equipment and First Aid chapters).

5) Practice basic survival techniques.

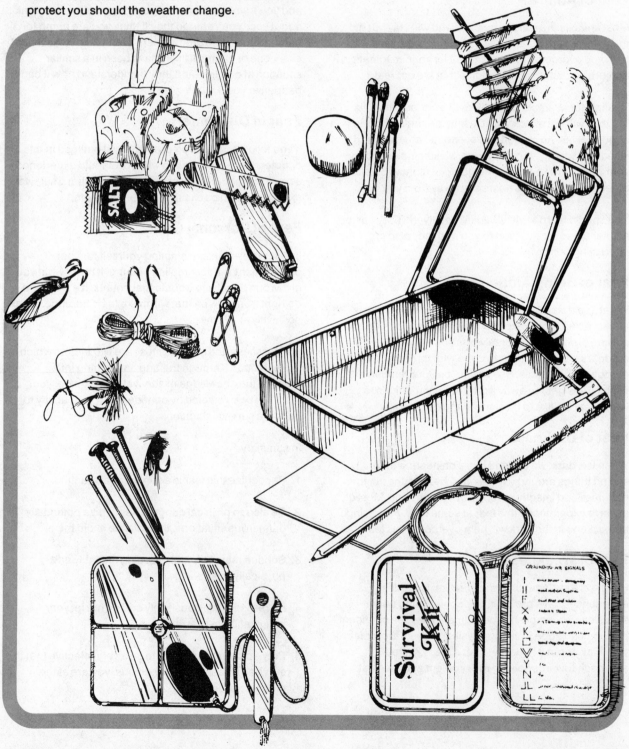

Field Survival Techniques

First Aid

First, treat any injuries by following the procedures outlined in the first aid chapter of the manual.

Fire Building

Fire is a basic need for survival. With fire, a person can warm himself, dry clothing, signal for assistance, cook a meal and enjoy a safe and comfortable night. Fire provides security, comfort and has a way of putting fear and apprehension out of the mind. Always carry the means to light a fire with you when hunting.

Ignition

Long wooden matches of the "strike-anywhere" variety, are the most practical matches for lighting fires. A waterproof, unbreakable container will help keep your matches dry.

To prevent matches from accidentally catching fire inside the container:

a) place half of the matches upside-down to keep their heads from rubbing together;

b) dip the matches in paraffin wax (this will also waterproof them and make them burn longer);

c) pack cotton batting into the container to keep them from striking against each other (the cotton will also make a good tinder).

A second way to start a fire is with flint and steel. Cold, wet, windy or stormy weather will not affect the use of this fire starter.

Other methods of igniting a fire are far less reliable and are not recommended.

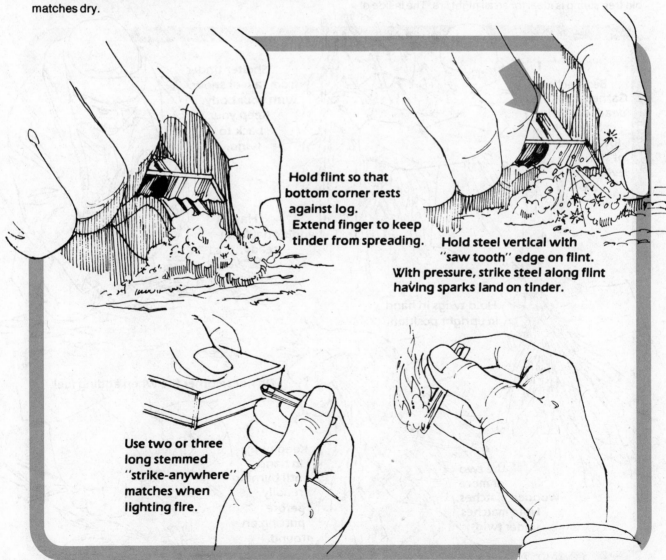

Hold flint so that bottom corner rests against log. Extend finger to keep tinder from spreading.

Hold steel vertical with "saw tooth" edge on flint. With pressure, strike steel along flint having sparks land on tinder.

Use two or three long stemmed "strike-anywhere" matches when lighting fire.

Fuel

Before attempting to light a fire, have two kinds of fuel available—tinder and kindling.

Most fires will not burn without first lighting some easily flammable tinder. In forest areas, you will find tinder readily available. Gather the fine dead twigs from the lower limbs of standing trees or from dry windfalls. They make excellent tinder.

Thin layers of birch bark torn into shreds is also good tinder. Other material such as dry grass, fur balls found in the nests of mice and birds, shavings, dry leaves, hornet nests and even lint scraped off your clothing with a knife or sharp rock make good tinder.

For kindling, gather dry, standing, dead wood. Because of its highly flammable resin, the dry wood of most evergreen trees makes good kindling.

The thicker the logs, the longer they will burn. A large, old tree stump is ideal for an all night fire. The inside of tree trunks and large branches may be dry though the outside bark is wet.

Fire Location

The location of your fire pit should be carefully selected. Do not build a fire under a tree as the tree could catch fire. The heat of a fire should also melt snow on the tree's branches, soaking the fire and putting it out. If you must build a fire on snow, construct a platform on the snow made of green logs or stones. Avoid using wet porous rocks as they may explode when heated.

If the ground is dry, scrape away all grass and debris and build the fire on bare dirt to avoid starting a grass or forest fire.

If possible build the fire against a rock or wall of logs to reflect the heat towards you and your shelter.

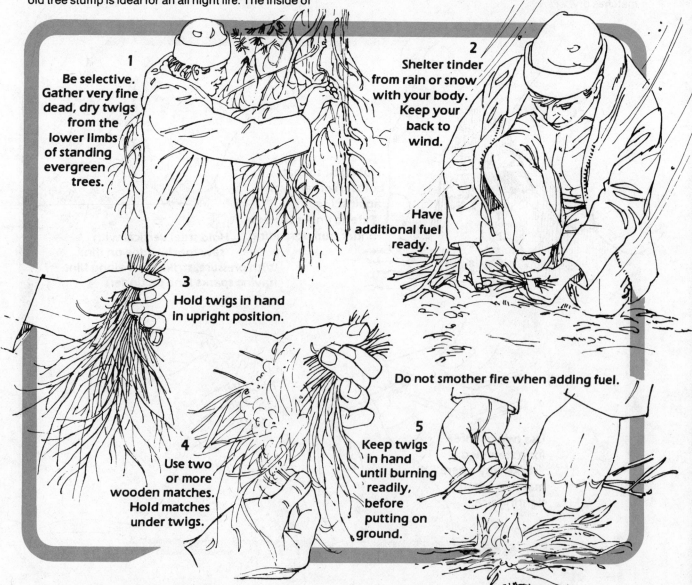

1 Be selective. Gather very fine dead, dry twigs from the lower limbs of standing evergreen trees.

2 Shelter tinder from rain or snow with your body. Keep your back to wind.

Have additional fuel ready.

3 Hold twigs in hand in upright position.

4 Use two or more wooden matches. Hold matches under twigs.

Do not smother fire when adding fuel.

5 Keep twigs in hand until burning readily, before putting on ground.

Shelter Building

Choose the most protected spot you can find for your shelter site. A cave, rock outcrop or fallen tree will provide shelter for the night. If it isn't sufficiently sheltered, use whatever is at hand to make it better. It is of vital importance to stay warm when lost or stranded. Your shelter should protect you from the wind and cold and keep you dry to prevent loss of body heat. Choose a shelter site that will allow you to locate a fire in front of it.

Build the best shelter you can. However, do not waste valuable energy needlessly.

Fallen Tree Shelter

If you are among trees, the quickest and easiest form of shelter is one made from a fallen tree that has ample space between the trunk and the ground. Often all that is necessary is to cut away some of the branches and lean them against the trunk to form a crude type of roof. Be careful not to cut off any of the limbs underneath that may be supporting the tree.

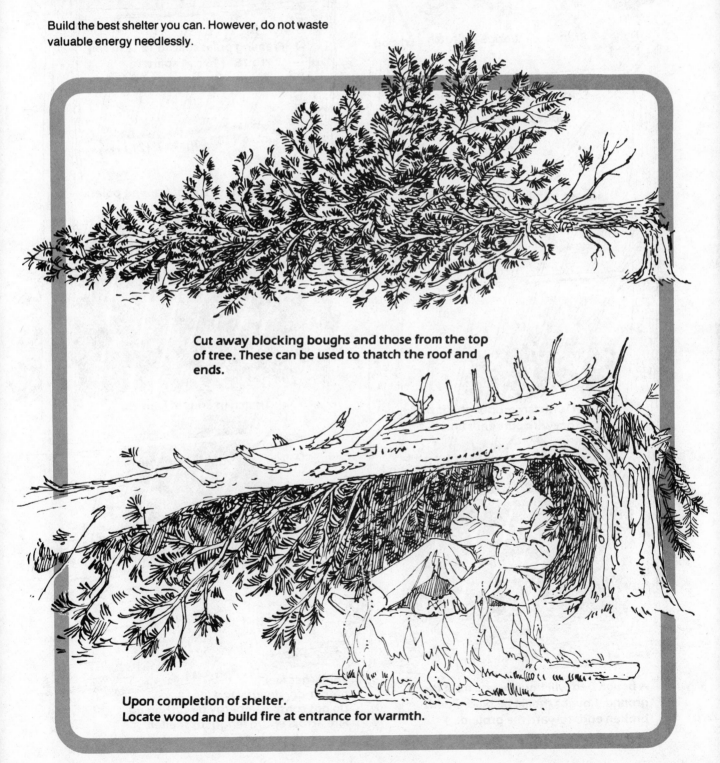

Cut away blocking boughs and those from the top of tree. These can be used to thatch the roof and ends.

Upon completion of shelter.
Locate wood and build fire at entrance for warmth.

249

Lean-To Shelter

One of the easiest shelters to build is a lean-to. A bed made of boughs about eight inches (20 cm.) deep, will provide good insulation from the cold ground. Boughs should be placed in rows with the butt ends toward the ground.

Attachments for Ridgepole

Tie   Branch   Wedge   Crotch   Tri-pod

1

Select sturdy support ridgepole.

Ridgepole with forked stick.

Locate suitable spot for shelter.

2

Place ridgepole and framing poles so that weight is against tree trunk.

Approx: 4' (122 cm)

Framing poles spaced 12" (30 cm) to 18" (46 cm) apart.

3' (91 cm)   6' (183 cm) to 7' (213 cm)

3

Start with largest boughs at the bottom with butt ends up.

4

Thatch boughs to top of framing poles.

Thatch in ends of lean-to.

5

6" to 8" (15 cm to 20 cm)

A bough bed will insulate you from the ground. Boughs should be placed with broken ends toward the ground.

6

For larger fuel, gather dry dead wood. Do not consume energy by cutting up. Fire across entire length of shelter.

Snow Cave Shelter

Snow caves are difficult to dig without getting wet. For this reason, they are less desirable than other types of shelter. However, snow is a good insulating material that can keep you warm in a survival situation.

A snow cave should be deep enough to sit in. When shaping a snow cave, arch the roof inside so moisture from melting snow will run down the sides of the cave and not drip on you. Do not make the cave's roof exceptionally thick. The cave should be shallow enough and the roof thin enough so you can break through the snow and stand up if a cave-in should occur.

Punch a ventilation hole in the roof. Keep it open by ramming a stick through it occasionally. It is very important to clear drifting or blowing snow from the vent so fresh air keeps circulating within the cave.

Chop a roomy bench or sleeping shelf at least one foot (30 cm) above the cave entrance and cover it with tree branches.

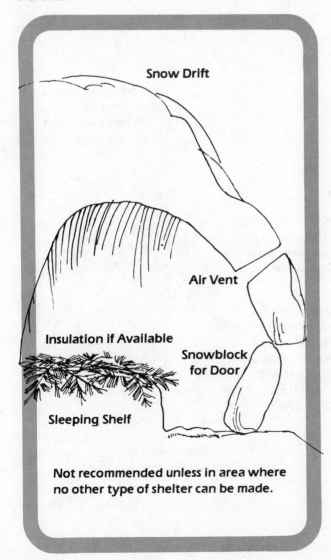

Snow Drift

Air Vent

Insulation if Available

Snowblock for Door

Sleeping Shelf

Not recommended unless in area where no other type of shelter can be made.

Rescue Signals

Once your needs for first-aid, fire and shelter have been dealt with, consider how to attract other people's attention to your location. Various types of signals can be used. Although the International Emergency Distress Signal is three signals of any kind (i.e. three shots, three whistle blasts, three fires in a triangle), a single signal is better than none at all.

Flare Signals

To attract searching aircraft, flare signals are best. Flare cartridges are available which can be fired from a rifle or shotgun. Also, small, flare signalling devices may be purchased and included in your survival kit.

Hold Firmly

Fire first flare immediately upon sighting aircraft.

When among trees aim through a clearning in the canopy.

Turn face away from flare gun.

Fire Signals

The best signals are fires. A large bright fire at night or a smoky one by day can be easily seen. Be careful to keep your fire under control because an uncontrolled fire could destroy your camp and threaten your life.

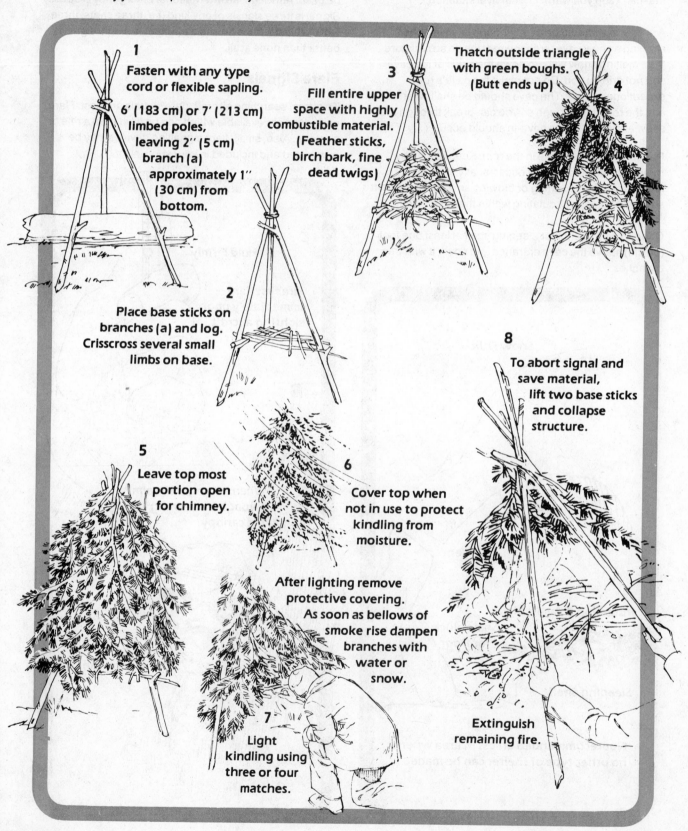

1 Fasten with any type cord or flexible sapling.

6' (183 cm) or 7' (213 cm) limbed poles, leaving 2" (5 cm) branch (a) approximately 1" (30 cm) from bottom.

2 Place base sticks on branches (a) and log. Crisscross several small limbs on base.

3 Fill entire upper space with highly combustible material. (Feather sticks, birch bark, fine dead twigs)

4 Thatch outside triangle with green boughs. (Butt ends up)

5 Leave top most portion open for chimney.

6 Cover top when not in use to protect kindling from moisture.

After lighting remove protective covering. As soon as bellows of smoke rise dampen branches with water or snow.

7 Light kindling using three or four matches.

8 To abort signal and save material, lift two base sticks and collapse structure.

Extinguish remaining fire.

Mirror Signals

The signal mirror is an excellent device for attracting attention. On a clear day, mirror signals may be seen for up to ten miles (16 km) at ground level and at much greater distances from an aircraft.

Sound Signals

Carry a shrill whistle like that used by police forces and mountain rescue teams. It has a loud, distinctive noise. If you do not have such a whistle, improvise one by blowing across the mouth of an empty cartridge case.

Carefully consider using your firearm to attract attention. Resist the urge to fire more than one or two shots on the first day you're lost because others will likely think you're shooting at game and ignore your signal shots. However, if you're seriously injured and bleeding heavily, fire your ammunition off in groups of three shots at a time with 10 seconds between each shot. Wait 10-15 minutes for an answering signal shot. If nothing is heard, fire a second group of three shots. Repeat this procedure as long as your ammunition supply will allow.

If you're not seriously injured, limit your signal shots to the late evening or night of the first day you're in trouble. Fire single shots spaced an hour or more apart through the night. Conserve enough ammunition to shoot game for food in case you must survive for a week or more (five or more cartridges).

Sound carries best during the evening quiet, just before dark. This is the best time to use a sound signal.

Information Signals

If you decide to leave your place of shelter, be sure to leave a message indicating the direction you're going. Make a large arrow on the ground from any available material—stones, tree branches, brush, trampled down grass or snow, or earth—so that search aircraft passing overhead will know which direction to look. Ground searchers will also be guided by such signals. If possible, leave a note explaining where you are headed and what time you left camp.

As previously indicated, your best chance of survival is by staying put at one location. To signal your location to airborne searchers, besides using a fire, you should mark a large "X" in a clearing near your survival camp. Use heaps of stones or earth, piles of brush, tree branches or trampled down grass or snow. Lay branches beside the lines of the X to create shadows and make your signal more visible from the air. Such signals can even be seen in the moonlight from aircraft.

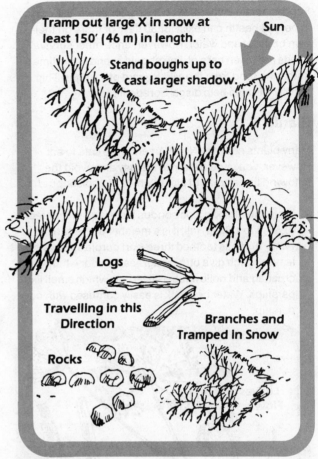

Tramp out large X in snow at least 150' (46 m) in length.

Sun

Stand boughs up to cast larger shadow.

Logs

Travelling in this Direction

Branches and Tramped in Snow

Rocks

Water

While a person can survive for several days without water, locating water is generally not a problem. It is readily available from rivers, streams, lakes, sloughs, small pools of rainwater or snow.

If possible, water should be purified before drinking. Boiling is the safest way to purify it. Dirty water should be filtered through several layers of cloth or allowed to settle beforehand. The taste can be improved by shaking it vigorously to aerate it.

Don't melt snow or ice in your mouth to quench your thirst as this will cause dehydration and loss of body heat. Melt the snow or ice over a fire first to obtain water. Conserve energy by drinking hot liquids instead of cold whenever possible.

Remember that the body requires two or three quarts (2.27 liters or 3.41 liters) of water a day, even in cold weather. Drink even though you may not feel thirsty. Do not ration water by sipping. It will do more good to drink as much as possible when it is readily available. If your water supply is limited, restrict your activity and movement, particularly during the heat of the day.

Food

Food is not an immediate necessity for survival. People in normal health can exist for 30 days or more on their own body fat and water. However, once other survival needs are taken care of, you should spend some time gathering food from the wild to ward off hunger. This activity will also help dispel boredom.

Plants

Many plants native to North America are safe to eat. However, you should learn to identify and avoid the following three types of plants which are poisonous:

a) Water hemlock is a poisonous plant, two to four feet (0.60 m to 1.22 m) tall, it is a member of the carrot family and has toothed three-part purple streaked leaves which give off a disagreeable odor when crushed and hollow tuber-like roots which smell like parsnips. Water hemlock is easily confused with cow parsnip.

Leaves and Flowers

Hollow Tuberlike Roots

Water Hemlock

Can easily be confused with Cow Parsnip.

b) Baneberry is a bushy perennial two or three feet (0.60 m to 0.91 m) tall. It has small white flowers in a short thick cluster at the top of the stem. Red or white berries replace the flowers in the fall and resemble dolls' eyes in appearance. Avoid all berries growing in clusters.

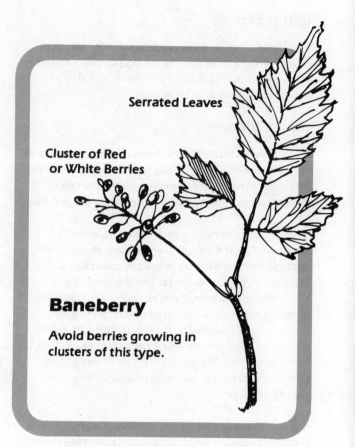

Serrated Leaves

Cluster of Red or White Berries

Baneberry

Avoid berries growing in clusters of this type.

c) Mushrooms of all kinds should be avoided as some kinds are poisonous and they are difficult to identify from those that are edible.

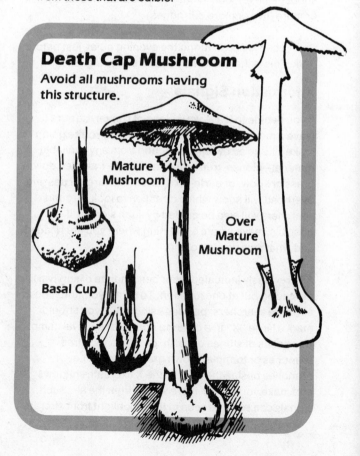

Death Cap Mushroom
Avoid all mushrooms having this structure.

Mature Mushroom

Over Mature Mushroom

Basal Cup

Animals

All animals in North America are edible and will provide excellent nourishment. They should be boiled and eaten as a stew or soup to maximize their value as food. You can obtain animals for food by shooting, spearing, snaring, trapping or hooking them. Special skills are required to trap animals and catch fish.

Remember, traps, snares and set-lines for fish work for you 24 hours a day whereas hunting does not.

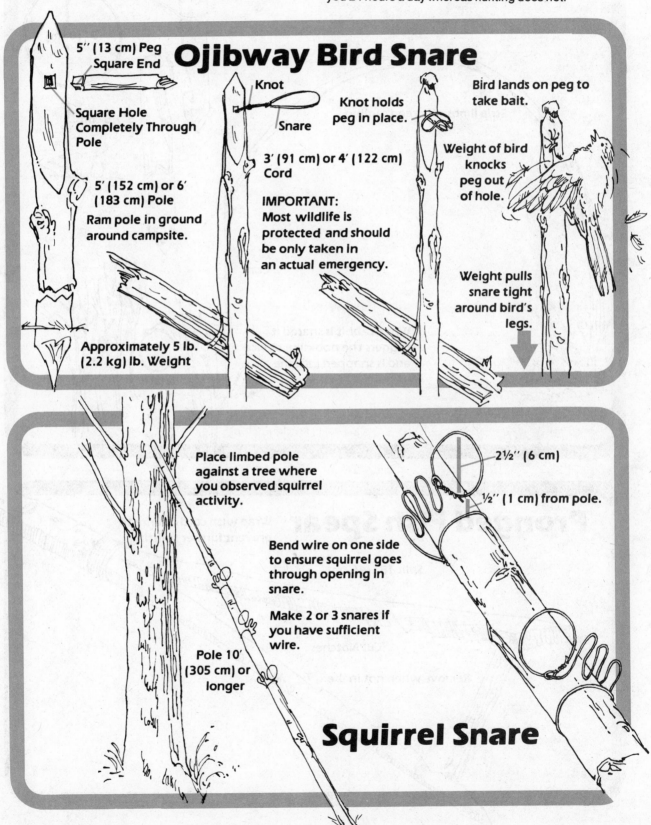

Ojibway Bird Snare

5" (13 cm) Peg
Square End

Square Hole
Completely Through
Pole

5' (152 cm) or 6'
(183 cm) Pole

Ram pole in ground
around campsite.

Approximately 5 lb.
(2.2 kg) lb. Weight

Knot

Snare

3' (91 cm) or 4' (122 cm)
Cord

IMPORTANT:
Most wildlife is
protected and should
be only taken in
an actual emergency.

Knot holds
peg in place.

Bird lands on peg to
take bait.

Weight of bird
knocks
peg out
of hole.

Weight pulls
snare tight
around bird's
legs.

Place limbed pole
against a tree where
you observed squirrel
activity.

Bend wire on one side
to ensure squirrel goes
through opening in
snare.

Make 2 or 3 snares if
you have sufficient
wire.

Pole 10'
(305 cm) or
longer

2½" (6 cm)

½" (1 cm) from pole.

Squirrel Snare

Snap-up Rabbit Snare

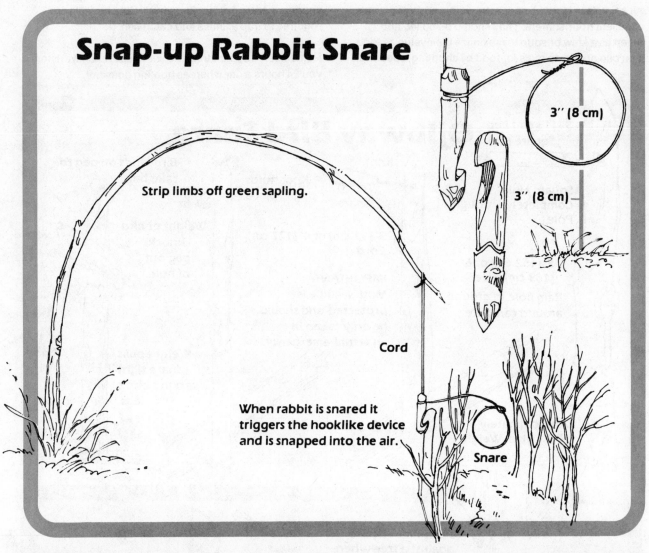

Strip limbs off green sapling.

3" (8 cm)

3" (8 cm)

Cord

When rabbit is snared it triggers the hooklike device and is snapped into the air.

Snare

Pronged Fish Spear

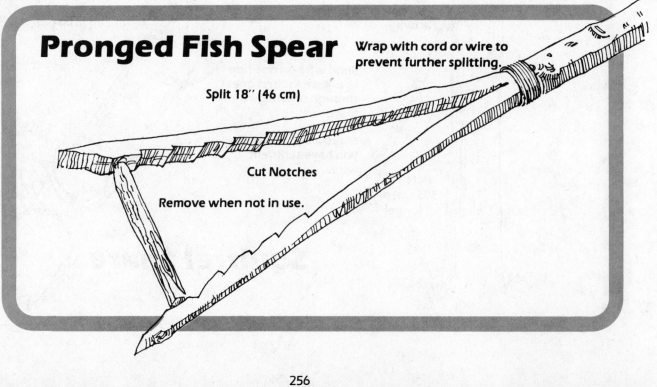

Wrap with cord or wire to prevent further splitting.

Split 18" (46 cm)

Cut Notches

Remove when not in use.

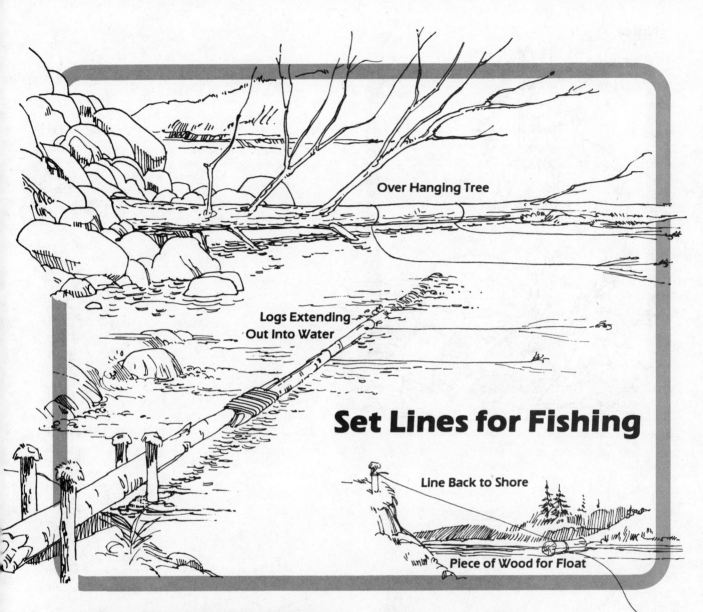

Over Hanging Tree

Logs Extending Out Into Water

Set Lines for Fishing

Line Back to Shore

Piece of Wood for Float

Deadfall

Heavy Log

Bait

Summary

In summary, the step-by-step procedure to survival is:

1) Treat for first aid

2) Build a fire

3) Build a shelter

4) Construct a signal

5) Locate water

6) Find food

Hypothermia

Introduction

Hypothermia is a condition which occurs when inner body temperature drops to a subnormal level. It impairs a person's ability to think and act rationally and can cause death.

Hypothermia is a major cause of death among outdoor recreationists. When a person is said to have died from "exposure", often the actual cause of death was hypothermia.

Development of Hypothermia

Hypothermia is caused by exposure to cool air or water. It is accelerated by wet or damp clothing, wind, exhaustion, or sudden contact with cold water.

A person's normal core (inner body) temperature is 98.6°F (37°C). When the body begins to lose heat, a person will react in two ways to stay warm:

1. He will shiver.

2. He will probably stamp his feet and move about.

Both these actions drain energy and slowly lead to exhaustion.

If this continues, the body's energy reserves will be depleted. The body will lose heat faster than it can produce it and the core temperature will drop. As body temperature decreases, the vital internal organs—brain, liver, heart—lose their ability to function. Cooling of the brain seriously impairs judgment and reduces reasoning power. This is hypothermia.

Hypothermia victims first experience uncontrollable shivering, then confusion, loss of memory and finally unconsciousness and may die.

Detection of Hypothermia

Whenever you are outdoors, think about hypothermia. Watch for symptoms of hypothermia in yourself and others.

The following are symptoms of hypothermia:

1. Uncontrollable spells of shivering

2. Slurred or slow speech, incoherent and vague statements

3. Memory lapses

4. Fumbling hands, frequent stumbling, lurching gait

5. Drowsiness

6. Exhaustion, inability to get up after a rest.

Treatment of Hypothermia

General Exposure

A victim of hypothermia may deny he is in trouble. If a person shows symptoms of hypothermia, believe what you see, not what he says. Even mild hypothermia requires immediate treatment.

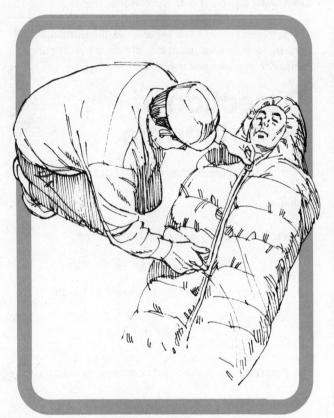

1. Move the victim of hypothermia to shelter and warmth as quickly as possible. If shelter is not readily available, immediately build a fire to warm the patient.

2. Remove the patient's wet clothes.

3. Apply heat to the patient's head, neck, chest and groin.

a) Use warm, moist towels or other cloth material, hot water bottles or heated blankets to warm the patient. As the heated materials cool, replace them with other warm packs.

b) If a sleeping bag or blanket is available, place the naked patient in it. Remove your clothing and lay close to the person, inside the bag, allowing the heat from your body to warm the patient.

c) As the patient recovers, give him warm drinks. This will help raise the core temperature. Don't give a hypothermia victim alcohol.

Hypothermia and Drowning

If the victim appears dead:

1. Clear the air passage and begin mouth-to-mouth respiration immediately (see First-Aid). Do not worry about getting water out of the patient's lungs.

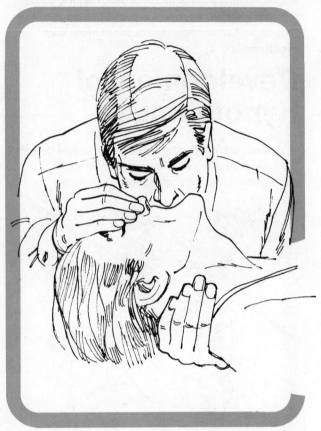

2. When the patient has begun to breathe on his own, place him in a sleeping bag or blanket to prevent further loss of body heat, but do not attempt to rewarm him. Warming will cause cold blood from the extremities to return to the core of the body. This may further lower core temperature and kill the patient.

3. Get the patient to the nearest medical facility. Do not permit the patient to walk. Transport him gently and keep him lying down, as still as possible.

4. If the patient does not start breathing, continue mouth-to-mouth respiration. Do not give up. Sometimes resuscitation takes a long time before a drowning victim will respond. Drowning victims look dead. Their skin is blue and cold to the touch. There may be no detectable heartbeat, breathing or any other sign of life. If other people are available, respiration can be continued while the patient is being transported to the nearest medical facility.

Prevention of Hypothermia

Prevention of hypothermia requires planning before going hunting:

a) Appoint a "foul weather" leader. This person's responsibility is to watch for danger signs and symptoms of hypothermia in himself and others.

b) Choose clothing that will keep you dry and warm.

c) Check weather conditions before you leave.

d) Prepare and pack a survival kit to carry in your jacket pocket.

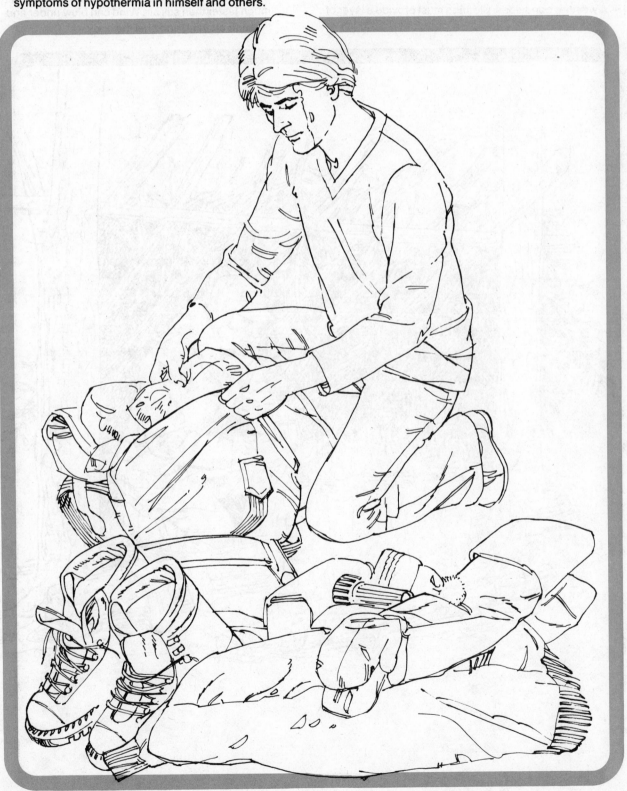

Hunting on Land

1. Pace yourself. Do not drive yourself to the point of exhaustion. Concentrate on building a fire and making camp while you still have a reserve of energy.

2. Stay warm and dry. Wearing proper clothing will keep you comfortable and warm even under poor weather conditions. Clothing must provide a layer of insulation, be thick enough to absorb perspiration and be able to shed rain and cut the wind. (see Equipment).

3. Get out of the wind. Wind multiplies the problems of staying warm. Even a slight breeze cools the body much faster than still air. Wind can blow under and through clothing and chill the body.

Hunting on Water

1. Avoid exposure to cold water. Make certain your
   boat is loaded in such a way that the weight is evenly
   distributed. Always wear a life preserver when in a
   boat. Do not stand or move around in small boats.

2. If you fall in or your boat capsizes get out of the water as quickly as possible. Climb into or on the boat. Most boats will float even when capsized or swamped. If you can't get out of the water remain still. Curl your body into the fetal position, or heat escape lessening posture (HELP). This will increase your survival time.

Because 50% of body heat may be lost from the head, do not use the "drownproofing technique" which requires that your head be in the water.

Wait until help arrives.

3. Stay off ice that is less than 2 inches (5 cm) thick. If you break through the ice, extend your arms flat on the ice surface and kick your feet to the surface of the water. Try to squirm the upper part of your body onto the ice. Roll quickly to one side away from the edge. You may have to break the thin ice ahead of you to reach ice thick enough to hold your body weight. Once you are out of the water, immediately get to shore and build a fire to warm yourself and dry your clothing.

Ice Claws

Notes

First Aid

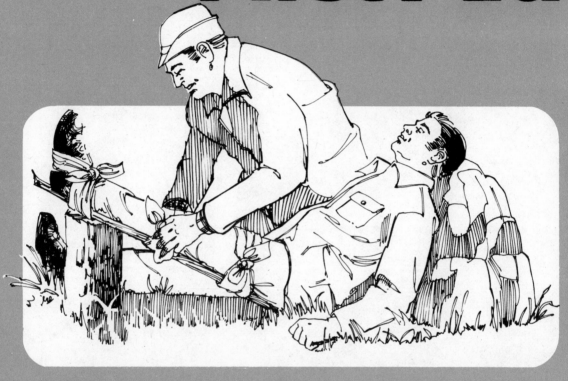

What is First-Aid?

First aid is the immediate assistance given to someone who is hurt or suddenly becomes ill. it is intended to help the person only until medical aid can be provided.

First aid does not take the place of a doctor's treatment but it can help save lives and prevent further injury.

The basic objectives of first aid are:

1.) to preserve life
2.) to minimize the effects of injury
3.) to relieve pain and suffering

Examine the Victim Quickly Using the Following Step by Step Procedure:

1. Check to make sure the victim is breathing.

2. Locate all wounds and stop all bleeding.

3. Check for lumps on the head.

4. If the victim is conscious, ask him where it hurts and what happened.

5. See if he can raise his head and move his neck—if not, do not move him.

6. If his head, neck and spine are okay, check his arms and legs.

7. If conscious, have the victim take a deep breath and cough to determine whether he has chest injuries.

8. Check for internal injuries by asking him to pull in his stomach and let it out again.

9. Check for spinal injuries by running your hand firmly down his back to detect tenderness or pain.

General Procedures

If a person appears seriously injured, don't try to move him. If you don't know exactly what the injury is, keep the victim lying down with his head level. Don't allow him to move around.

Fear, anxiety and sometimes panic, are often the reactions of those involved in emergencies. If you act frightened or upset, you will make the victim even more excited and afraid.

Be calm. When examining and treating an injured or ill person, do what needs to be done carefully, efficiently and quickly. Be as soothing and cheerful as you can. This attitude will calm the person who is hurt or sick and make him feel he is being well taken care of until the doctor comes.

If an accident occurs where there is danger of further harm coming to the injured person from exposure to severe weather, falling rocks or trees, fire or other dangerous conditions, then the patient must be moved to a safe place. Be careful not to put yourself in danger while trying to help.

Artificial Respiration

Clear the Air Passage

If the air passage to the lungs is blocked, two things could happen. The victim may become unconscious and he may stop breathing.

Blood, vomit or saliva in the mouth may block the back of the throat and prevent air from passing to the lungs. Sometimes an unconscious person's tongue will partially block off and limit the amount of air which can reach his lungs.

It is vital to get air moving in and out of the lungs at once. Tilt the victim's head back as far as possible. Pull his jaw upward and forward into a jutting-out position. If you can see anything in the victim's mouth that may obstruct the air passage, clear it out with your fingers.

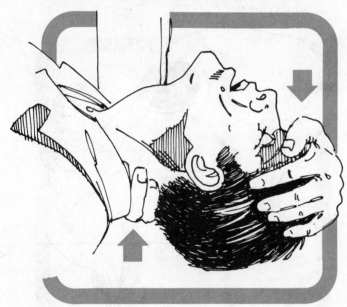

If a fractured neck is suspected, do not force the person's head back. Instead, hook your thumb over his lower teeth and grasp his chin with the fingers of the same hand. Lift the chin upward, open his mouth and remove any visible obstruction.

If he does not start to breathe immediately, apply artificial respiration, using one of the following methods:

Mouth-to-Mouth Method

1. Clear the air passage.

2. Open your mouth wide and take a deep breath.

3. Place your mouth over the victim's mouth forming a tight seal. Pinch his nostrils closed with your fingers and blow into his mouth vigorously.

4. Take your mouth away, turn your head to the side and take another deep breath and repeat the blowing in procedure.

5. Don't stop until he starts breathing by himself, or the doctor arrives.

If the victim is an adult, blow 12 breaths a minute; if a child, blow about 20 shallow breaths a minute. When giving mouth-to-mouth respiration to a small child, place your mouth over both his nose and mouth while blowing.

Chest Pressure—Arm Lift Method

If the victim has mouth or facial injuries, the mouth-to-mouth method may not be possible. In this case, the chest pressure-arm lift method of artificial respiration is more practical.

1. Clear the air passage.

2. With the victim lying face-up on his back, place a pillow, rolled blanket or whatever is immediately available under his shoulders. This will raise the shoulders and chest several inches and the head will drop backward. Turn the head to one side.

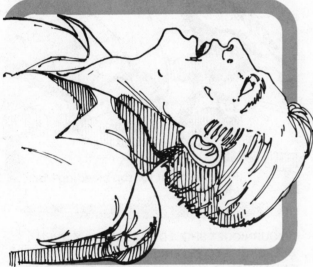

3. Kneel at the top of the victim's head facing his feet. Grasp his wrists and cross them over the lower part of his chest.

4. Still holding his wrists, lean forward until your arms are approximately at right angles to his chest. Allow the weight of your upper body to exert steady, even pressure downward. This will cause air to flow out of the person's chest.

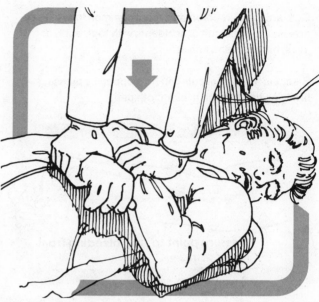

5. Release pressure by rocking back on your heels, pulling the victim's arms outward and upward as far above his head as possible. This action will cause air to flow into the victim's lungs. Each complete cycle should take five seconds.

6. Repeat these movements without stopping, keeping a steady even rhythm of 12 cycles per minute.

7. Check inside the victim's mouth often to see if any obstructions have appeared. Remove any obstructions to the air passage.

8. Don't give up. It sometimes takes hours of continuous effort before the victim will begin to breathe by himself.

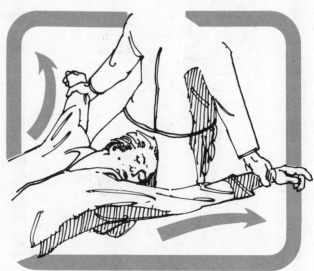

273

Bleeding From Cuts

Cuts are the outdoorsman's most common injury. They are usually the result of accidents with tools such as axes, hatchets and knives.

Bleeding from most cuts can be stopped by pressing firmly on the cut with a thick cloth pad.

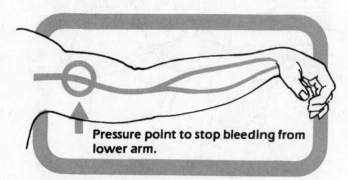

Pressure point to stop bleeding from lower arm.

It is vital to stop all bleeding as quickly as possible. Use whatever cloth is handiest—a handkerchief, even a piece of clothing such as an undershirt—if a sterile compress isn't readily available.

Press the pad firmly, directly over the wound and hold it there until the bleeding stops. Keep pressing for at least five minutes. Do not dab at the cut and do not keep looking to see if the bleeding has stopped. If you release the pressure too soon the bleeding will start again.

If the cut is on an arm or leg, keep it elevated to help stop the bleeding.

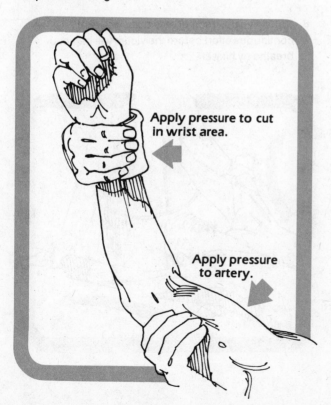

Apply pressure to cut in wrist area.

Apply pressure to artery.

If blood is coming in spurts, it means an artery has been cut. Bleeding from an artery can cause death in just a few minutes if it is not stopped quickly. To stop bleeding from a severed artery, keep pressure directly over the wound AND apply additional pressure at pressure points. If the cut is in the lower arm, blood flow can be controlled by applying strong pressure on the inside of the arm, halfway between the elbow and shoulder. If the cut is in the leg, blood flow can be controlled by applying strong pressure in the groin area.

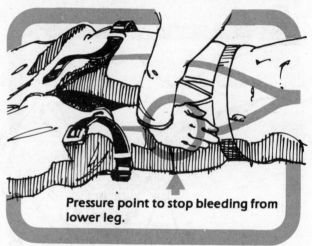

Pressure point to stop bleeding from lower leg.

A TOURNIQUET SHOULD BE USED ONLY WHEN BLEEDING IS SO SEVERE THAT THE VICTIM'S LIFE IS ENDANGERED, because the tourniquet could result in the loss of a limb. Never use wire or string to make a tourniquet, use a belt, strips of cloth or a rolled handkerchief. The tourniquet should be tied loosely, as close to the wound as possible and between the wound and the heart.

Insert a stick in the knot of the cloth or belt and twist to tighten the tourniquet. It should be tight enough to stop the bleeding but not so tight that it cuts off blood circulation.

Once the bleeding has stopped, the wound should be cleaned. Wash the wound with clean water and soap. Be very gentle or the bleeding may start again.

Antiseptics and alcohol should not be used to clean wounds. Although these products do kill germs, they can also destroy tissue which could delay healing.

After the wound has been carefully cleaned, apply a sterile bandage or gauze compress and hold it firmly in place with adhesive tape.

As a precaution against serious infection, anyone planning a hunting or camping trip should receive an anti-tetanus toxin injuection before starting out.

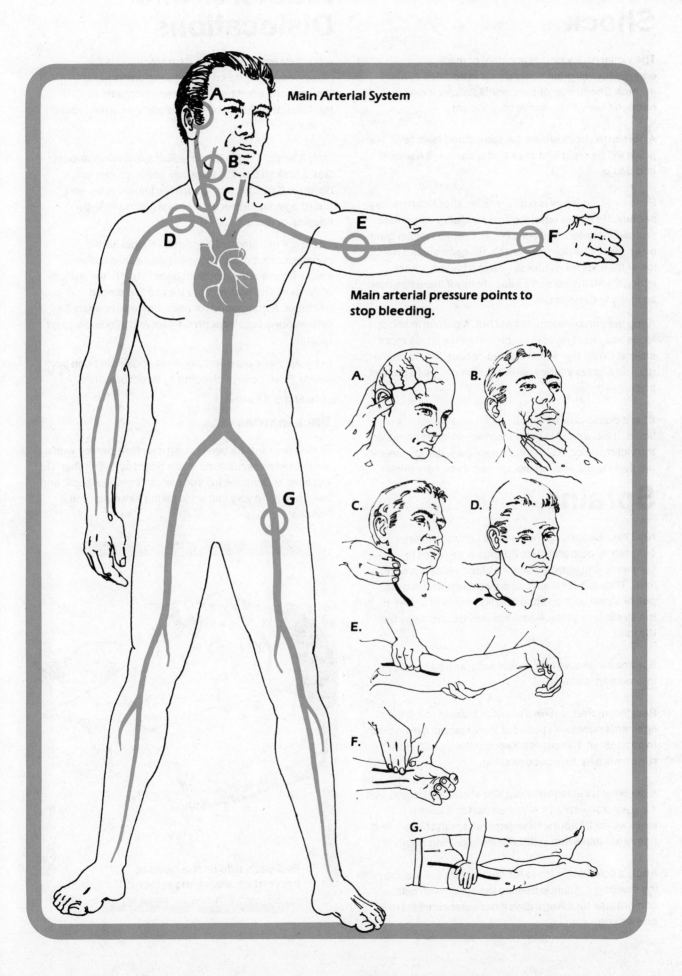

Main Arterial System

Main arterial pressure points to stop bleeding.

A.

B.

C.

D.

E.

F.

G.

Shock

The victim of any kind of accident or medical emergency will often suffer shock in addition to his injuries. Shock may occur immediately, or it may happen several hours after an accident.

A person in shock is pale, perspiring and feels faint. His pulse will be rapid and weak and his skin will feel cold and damp.

Even when an injury is not extensive, shock can be very serious. No matter what the accident, after immediate first-aid treatment has been given, keep the victim lying down even if he doesn't want to. His head should be lower than his body, unless he has a head or chest injury. Raise the person's head slightly if there has been an injury in these areas.

Keep the person warm, but not hot. A person in shock loses body heat rapidly, which makes the shock more severe. Cover him with a blanket or coat. If he is on the ground and his injuries permit movement, put a blanket underneath him.

If he is conscious, he may be given small amounts of liquid. If the wound is in the stomach or lower chest, or if the victim will obviously require surgery, do not give him anything to drink, even though he may be very thirsty.

Sprains

Next to cuts, sprains are the most common injury suffered by outdoorsmen. Sprains are injuries to ligaments and muscles and the blood vessels around a joint. They almost always occur as a result of excess pull or strain on the supporting ligaments of a joint. If the stress is extreme, ligaments may be torn away from the joint.

Sprains cause swelling, tenderness, and pain if the injured part is moved.

Rest the injured part on a pillow or blanket roll. If the ligaments have been pulled or torn, rest will permit them to strengthen themselves. Keeping the injured limb raised will help to reduce swelling.

A severely sprained wrist or ankle should be treated as if it is fractured—splint the injured part and keep it elevated for 24 hours. Newspapers or magazines rolled tightly will make firm splints for immobilizing a limb.

Apply a cold compress to the sprain. This will reduce the swelling. Continue treating the sprain with cold compresses for several days if necessary until there is no swelling.

Fractures and Dislocations

A fracture is a broken bone. A dislocation is the displacement of the end of a bone from its joint. Dislocations often have the same symptoms as fractures and should be treated as if they were broken bones.

Only a doctor or qualified medical practitioner should 'set' a broken bone. If someone has fractured or dislocated a bone, immobilize the injured area, and guard against further injury while getting him to a hospital or doctor.

There are two kinds of fractures—simple and compound. A simple fracture is also called a closed fracture because the broken bone is under the surface of the skin. Dislocations are treated like closed fractures. A compound, or open fracture, is when the broken bone cuts through the skin and makes an open wound.

In treating an open fracture, do not push the bone back inside. First, control bleeding by direct pressure.

Give first-aid for shock.

Back Injuries

Great care must be taken when moving a person with a suspected back fracture. Use a board as a stretcher. Do not twist or bend the injured person's neck or back, and keep him lying very still while taking him quickly to a hospital.

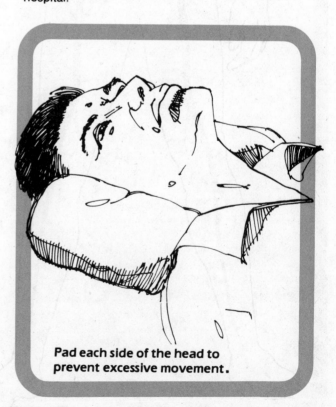

Pad each side of the head to prevent excessive movement.

Upper Arm Fracture

When there is a fracture of the upper arm, tie splints securely, one on each side of the break. Put padding in the injured person's armpit to make a cushion and prevent chafing. Support the arm with a sling. Then bind the arm to the chest to keep it still.

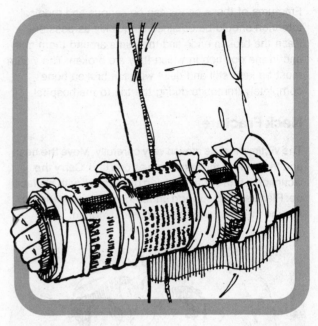

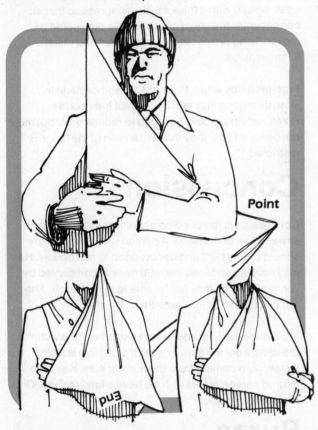

Point

Elbow Fracture

When an elbow is fractured, do not move the joint to a different position. Splint the elbow in the same position it is in after the break. The victim should be treated by a doctor as quickly as possible to prevent damage to the hand and other complications.

Forearm Fracture

There are two bones in the forearm. Very often, both bones will be broken in an accident. Splint the entire forearm to immobilize the arm.

Wrist Fracture

A broken wrist is often the result of falling on an oustretched hand. Until the wrist can be properly set, it should be immobilized with splints and kept in an elevated position.

Ankle Fracture

Splint the ankle without attempting to change the position of the broken bone. A tightly rolled blanket or pillow can be used to splint a broken ankle. With the injured foot placed on the center of the blanket roll or pillow, bring the roll up each side of the ankle and strap or tie securely.

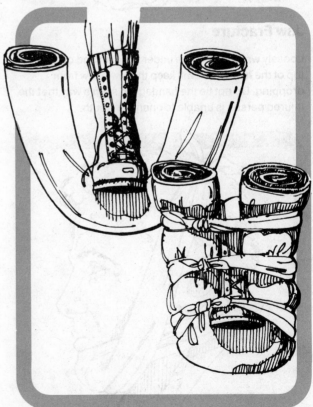

Hip, Pelvis, Thigh and Lower Leg Fractures

Fractures of these bones can be serious and medical attention should be obtained as quickly as possible. Keep the broken ends and the joints around them still and in the position in which they are broken. The victim must be kept still and quiet with the broken bone completely immobile during the trip to the hospital.

Neck Fracture

The victim must be moved very carefully. Move the head and the body at the same time as one unit. Carry the victim on a firm stretcher, lying on his back with his face up. Place a small support under the neck and padding around the head and neck to prevent motion.

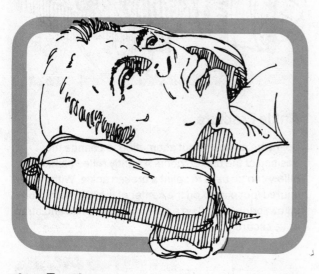

Jaw Fracture

Loosely wrap a bandage under the chin and over the top of the head. This will keep the lower jaw from dropping. Do not tie the bandage in such a way that the injured person is unable to open his mouth.

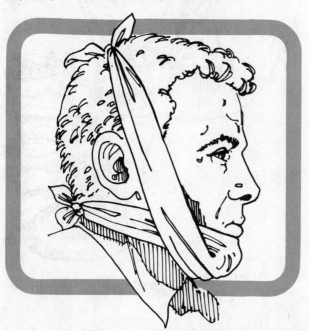

Fractured Ribs

A fractured rib can be dangerous because the broken bone could puncture the lung or some other internal organ.

If a fractured rib has broken through the skin, cover the open wound with a thick sterile compress so that air cannot enter the chest cavity. The victim should be moved, lying on his back with his head and chest slightly raised.

Fractured ribs which have not caused damage to internal organs may mend and heal themselves. Fractured ribs should be taped to reduce pain, but must not be taped so tightly that expansion of the lungs is restricted.

Concussion

Concussion is the swelling of brain tissue following a severe blow to the head. A person with a head injury should be kept still and encouraged to rest quietly. He may have a headache and stiff neck accompanied by vomiting and he may not be able to think clearly. The pupils of the eyes may be different in size.

Immediate medical attention is essential if the victim is bleeding from the ears or mouth or if there is a clear, watery fluid coming from the nose or ears. Keep the injured person at rest with his head slightly raised. Give first-aid for shock.

Burns

Do not ignore a burn, even if it is minor. If left untreated, a burn could become infected.

If someone is badly burned you must relieve the pain, prevent infection and treat for shock until you are able to get the victim to a hospital. Shock is the greatest danger after a severe burn.

The severely burned person may be given small sips of a weak solution of salt water or small sips of a mixture made of 1 teaspoon of salt and ½ teaspoon of baking soda added to 1 quart (1.13 liters) of water.

Do not try to clean a burn or strip away any clothing that is sticking to the burn. Immerse the burned area in cold water. This will relieve pain. If a blister forms, do not break the blister.

Cover the burn with a clean dressing. This will relieve the pain by keeping the air away from the burn. It also reduces the chance of infection. If a very clean dressing is not available, leave the burn uncovered.

Do not use antiseptic or iodine on a burn and never apply grease or butter. If the burn is very minor, burn ointment or Vaseline may be used to relieve the pain on the first day.

A person exposed to a flash or forest fire may suffer damage to the lungs from breathing in smoke and heat. He should be taken to the hospital as quickly as possible.

Blisters

Inspect your feet frequently for tender red patches which are the beginnings of blisters. Cover these areas with adhesive tape to protect the skin from being rubbed by your shoe and forming a blister.

Once a blister has formed, make a donut bandage—which is a round pad with the center cut out—to protect the blister.

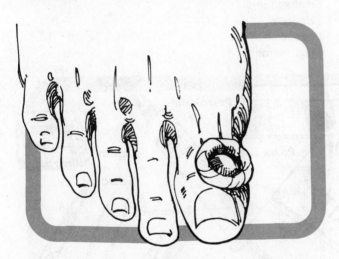

Do not break blisters. This increases the chance of infection and makes them more painful. Instead, cleanse the area around the edge of the blister and, with a sterilized needle, prick a tiny hole in the side of the swelling. Very gently ease the fluid out through the pinprick. When the blister is empty, cover the area with a sterile dressing or adhesive tape. If tape is applied over the blister, it should remain in place until a new layer of skin has formed.

To relieve pain and inflammation, soak the blistered area in hot water for 20 to 30 minutes, three or four times daily. After each soaking cover the tender area with a sterile dressing.

The ragged dead skin of a broken blister should be trimmed carefully to prevent damaging new tissue, but should not be completely removed until the new skin has formed and toughened.

Frostbite

Frostbite is the freezing of a part of the body; most often the nose, ears, cheeks, fingers, or toes.

When frostbite occurs, the skin is first flushed, then changes to a shiny white or grayish-yellow. Occasionally there is pain with frostbite, but usually the affected areas are numb.

If you suffer frostbite, do not rub the frozen part. Warm forstbitten skin by putting the affected area against a warm part of your body—cup your hand over a frostbitten ear, warm frostbitten fingers under your armpit.

As soon as you are indoors, immerse the frozen part in lukewarm, body-temperature water. Do not use hot water.

After thawing, cover the affected part with some warm material. Drink hot nourishing liquids such as soup and hot chocolate.

After the skin thaws, do not allow it to become frostbitten again soon afterward. Refreezing will kill skin tissue.

A hunter whose feet are frozen would be better to walk for help on frozen feet than to thaw his feet and proceed later, taking a chance on having his feet freeze a second time.

Bites

Animal Bites

If you are bitten by an animal, wash the wound with soap and water. Cleanse thoroughly to prevent infection. Use firm pressure with a clean cloth to stop bleeding. Have a doctor examine the wound as soon as possible.

Wild animals can carry rabies which can be fatal to humans unless treatment is started as soon as possible.

Animal bites may also cause tetanus in a person who has not been immunized against this infectious, sometimes fatal disease. To guard against tetanus, an anti-tetanus inoculation is recommended before taking an extended hunting trip into remote country.

Insect Bites

Ticks burrow into the skin. Pulling them off often leaves their heads beneath the skin, later causing infection. Dabbing ticks with Vaseline, kerosene or gasoline, or bringing the tip of a hot stick near the insects, will make them let go.

Spider bites can cause swelling and redness. Cold compresses applied to the bite will reduce swelling.

Bee and wasp stings can be very serious. If a person is stung by many bees or wasps, he may become quite ill. Some people are allergic to bee or wasp venom and will have severe reactions if stung.

Multiple stings or allergies may cause a person to have difficulty breathing, go into shock and

unconsciousness. Cold compresses will reduce swelling and a paste made of starch or calamine lotion will lessen the itching.

First Aid Kit

A first aid kit is an essential part of every hunter's gear. The hunter should never go into the field without a first aid kit. The kit should contain basic, effective first aid items and the hunter should be completely familiar with and know how to use its contents.

A first aid manual should be part of the kit. Size and shape of the kit will depend on how the kit will be carried—backpack, jacket pocket, belt.

Essential Items Include:

First aid handbook
Bandaids—approximately 6-12
4 × 4 inch (10 cm × 10 cm) sterile bandage
Roll of gauze bandage—1 inch (2.5 cm)
Adhesive tape—½ inch × 5 yards (1 cm × 1.5 m)
Petroleum gel
Antiseptic
Razor blade
Small scissors
Tweezers
Eye snare
Small mirror

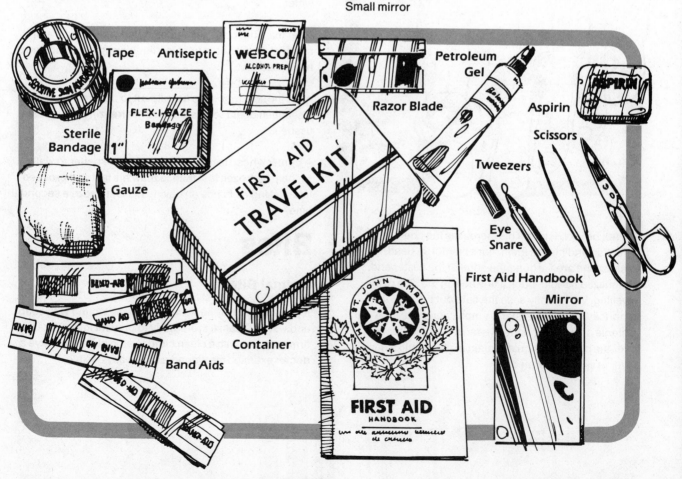

Your family doctor may suggest that some special drugs be included in your first aid kit.

Tape around the rim of the first-aid kit's container. This will keep the kit water-tight and, although the tape is not sterile, it may be useful if extra tape is needed for any purpose.

Your first aid kit, like your survival kit, should be completely familiar to you. Know what it contains and how to use each item properly.

Learn enough basic first aid so that you can help yourself and your companions should an emergency occur.

Responsibilities After First Aid

After first aid treatment has been given, other actions may need to be considered.

Moving the Injured Person

Give careful thought to:
1. Nature of injury
2. Distance from help
3. Discomfort and complications associated with the injury.
4. Type of terrain
5. Weather conditions
6. Time of day
7. Is medical help available at destination.

Leaving Victims To Go For Help

Consider the following:
1. State of mind (is victim capable of staying alone?)
2. Is casualty out of shock?
3. Weather conditions (Will the injured person be comfortable while you are away? Is he sheltered from sudden storms?)

Areas of Concern For Yourself:

1. Do you know your destination and route thoroughly?
2. Are you mentally and physically capable of arriving at destination in the time you plan?
3. Should the weather change for the worse, will you still be able to reach help?
4. Be certain you can direct help to the exact location of injured person.

Consider these points carefully before you take action and always keep in mind that it is your responsibility to try and save a life without endangering yourself or others.

Preparing Yourself to Provide First Aid for Field Emergencies

Proper training is the best way to prepare yourself to aid someone who is injured or becomes ill while they are in the field. First aid is easily and quickly learned from a qualified instructor. With the knowledge and practice gained from a course in first aid and the contents of a properly equipped first aid kit, you will be ready to handle minor mishaps and injuries. You will also be able to give life preserving assistance in the event of more serious injury.

Cardio Pulmonary Resuscitation (CPR) techniques also are most easily learned in a formal course of instructions and practice given by a certified teacher. Such training can be called on in dealing with breathing or cardiac emergencies. Training in first aid and CPR is readily available in most localities through classes sponsored as a public service by local Red Cross units, sportsmen's clubs or various other community organizations. For your own well being and that of your companions' you should enroll in a first aid and CPR training course and periodically updating your knowledge and re-enrolling in such classes. This is the easiest and surest way to be prepared to handle emergencies in the field.

Notes

Vision and Physical Fitness

Introduction

The wise hunter has a complete medical examination each year before the season starts because he knows he must be in good physical condition to enjoy the walking, climbing, and other exercise he will do while hunting.

Too often, however, sportsmen fail to have their eyes examined as well.

Vision

Correct eyesight is extremely important to the hunter. No matter how well he knows the rules of safe hunting, if his vision is impaired and he cannot distinguish objects clearly against a background of trees and brush, he is a danger to himself and to others. Corrective lenses can almost always help defective eye-sight and it is seldom that a person who wears glasses has to give up hunting.

Knowing your visual limitations and adjusting your hunting habits to compensate for them can help avoid accidents. If you know you don't see well at dusk or in the early dawn, hunt only during bright daylight. If the sun's glare impairs your vision, wear sun glasses. If you normally wear glasses, then be sure to wear them when hunting.

Even hunters who do not need corrective lenses should wear plain glasses while hunting to protect their eyes from branches, brambles and twigs, dirt and other debris.

Visual Abilities

Distance Acuity

The ability to clearly see a distant object in detail is called distance acuity. A person who has normal distance acuity can focus on an object at least 20 feet (6 m) away and will be able to see the object in detail under a variety of lighting conditions.

Game is usually well camouflaged by its natural coloration which blends with the landscape. Often, the only sign that game is present is the blink of an eye or the flick of a tail. The hunter must be able to clearly distinguish the form of the animal to recognize it.

Nearpoint Vision

The hunter must also have nearpoint vision—the ability to focus clearly at close range. If close-up objects appear blurred or fuzzy, or if you have difficulty in aligning iron sights, your nearpoint vision may not be as sharp as necessary for safe and accurate shooting. Glasses will help this condition or a telescopic sight may solve the problem of sighting.

Depth Perception

Depth perception is the ability to judge distance accurately. If you consistently misjudge distance, it could be that your depth perception is inadequate. An eye examination will identify if this is so and what can be done to correct the problem.

Peripheral Vision

A hunter needs to see more than what is immediately in front of him. He must be able to see things moving on either side, above and below him, and be aware of any objects within the immediate area of the target. This wide field of vision is called peripheral vision. Good peripheral vision allows the hunter to see objects within the target area without having to move his head or body.

Concentrated Line of Sight —————————
Peripheral Vision - - - - - - - - - - - - - -

Binocular Coordination

Binocular coordination is when both eyes are working together in balance. A person who has good depth perception and adequate peripheral vision plus binocular coordination will be able to see his target clearly even against a background of brush or trees.

Light Gathering Ability

The ability of the eye to form images and detect color under a variety of light conditions is important. This ability may vary greatly from one person to another.

Tinted glasses can help the hunter to see his target clearly under varying light conditions. For persons who are sensitive to the sun's glare, polarized sun glasses tinted green, brown, or smoky in color are recommended. Some lenses are specifically designed to help the wearer see better under dim light conditions.

Color Vision

Color vision is the ability to distinguish between colors and detect a range of colors within the visible light spectrum.

Many hunters are unaware that their color vision is defective. When a hunter is aware that he has a color vision problem, he can take extra precautions to overcome this problem. An eye examination will quickly detect any abnormality in color vision.

Blaze orange is one of the most visible colors to wear in the woods. Tests have proved that fluorescent colors, especially blaze orange, are seen readily under almost all light conditions. Even persons with color vision defects are usually able to distinguish blaze orange.

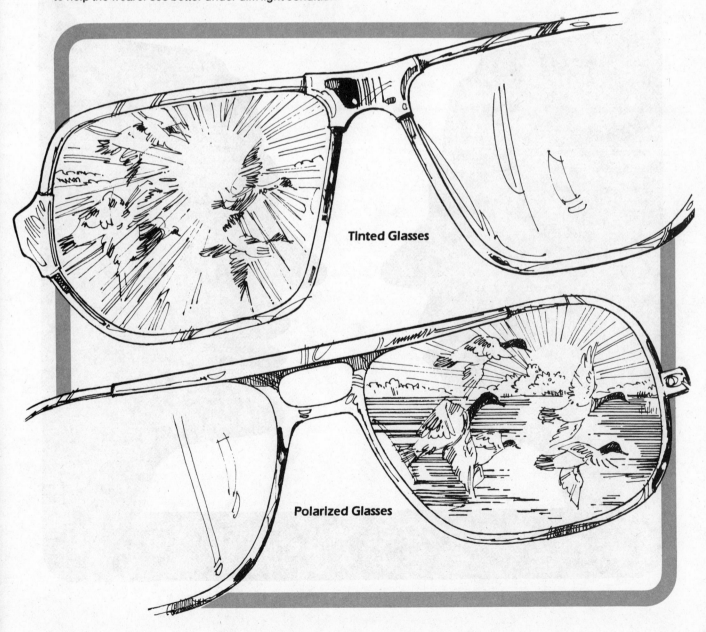

Tinted Glasses

Polarized Glasses

Perception

The way we see and the way we react to what we see is called perception. Understanding perception is very important to a hunter.

Our eyes often play tricks on us. Our minds can register what we want to see and not what is actually there. Most hunters have on occasion mistaken a tree stump for a deer, or been positive they saw a deer where there was none.

Hunters are often exposed to seeing, first a blur and then the actual object. The blur caused by early morning mists and the gray-blue twilight at dusk, coupled with the intense desire to see an animal target, can trick you into believing that you see what isn't there. To eliminate a blurred image, it is often useful to look away from the object and think about something else. Then look back at the original object.

It is possible for two people to look at the same object and see entirely different things.

In the illustration, do you see a white vase, two faces or something else?

When you see a vase in the picture, the white portion of the picture has taken form and the gray portion appears as formless background. When you perceive two faces, the gray portion has form and the white portion appears as background.

Our eyes can also play tricks on us in perceiving the size of objects. When you look at the illustration, do you see a short middle section and a longer middle section? Both are actually the same length.

Our eyes can deceive us by seeing some objects brighter than others when in fact they are the same. In this illustration the circle appears to be a uniform gray color, which in fact it is. But if you place a pencil on the line separating the black and white sections, the gray portion against the black background appears to be brighter.

Move the pencil across the figure to the right and the brighter gray extends into the white. Move it to the left and the darker portion appears to recede into the black.

Our minds may also tell us we see movement although the object is still. Motion pictures and television are examples of this illustration. The movement we see in movies and television is actually a series of still pictures—each projected separately for a fraction of a second.

You can create the same effect by placing your index finger about three inches in front of your nose. Wink each eye alternately—your fingers will appear to move from side to side.

Light and shadow also affect perception and create illusion. In the illustration, there is a section of boiler plate with several dents in it. If the illustration is turned upside down, the dents will appear as bumps. The reason this illusion occurs is because we are accustomed to living in a world where most light comes from above us.

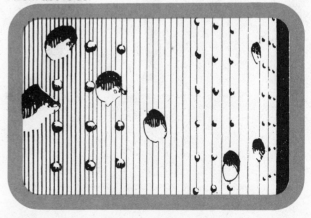

Shadow can also play tricks on your eyes when you are hunting.

Look at the deer in the illustration. Read all the words aloud. Did you miss the extra "a"? Most people do because their mind tells them what they should see before their eyes can register what they actually see.

Considering the many factors that may affect your perception while hunting, it is important to take a second and third look at your target before you start.

Are you sure
this is a
a deer?

Improving Vision Through Eye Training

No matter how good your vision is, it can be improved. There are several eye exercises which will sharpen and train the eyes to see clearly and perceive accurately.

Before the hunting season starts, it is wise to spend time outdoors as if you were actually hunting. Try to find as much wildlife as possible, stalking it within range before it becomes aware of your presence. Make several such trips at different times of the day and under different weather and light conditions.

On these expeditions, take note of your surroundings and commit the scene to memory. Notice the fine detail of the landscape and look for animal tracks and droppings.

Look for movement. Few animals stand motionless for a long period of time. The tail of an animal is usually seen first. However, slight head or body movements may also be detected. Notice which way the wind is blowing from the movement of the leaves.

Even though it may be impractical for you to go into the woods before hunting season starts, you can practice eye exercises. While riding in a vehicle, focus on distant objects and try to define as much detail as possible. Keep your eyes moving. Practice reading road signs as far down the road as possible and try to identify the license numbers of passing vehicles. See how much information you can retain.

Color slides are an excellent aid to train your eyes to see and register objects accurately. Flash the slides on and off the screen. Then try to recall everything you saw in the slide. List everything you can remember—colors, objects, activities. Try to increase your speed of recognition by flashing slides on and off the screen more quickly.

Vision Rules for Hunters

Improving Vision
Through Eye Training

1. If you normally wear glasses, wear them when you hunt. A tiny amount of wax on the surface of the lens—rubbed up to a high gloss—will help eliminate fogging. Or you can buy commercial preparations for this purpose.

2. Every hunter should wear safety glasses to protect his eyes to prevent injury from twigs, branches and other debris as he moves through the bush.

3. Always double-check your target. You can train yourself for this by working on your ability to distinguish figures against backgrounds that blend with their natural color.

4. Blaze orange is the easiest color to see. Make it part of your clothing.

5. If you know you are color blind, take precautions to overcome any problems which could occur as a result of this condition.

6. Before aiming at a game animal, check to ensure nothing will move in the way of your shot.

7. Have your eyes checked at regular intervals, preferably once a year. The hunter should have his examination just prior to the hunting season.

8. Remember your eyes can play tricks on you. Be sure you see what you "think" you see.

Physical Fitness

Your physical condition has a great deal to do with how well you will hunt and how much you will enjoy hunting. Always get in condition before going out into the field. Know your limitations and stay within them.

Visit Your Doctor

See your doctor before the hunting season begins and follow his advice.

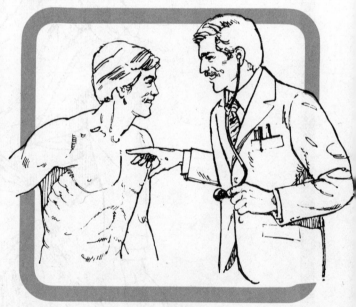

See Your Dentist

A toothache can be as immobilizing as a sprained ankle. Be sure to have a check-up before the season starts.

Body Conditioning

All people are not the same physically. Ask your doctor to suggest a program of conditioning specifically for you. If you are not "in shape" or are "out of condition", take it easy for the first day or two of hunting. Build up your endurance and fitness level by degrees.

Rest

Rest is vital to a person's well-being. Lack of sleep and proper rest will limit your enjoyment of the hunt.

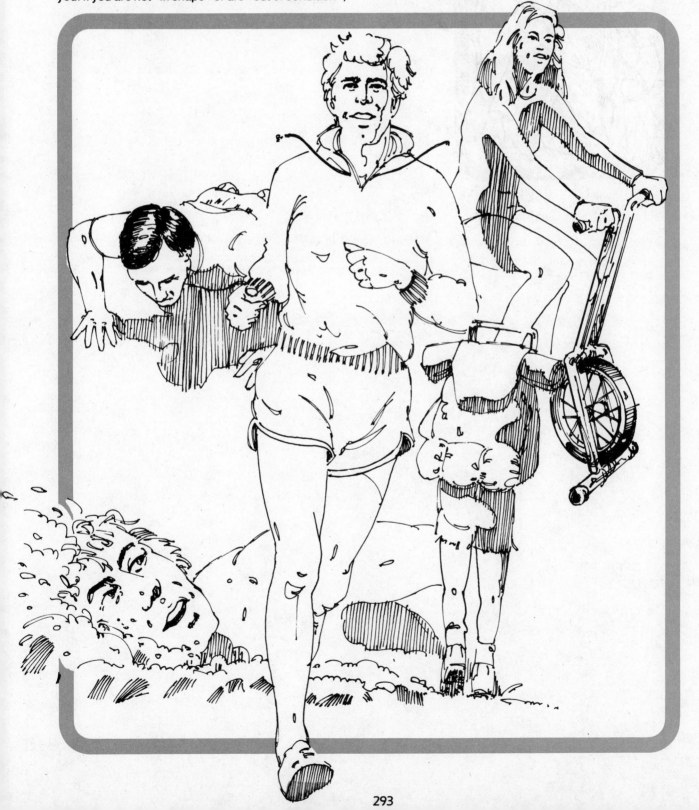

Notes

Legal Responsibilities

Introduction

Hunting by early Indian peoples in North America was not governed by legislation or written laws but by many "unwritten laws" or rituals based upon their dependence for the land and its wildlife. As they were relatively few in number and their hunting implements were primitive (they had no firearms), Indian "subsistence hunting" had very little impact upon wildlife populations.

With the coming of white men with new technology (steel traps, firearms) during the 18th and 19th centuries came a noticeable change. Early explorers, fur traders and settlers commonly abused the opportunity to hunt and trap in a land where game was plentiful and laws were nonexistent. The right to hunt freely without restriction imposed by laws or landowners was one of the basic freedoms sought by settlers in the New World. Considering many of these pioneers were denied the privilege of hunting in their former homeland, perhaps this was to be expected. Even today in most European countries, hunting opportunities are restricted to a small group of wealthy and influential people.

In North America the drastic decline in numbers of many wildlife species due to changing land uses and over exploitation by both whites and Indians during this period, prompted concern by many people to have the government enact laws to control abusive killing and indiscriminate shooting. As early as 1825, Maine had a closed season on deer and moose. In 1844, a group of sportsmen—conservationists in New York State began to call for laws which would control the harvesting of game. In 1864, Utah passed a law prohibiting the killing of buffalo. In 1895, poaching of buffalo became a federal offense. In 1900, a law was enacted which prohibited the interstate transportation of any game animal or bird killed in violation of state law.

The preceding paragraph illustrates the slow, but steady, enactment of laws to protect game. What it does *not* show, however, is that it was the hunter-sportsman who was the driving force in getting these laws on the books. It is commonly thought that the stimulus for wildlife conservation laws came from those who held high office and wanted to protect wildlife from the hunter. Actually, it was the other way around. These laws were passed at the insistence of the hunter in order to conserve a natural resource and to save the sport of hunting.

So it is today. With few exceptions, hunters view wildlife as a resource which, if properly managed, will thrive indefinitely and in spite of the many adaptions which have been required of most species. Wise management, largely possible due to the annual contribution of millions of dollars from hunters through the purchase of licenses, has brought about a complete reversal of the situation which existed only 50 or 60 years ago. Deer now thrive in places where they were thought to be extinct in 1900. This was the case in Pennsylvania, for instance, but in 1980 just under 135,000 deer were taken by hunters in that state.

Levels of Government

Wildlife laws in North America are made at various levels—federal government, state and provincial governments and county, municipal or local government.

Each level of government has been given specific responsibilities. Federal government wildlife laws are concerned with many things such as; the management and regulation of wildlife species that are classified as migratory, the regulation of interstate commerce of wildlife, establishing treaties with other countries pertaining to the management of wildlife, endangered species and others.

State and provincial Fish and Wildlife Divisions are concerned with wildlife laws pertaining to the management of wildlife species found within their boundaries.

County, municipal and local wildlife laws usually concern wildlife species found within boundaries of these governments.

In matters of overlapping legislative jurisdiction, federal law cannot be replaced or countered by state or county laws.

Each hunter has the responsibility to know the laws governing the hunting of the species he is hunting as well as the laws for the area he is hunting in.

Laws to protect life and property

(a) It is unlawful to discharge a firearm or cause a projectile from a firearm to pass within 200 yards (180 m) of an occupied building.
(b) No person shall have a loaded firearm in or on a motor vehicle.
(c) Big game hunters using firearms must wear blaze orange.
(d) No person is allowed to shoot along, across or off a highway.
(e) No one shall hunt while impaired by drugs or alcohol.
(f) It is unlawful to hunt waterfowl using a single ball cartridge.
(g) It is unlawful to discharge a firearm from a developed road.

Laws to protect and conserve wildlife

(a) All regulations pertaining to hunting seasons and bag limits are intended for this purpose.
(b) No one shall hunt or molest big game while the animal is swimming.
(c) No one shall hunt in a wildlife or bird sanctuary, without a permit to do so.
(d) No one shall hunt using an aircraft.
(e) It is unlawful to buy or sell wildlife, or to keep wildlife in captivity, unless a special permit has been obtained.
(f) It is unlawful to release any exotic wildlife to the wild.
(g) No one shall hunt during the hours between one-half hour after sunset and one-half hour before sunrise.
(h) Certain game animals must be registered with the State Conservation Agency so that biological data necessary for wildlife management purpose may be obtained.

Laws governing hunter behavior

The concept of "fair chase" provides the basis for most regulations in this category.

It is unlawful to hunt using:
(i) poison or drugs

(ii) any fully automatic firearm
(iii) snares, traps or nets
(iv) vehicles to chase game
(v) any bait or live decoy
(vi) recorded or electrical wildlife calls
(vii) a dog for big game (except cougar, black bear and white-tailed deer in some areas)

Understanding Hunting Laws

It is the responsibility of every hunter to know the federal and state laws which apply when hunting.

State Conservation Agencies publish pamphlets called "game regulation summaries" that outline the main regulations governing hunting. This information is updated each year to reflect recent changes in the law.

Hunters should obtain copies of the summaries and study them before going into the field. If a hunter has questions concerning hunting regulations which are not answered in the summaries, or if any of the information is unclear, he should contact the nearest Conservation officer or wildlife agency office for clarification.

Creating or Changing Laws

Only duly elected legislatures have the legal capability to create or change laws. However, avenues are available to the public to influence legislation. If you want to see a new law enacted or an existing law changed, you should make your elected representative to the government aware of your thoughts.

If you are convinced the law is wrong, work to change the law but do not disobey it. Many people have found that as they considered their reasons for wanting a law changed, the purpose behind the law became evident. Studying the law will provide an in-depth understanding of why the law is in place.

Citizens have several avenues open to them to create or change hunting laws in North America.

Enforcing Laws

Hunting laws are enforced through various government agencies. In most states, conservation officers have the primary responsibility to enforce laws which apply to wildlife. However, other federal and state personnel also have authority to enforce hunting regulations.

When a hunter is caught breaking the law, he is either warned of his offense or charged. A "charge" is an accusation in legal terms. If charged, he may be issued a voluntary payment ticket, taken into custody or advised of the date when he must appear before a judge. If he appears before a judge the judge will then hear the charges made by the enforcement person and hear the plea of the person charged (guilty or not guilty). After hearing the evidence from both sides, he will make a decision. If the person is guilty, he will establish a penalty for the violation as provided for by the legislation applicable to the offense. The penalty will usually involve the payment of a fine and may result in the loss of hunting privileges.

Some offenses have a provision for payment of a fine on a voluntary basis. This means that the amount of the fine has been established by law for these offenses. The accused has the option of paying this fine if he considers himself guilty or processing the charge through court if he prefers.

In summary, governments make laws, enforcement agencies enforce them, a judicial system establishes guilt or innocence and a penal system administers the penalties.

Hunter Responsibilities

It is the duty of every citizen to obey laws governing his own conduct and to see that laws are upheld by others.

Responsible hunters should set a good example for others to follow. Adherence to all laws by hunters will assure the opportunity to hunt in the future.

Report Law Breaking

It is the responsibility of every hunter who sees someone breaking the law to report the offense to a conservation officer or to any law enforcement personnel having jurisdiction. They will take whatever action is required to have the offense investigated.

It can be particularly difficult to report a lawbreaking incident when the person who has committed the offense is a member of your own hunting party, perhaps even a relative. An individual's personal code of ethics will determine what to do. At the very least, the offender should be made to realize his actions are wrong and that his wrongdoing can damage the reputations of the other members of the hunting party. A person aiding and abetting another person in the commission of an offense may be charged with the principal offense.

Accidental Violations

Each year some hunters are involved in accidental violations. Perhaps a hunter shoots at a buck and inadvertently kills a doe. He should report the accident

to the proper authorities who will attempt to determine what degree of negligence was involved. The hunter may be charged with the offense and processed through the courts if, in the officer's view, he was unduly negligent in causing the accident.

Providing Biological Data

Wildlife biologists are constantly studying wildlife to learn more about this natural resource. Marking and tagging programs help provide wildlife management personnel with migration and movement data necessary to understand and conserve wildlife. Hunters are asked to report locations where tagged game is taken. Information from leg bands or neck collars taken from any harvested game should be reported to the nearest conservation agency office.

The success of any of the marking program depends on hunters sending in a band collar to the nearest Fish and Wildlife office and providing whatever additional information is requested.

In some states hunters are required by law to personally register the kill of certain animals; caribou, cougar, elk, grizzly bear, goat or trophy sheep; at an official checking station or with the state's conservation agency.

Sometimes a questionnaire is supplied with a hunting licence which should be completed by the hunter and returned to the conservation agency. Questionnaires may also be sent to hunters whose license numbers have been selected at random by computer.

Interpretation of the Law

Laws should be written so they are interpreted the same way by everybody. However, in practice, this is a very difficult goal to accomplish. Because people may interpret some laws differently or rely on misinformed sources of information, they can become confused about what the law allows and what it does not. Areas of law that are particularly confusing to many hunters yet which they need to interpret correctly are laws regarding trespass, access to public and private land and firearms use.

It is the responsibility of the hunter to know the hunting regulations and firearms laws for the area in which he is hunting and for the game species he is hunting.

Notes

300